Learning Ecologies
in Architecture

Learning Ecologies in Architecture

Edited by Deen Sharp

Table of Contents

30
Foreword: Investing in Education
Farrokh Derakhshani

34
Learning Ecologies in Architecture
Deen Sharp

MAKING SPACE FOR EDUCATION

42
Learning Spaces in Africa: From Missionaries to Development Hubs
Ola Uduku

56
Building Education in Africa
Tubi Otitooluwa, Justicia C. T. Kiconco, Timothy Latim, and Jonathan Kplorla Agbeh

76
Hybrid Rhythms: Alioune Diop University Teaching and Research Unit
Deen Sharp

ARCHITECTURE AND THE MATERIALS OF SOCIAL ENGAGEMENT

110
Connecting Every Curve: The Architecture of Community at Kamanar Secondary School
Deen Sharp

128
Local Community: Voices from Kamanar
Lamine Sambou
Oumy Sagna
Gaston and Tanta

156
Socially Engaged Architecture as a Pedagogical Practice
Farhan S. Karim

174
Building Earthbound: Notes from Accra and Freetown
Katherine Dawson

184
Building Learning Spaces with Communities
In Conversation with Anna Heringer and Christian Paul Zigato Agboada

LEARNING ECOLOGIES

196
Architecture's Ecology: Translation, Participation, Collaboration
Lesley Lokko

202
Creating a School for Architecture
Mamadou Jean-Charles Tall

208
Structures of Hope: Architecture, Education, and African Futures
In Conversation with Christian Benimana

218
Designing Education: Reflecting on the Aga Khan Award for Architecture
Christian A. Hedrick

238
Epilogue
Souleymane Bachir Diagne

246 Contributor Biographies
255 Image Credits
256 Imprint

The Alioune Diop University Teaching and Research Unit in Senegal is part of an effort to encourage youth to stay in rural areas and to equip Senegal's next generation with tools to achieve food security and sustainable development.

The southern facade of Alioune Diop University is made up of 20,000 triangular concrete pieces.

The eastern entrance to Alioune Diop University invites users into the building with the offer of shade. Irregular steel V-shaped branches support the large external roof.

An external corridor runs along Alioune Diop University's northern side. Temperatures can reach 40 degrees centigrade in this arid region of the country.

Behind the southern exterior facade of Alioune Diop University runs a corridor, allowing sun-heated air to rise and esca
The architects used shade and cross-ventilation to achieve cooling and airflow with minimal energy consumption.

The southern facade of Alioune Diop University. It took over a hundred workers six months to construct the latticework.

The catenary vaults of the Kamanar Secondary School were constructed with stabilised rammed earth by local masons. Excavation for the earth was on site and the quarry was subsequently turned into a sunken sports field.

The modular vaulted structures of the Kamanar Secondary School. Each structure is called an *awla*. It is covered with a metal sheet to protect the clay from the rain and provide an air chamber.

The interior of an *awla*. Wooden lattices provide passive cooling, and the floor is laid with reused ceramic tiles.

Existing trees became an organising element for the school, and the shade they provide was maximised throughout the design. More fruit trees were planted to provide further shade, and also potentially income for the school.

The furniture for the classrooms at Kamanar Secondary School was made on site in collaboration with local craftspeople.

The entrance to Kamanar Secondary School, located in Senegal's southern Casamance region. Communities across Casamance place a high value on education and have actively sought to expand access to formal schooling.

Foreword:
Investing in Education
Farrokh Derakhshani

The quality of educational buildings has an important impact on the formation of future generations, as children and youth spend most of their days in buildings that are not their home, refining their identity and also a sense of belonging to their roots. In these formative years, they not only acquire education but establish their collective memories.

It is important to bear in mind that – above and beyond the students who are transitional in such facilities – these rooms are also working spaces for teachers and staff, who spend years of their lives there.

Over the past century, new educational facilities have also been a symbol of progress and development in rapidly changing societies and nascent nations. Often erected as the first institutional buildings in villages and urban neighbourhoods, they sometimes become construction models for other domestic architecture. Population growth in the Global South requires the building of more and more schools and universities. However, as educational systems change at a rapid pace, old formulas cannot adequately address the problem and thus new building types are required.

In establishing the Aga Khan Award for Architecture (AKAA), the major hope – since its early days almost five decades ago – has been to present models that could inspire those who were eagerly looking for better solutions in building their future societies. Schools have been of utmost priority in this process. During the 1st Award Cycle in 1980, the Agricultural Training Centre in Nianing, Senegal, was honoured by the AKAA Master Jury for its "development of a labour-intensive building system into complete architectural language, revitalising masonry construction and providing a model for a number of projects in Senegal."[1] This rural training centre was conceived on recommended principles in the 1970s to bridge the architectural and social gap in colonial and postcolonial architecture, promoting regional and local self-reliance in school construction and furthering on-site training, local expertise, and technical leadership. All of these principles are still a goal now, half a century later.

Established in 1977 by His Late Highness the Aga Khan IV, the Award has consistently aimed to recognise exceptional achievements in recent architectural projects that contribute to the quality of life of its users and have an impact on its context. Numerous educational facilities have been recognised during the past fifteen triennial cycles of the Award. Two winning projects in Senegal stand out – Kamanar Secondary School and Alioune Diop University Teaching and Research Unit – in that they address many different concerns at once: climatic responsiveness, elevation of local construction know-how, intelligent use of local human and material resources, and creation of attractive architecture that can enable teachers and staff to offer better education in an excellent environment!

The publication at hand, *Learning Ecologies in Architecture*, emerges at a critical moment in the intertwined histories of architecture and education. The title is particularly apt: the notion of an "ecology" directs our attention not only to the physical environment but also to the myriad social, cultural, and material relationships that sustain learning. It reminds us that education is not an abstract endeavour that can be detached from place, climate, culture, or community. It is deeply situated – and so must be the architecture that serves it.

Yet the educational systems themselves have evolved rapidly, demanding new architectural responses. No longer is a school simply a collection of classrooms. Educational philosophies increasingly call for spaces that encourage active, collaborative learning, creativity, and community engagement. At the same time, the climate crisis imposes an urgent imperative to design sustainably, using local resources and methods that reduce energy consumption and environmental impact.

The projects presented in this volume underscore an essential conviction of the Aga Khan Award for Architecture: that architecture must be context-sensitive, as well as responsive to climate and site, on the one hand, and to social and cultural realities, on the other. The buildings documented here do far more than simply shelter learners. They participate in creating resilient learning ecologies – networks of relationships among people, place, and knowledge. They are acts of care.

The notion of care has become increasingly significant in architectural discourse, as the essays in this book demonstrate. Care implies maintenance, stewardship, and responsibility. It is about how buildings age, how they are adapted, and how they continue to serve evolving needs. This principle resonates strongly with the work of the Aga Khan Development Network (AKDN), which, alongside the Award, has built and supported numerous educational facilities throughout the world – from primary schools in East Africa to the Aga Khan Academies, which integrate climate-sensitive architecture with pedagogical innovation.

Another critical theme woven through the pages of this volume is climate. Architecture today cannot ignore the realities of a warming planet. Educational facilities, especially in regions where temperatures may exceed 40 degrees centigrade, must minimise energy consumption while ensuring comfort and usability. Both Senegalese projects demonstrate how intelligent design can achieve this balance. Passive cooling, careful orientation, and use of local materials – such strategies are not mere technical details but profound ethical choices. They show that architecture, even in modest school buildings, can be a tool for environmental stewardship.

This environmental responsibility is part of a broader ethical commitment inherent in the mission of the Aga Khan Award for Architecture. From the earliest days, the Award has sought to promote architecture that enhances quality of life, respects cultural heritage, and addresses the pressing social and environmental issues of its time. Educational architecture has been central to this mission, precisely because it sits at the intersection of so many critical concerns: community, climate, culture, and the future.

Over the fifteen triennial cycles of the Aga Khan Award, numerous educational facilities have been recognised. Each project becomes part of a growing archive, a collective resource of ideas and precedents from which architects, educators, and communities can draw inspiration. As Christian A. Hedrick notes in his essay, the Award's archive is not merely a record of built works; it is a veritable repository of lessons about how architecture can embody values and respond creatively to complex challenges.

As the world confronts an era of overlapping crises – environmental, social, technological – the lessons from these projects become ever more urgent today. We need architecture that does more than solve technical problems; we need architecture that builds relationships, nurtures knowledge, and fosters a sense of belonging. Indeed, we need learning ecologies that are sustainable not only environmentally, but culturally and socially.

---

1 Renata Holod and Darl Rastorfer, eds., *Architecture and Community: Building in the Islamic World Today* (New York: Aperture, 1983), p. 14.

Please scan the QR code to view the Aga Khan Award for Architecture film portraits of the Kamanar Secondary School, Thionck Essyl, Senegal (AKAA 2022), and the Alioune Diop University Teaching and Research Unit, Bambey, Senegal (AKAA 2019).

Learning Ecologies in Architecture

Deen Sharp

Learning, Ecologies, and Architecture

The content and purpose of what we teach our children and young people in schools and universities is undergoing profound transformation. What skills are required and taught, how they are acquired, and to what end are all being challenged. This disruption is accelerated by the arrival of generative artificial intelligence (GenAI) and is compounded by the intersecting polycrisis of climate change, economic instability, and conflict – particularly in the Global South. Amidst all this change, the need remains to foster resilient connections between learners, communities, and their social-natural environments. These linkages are essential for establishing the broad and context-based skills – technical, analytical, and critical – so necessary for navigating a turbulent planet. The need for resilient learning ecologies has never been more urgent. Architecture, particularly the design of educational spaces, plays a critical role in cultivating these learning ecologies.

Ecology is about spatial relationships. Rooted in the Ancient Greek *oîkos* (meaning "house") and *logia* (the "study of"), the term was coined by the German biologist Ernst Haeckel in 1866 to describe how organisms relate to both their organic and inorganic environments – "the household of nature".[1] Traditionally understood as the scientific analysis of the interdependencies that shape natural systems, ecology has become increasingly relevant in the context of human-driven environmental transformation. It emerged, in part, as a scientific response to the upheavals and violence brought about by empire and industrialisation.[2]

Over time, the concept of ecology has evolved beyond the life sciences. In urban ecology, for example, scholars examine how cities and natural systems are mutually constitutive. This shift has also influenced architecture. Architectural ecology is not simply environmentally sustainable design or energy-efficient architecture but must also be understood as a complex, relational, socio-political framework.[3] No longer limited to mitigating environmental impact, architecture is now understood to actively shape, and be shaped by, ecologies that are material, political, and cultural.

This book presents a series of architectural projects focused on educational institutions that embody what I refer to as learning ecologies. Two educational buildings built in Senegal form the core of this book, for they exemplify an ecological approach to architecture and educational design, both designed by Spanish firms and recognised by the Aga Khan Award for Architecture: IDOM's Alioune Diop University Teaching and Research Unit in Bambey (14th Award Cycle) and Dawoffice's Kamanar Secondary School in Thionck Essyl (15th Award Cycle). Architecture in these two cases is asserted not only as the domain of professionals, but also as a set of collective practices through which built environments are shaped and inhabited.

These buildings serve as entry points into a wider exploration of how architecture can respond holistically to both environmental and social contexts. They address ecological concerns, such as carbon footprints, materials provenance, and passive energy strategies, while also engaging with the cultural values and with the everyday practices and economies of the communities they serve. This is where ecologies of care, maintenance, and relationships are shaped. The book *Learning Ecologies in Architecture* highlights architecture as a co-produced, context-sensitive practice, one that fosters networks of care, knowledge exchange, and shared responsibility in the creation and inhabitation of educational space.

Education and Its Architecture in Africa

In sub-Saharan Africa, formal education was deeply entangled and associated with colonial rule, used as a tool to cultivate a compliant elite, but it was never entirely contained by it. With the end of colonialism, formal colonial education was not dismantled but, to some extent, reimagined. Postcolonial states sought to transform an education system designed for subordination into one grounded in self-empowerment, cultural affirmation, and national aspiration. For leaders like Léopold Sédar Senghor, who served as President of Senegal from 1960 to 1980, education became central to the project of reclaiming African identity, heritage, and culture. Rather than reject European forms of knowledge outright, Senghor positioned education as a site of synthesis. He saw it as a space where the values of the Négritude movement, which he led, could flourish through this recovery and celebration of African heritage within a global intellectual framework. Similarly, leaders like the Ghanaian President Kwame Nkrumah saw no contradiction between embracing modernity and resisting its colonial manifestations. They envisioned education as a foundation for building a knowledge-based society that could respond to the enduring legacies of colonial exploitation and the transatlantic slave trade.[4]

Many post-independence leaders founded new universities or strongly upgraded existing institutions. To note just a few examples, Senghor significantly expanded the University of Dakar (now Cheikh Anta Diop University), Nkrumah founded the Kwame Nkrumah University of Science and Technology (KNUST), and Jomo Kenyatta in Kenya expanded the University of Nairobi and founded Kenyatta College (which later became a university). Many of these newly established or expanded organisations had a profound impact on the architectural and urban landscape of Africa. In this volume, the architectural collective Shared Heritage Africa highlights four educational projects: the Senate Building at the University of Lagos in Nigeria, the IWACU Centre in Rwanda, the Great Hall at KNUST in Ghana, and the Faculty of Technology at Makerere University in Uganda. The authors argue that all four projects have influenced African educational and institutional landscapes and the practice of architecture.

Continued attempts by African governments to keep up with the strong demand for formal education have resulted in an extensive building boom of educational institutions. Tens of thousands of schools and universities have been erected across the continent since independence. Both the Alioune Diop University Teaching and Research Unit and the Kamanar Secondary School are part of this expansionist trend. However, Ola Uduku – in her in-depth historical overview of educational buildings and programmes in Africa – remarks that such innovative design projects like Diop University and Kamanar are the exception rather than the rule. She laments the entrenched colonial school design in much of Africa and the mismatch between this inherited spatial model and the real educational conditions and contexts.

Learning Ecologies in Senegal

Alioune Diop University Teaching and Research Unit and the Kamanar Secondary School go beyond the construction of spaces for learning; they engage deeply with the broader environmental, cultural, and social contexts of their sites. Both respond sensitively to the natural environment, drawing inspiration from local flora and fauna and people's interaction with it, addressing concerns such as shade, water use, and ecological history. They prioritise passive cooling techniques, energy efficiency, and sustainability, while relying on cost-effective materials sourced locally whenever possible.

Their environmental attentiveness is matched by a strong commitment to social engagement. Both projects co-produced spaces of learning. IDOM collaborated with local craftspeople from the nearby town of Bambey to make the 20,000 triangular perforations, prefabricated on site, that form the striking lattice wall on the building's southern facade. Dawoffice, meanwhile, adopted a fundamentally collaborative and pedagogical approach. The Spanish team, comprising staff and volunteers, lived and worked with both the school and the broader local community. A charitable foundation was established by Dawoffice for the purpose of raising funds for this project and has continued to fund the maintenance and some of the operational lines of the school. Their work resulted not only in a school building, but also in a long-term partnership that became part of a wider educational process for students and residents alike.

At Kamanar Secondary School, the use of soil from the site to construct the simple catenary vaults illustrates not only the beauty of clay as a building material but also its capacity to bring communities together. Local craftspeople worked with the Dawoffice team to shape the structurally efficient vaults that define the school. This process embodies the socio-natural entanglements of materials, or what Katherine Dawson describes in her essay as geosocial worlds. Built environments, she argues, are not inert; they emerge through ongoing interactions between geological forces and social, political, and economic life. This perspective situates architecture beyond frameworks of form and function, placing it instead within the broader geosocial and planetary dynamics that shape our world.

Learning Through Making and Caring

Mud construction globally has long been central to socially engaged architecture. Farhan S. Karim, in his contribution, explores the emergence of socially engaged architecture in Bangladesh, where mud has played a key role in building practices. He analyses three exemplary projects that position architecture not merely as the design of physical structures, but as a tool for advancing social justice and equity. These projects share a non-hierarchical ethos, treating architectural form and process as mutually constitutive, and foregrounding "care" as a strategy for social engagement. One such project is the METI School in Bangladesh, designed by the German architect Anna Heringer. In this volume, Heringer is interviewed alongside the Ghanaian engineer Christian Paul Zigato Agboada, and they reflect on the intersections of education, materiality, and cultural identity. They also discuss their collaboration on the Earth Campus in Tatale, Ghana, which explores the transformative power of mud, emphasises the importance of local knowledge systems, and rethinks what educational spaces can, and should, be.

Architectural Education in Africa and Beyond

In the emphasis placed on context and the importance of local knowledge systems, the fact that both of the Senegalese educational projects were designed by Spanish architectural firms cannot be ignored or sidestepped. There is a deep frustration that exists in relation to the state of architectural education in Africa that is addressed in this book. Lesley Lokko, who is widely recognised for her efforts to expand architectural education in Africa, laments the state of the profession on the continent. In the whole of Francophone West Africa, Lokko notes, there is just one officially accredited architecture school, in Togo. Where meaningful architecture is produced, Lokko argues, healthy ecologies are evident. These ecologies are constituted by educational opportunities, in-depth scholarship, a culture of architectural critique, local and international awards, publications, and established state, public, and philanthropic institutions that promote dialogue and discourse. All the same, the green shoots of a healthier learning ecology for architecture are starting to become visible, as showcased in this book. This includes the establishment of architecture schools and training programmes, as well as improved architectural dialogue and research.

In a recent interview, the Rwandan architect Christian Benimana discusses how he founded the African Design Centre and its fellowship programme, aimed at cultivating the next generation of African architects who are attuned to the latest architectural skills but able to ground them in the particularities of the African context. Similarly, the Senegalese architect Mamadou Jean-Charles Tall, in his contribution, recounts his efforts to cultivate a richer learning ecology for architecture in the establishment of the Collège Universitaire d'Architecture de Dakar (CUAD), which he co-founded with Naby Kane and Annie Jouga. Tall describes how his university focuses on developing students' creativity, but also on addressing their understanding of architectural history and theory, dominated as it has been by references to Western architects. Tall wanted to push students to recognise that steel, glass, and cement are not the only materials capable of producing good architecture – that the students can learn from their own contexts and histories to create great and meaningful architecture. Indeed, the Aga Khan Award for Architecture, through its recognition of projects from mainly outside the West, has created an archive of architecturally significant examples of educational building. Christian Hedrick, in his contribution, provides a global view of educational projects that have won the Award throughout its history. He selects nine projects that are organised into three categories: classical formal education, learning by doing, and learning by example.

Towards a Pedagogy of Learning Ecologies

In an era marked by ecological crisis, technological disruption, and deep educational inequalities, *Learning Ecologies in Architecture* calls for a renewed understanding of how educational spaces can be imagined, built, and inhabited. The projects and perspectives featured in this volume underscore that architecture is much more than merely a backdrop for learning – it is a dynamic participant in the cultivation of knowledge, care, and community. From the clay vaults of Kamanar to the participatory latticework of Diop University, these examples show how architecture can embed local materials, social relations, and ecological intelligence into the very fabric of educational practice. At the same time, the limitations of architectural education across much of Africa remind us that nurturing resilient learning ecologies requires not only good buildings but also the broader institutional, cultural, and pedagogical infrastructures to support them. This book is thus both a celebration of architectural possibility and a call to reimagine the conditions through which education and architecture co-produce more just and sustainable futures.

1   Peg Rawes, "Introduction – Architectural Ecologies: Ethics, Aesthetics and Agency", in *Relational Architectural Ecologies: Architecture, Nature and Subjectivity*, ed. Peg Rawes (London: Routledge, 2013), p. 1.
2   Sharon Kingsland, "Conveying the Intellectual Challenge of Ecology: An Historical Perspective", *Frontiers in Ecology and the Environment* 2, no. 7 (September 2004), p. 369.
3   Peg Rawes, "Introduction".
4   Olúfẹ́mi Táíwò, *Against Decolonisation: Taking African Agency Seriously* (London: C. Hurst & Company, 2022), p. 122.

MAKING SPACE

FOR
EDUCATION

Learning Spaces in Africa: From Missionaries to Development Hubs

Ola Uduku

Sub-Saharan Africa's engagement with formal Western-style education spans over two centuries and started with the establishment of missionary organisations on the continent. Long before this, however, the continent possessed rich and diverse systems of traditional and religious learning, which predate Western models by many centuries. Missionary encounters with Africa began even before the large-scale development of the transatlantic slave trade, as Western sailors and merchants established trading links with coastal communities. These early missionaries played a central role in introducing Western education, founding some of the continent's first formal schools (fig. 1). By the time of the Berlin Conference (1884–85) and the subsequent carving up of Africa, all major Christian denominations had established mission stations across much of the continent.[1]

Major missionary organisations included the Church Missionary Society – the Anglican Church's mission arm – as well as the Presbyterian and Methodist missions, representing Scottish and English denominations. The Baptist Mission and the Sudan Interior Mission (SIM) were of American origin, while the Basel Mission was founded and funded by Swiss churches. These missions were involved in a wide array of activities beyond proselytisation and the construction of churches and chapels. They played a significant role in healthcare, especially in establishing dispensaries, clinics, and hospitals. Equally important was their contribution to education, which began with basic catechist training (the instruction given to local converts) and was then expanded to include higher education. Notable examples include Fourah Bay College in Sierra Leone and the Lovedale and Tiger Kloof missions in South Africa.

Figure 1. The Nursery of Infant Church School in Badagry, Nigeria, founded in 1843, is an example of the beginning of formal Western-style education across Africa.

The Roman Catholic Church has played a particularly prominent and historical role in both social development and proselytising across Africa. Key Catholic orders that established a presence on the continent included the Holy Ghost Fathers – active in the southern Sahelian areas of northern Ghana and into Burkina Faso – and the Jesuits, who were initially focused in North and Central Africa but are now also found in East Africa and the island nation of Madagascar.[2] These missions were originally staffed primarily by Catholic priests sent from countries such as Ireland, Portugal, the United Kingdom, and Italy.

Educational Buildings and Programmes

The influence of missionaries on Africa was far-reaching and has been extensively documented by historians and cultural commentators from the twentieth century to the present.[3] While the primary aim of most missions was proselytisation, the conversion of local populations to Christianity, their activities went far beyond religious preaching. Missionaries established a broad infrastructure that included churches, schools, and medical facilities. Among these, educational institutions arguably had the most lasting impact on the continent's development.

Though many schools were affiliated with specific religious orders, their educational offerings often extended beyond the respective faith communities. In practice, not all students educated in mission schools became converts. This was especially true in British-controlled territories, where the policy of "grants-in-aid" enabled government funding to be allocated to mission schools. These grants subsidised buildings, teachers' salaries, and educational materials, on the condition that schools were regularly inspected. Inspectors ensured that the institutions were well maintained, followed the British curriculum, achieved satisfactory outcomes, and admitted all eligible local students based on merit rather than religious affiliation.

Missionary schools were typically situated within a broader "mission compound", a spatial arrangement in which the chapel or church spiritually anchors the site. Archival accounts, such as those from the missionary Hope Masterton Waddell, offer detailed descriptions of the construction and organisation of these compounds – including the church, dispensary, and the schools – often built using local materials and labour.[4] Wattle and daub walls, thatched roofs, and community participation in building works were common in the early stages of missionary expansion.

An illustrative case is Adisadel School near Cape Coast, Ghana (fig. 2). Founded in the early twentieth century, the school followed the typical mission layout and was later incorporated into the Gold Coast's National School Buildings Programme during the 1950s.[5] This redevelopment was carried out by the modernist architects Maxwell Fry and Jane Drew. Over time, the materials used in school construction evolved, from wattle and daub to sun-dried clay bricks, and

Figure 2. The Adisadel School near Cape Coast, Ghana, followed a typical mission layout and was later redeveloped by the modernist architects Maxwell Fry and Jane Drew.

eventually to cement blocks, especially in the period after the First World War. These material shifts marked a broader transition towards permanence and standardisation in educational infrastructure across colonial Africa.

Much of Catholic missions' contribution to school architecture was more transnational in scope. Unlike Protestant missions, which often operated within defined colonial territories, Catholic missions frequently spanned multiple countries, reflecting the global reach of the church.[6] This transnational character was also evident in the architectural practices they employed. The planning and construction of Catholic mission schools often involved a diverse set of actors, including architects, building professionals, and others from the built environment, many of whom were drawn from religious orders or affiliated institutions based in Europe. These actors brought with them design knowledge, construction techniques, and aesthetic sensibilities that influenced the building of schools across different regions of Africa.

Colonial Schools

Following the territorial divisions of the Berlin Conference, colonial governments asserted control not only over land but also over the provision of social infrastructure, including education. As formal governance structures solidified, so too did the colonial administration's involvement in planning and delivering schooling across the continent.[7] By the 1960s, with the advent of independence across much of Africa and the institutional consolidation of religious missions, a gradual delinking of church and mission architecture began to emerge. One example of this shift can be seen in the Baptist Academy building in Obanikoro, Lagos. Although rooted in a religious educational tradition, it was designed through a UNESCO school-building programme in Nigeria.[8] This programme included consultancy workshops hosted at the Architectural Association (AA) in London and was co-led by the architectural partnership Robert Matthew Johnson Marshall (RMJM) alongside local firms such as Godwin and Hopwood Architects, based in Lagos.

The colonial or national contributions to school and educational infrastructure can be traced back to the early twentieth century, particularly in regions like Sierra Leone, the Gold Coast (now Ghana), and the southern areas of the former Niger Coast Protectorate (modern-day Southern Nigeria). These regions benefitted from substantial government investment in educational institutions at all levels, from primary schools to teacher training colleges. Architects involved in these projects often worked across colonial borders. A notable example is the modernist team of Maxwell Fry and Jane Drew, who were responsible for key educational buildings like schools in the Gold Coast (Ghana) and the University of Ibadan in Nigeria. Transnational influence extended beyond architectural firms to impact religious and commercial networks as well.[9] For instance, the British architectural firm Architects Co-Partnership (ACP) played a major role in planning social infrastructure in the newly independent country of Ghana. Their work included designing key facilities in Akosombo, such as community centres, hospitals, and schools, and thus supporting the social needs of the town's residents following the construction of the Akosombo Dam.[10]

As with earlier missionary schools, colonial school architecture was guided by official design standards. The British Building Research Establishment (BRE) developed *Colonial Building*

Figure 3. Achimota College in Ghana, established in 1924, was a landmark institution of the colonial era. It played a central role in expanding access to higher education in West Africa and produced many of the region's early leaders and intellectuals.

Notes – initially for public works before the First World War – which later evolved into the *Overseas Building Notes*.[11] These documents were disseminated to architects working across British colonies to promote uniformity in infrastructural design, including schools.

Symbolically, significant colonial-era school buildings – such as King's College in Lagos and Achimota College in Ghana (fig. 3) – were often located near administrative centres and featured elements like clock towers as a visual identifier of both the institution and the organisational legacy of the colonial school and administration.[12] Even after independence, design practices remained tethered to colonial-era guidelines, with little change to pedagogical models or spatial layouts despite the rise of African leadership in government and education ministries.

Following the Second World War, UNESCO helped to establish educational research centres across Africa. These centres created internationally informed guidelines for school design, many of which were adopted by national ministries of education during the 1960s to 1980s. In Nigeria, the International Development Association (IDA) funded the creation of "model" schools across the country's twelve post–civil war states (fig. 4). This initiative led to the establishment of Federal Government Colleges, designed by the Nigerian firm Ekwueme Associates, one of the country's pioneering Indigenous architectural firms, in collaboration with international consultants, like the British office RMJM.[13]

Private school networks also flourished during this period that pioneered new school design approaches. The "staff schools" attached to universities such as Ibadan and Kumasi were built

Figure 4. The Federal Government College (FGC) in Sokoto, Nigeria, designed by the Indigenous architectural firm Ekwueme Associates, was founded as one of the first "model" schools funded by the International Development Association.

initially to cater for the educational needs of expatriate and Nigerian academic staff. The International School of Ibadan exemplifies this model, designed by the British architectural firm Design Group and following the principles of tropical design. Also, in cities such as Lagos, private entrepreneurs set up the Corona Schools network in Nigeria starting in the 1960s, again initially to educate children of foreign professionals before their transfer to UK preparatory schools.

In East Africa, schooling was less likely to be "free-for-all" in the post–self-rule, independence era. The education model in most of East Africa remained underpinned by missionary educational institutions, and a few elite government and private schools providing education for the middle to upper classes. As with West Africa, prior to self-rule, all schools had grants in aid which helped the running of schools, but missionary and government schools charged nominal fees and expected students to purchase books and uniforms, which meant, for the poor, that education remained out of reach. The mass, "free" educational programmes launched in Nigeria and Ghana did not take place in East Africa, except for the Ujamaa Schools in Tanzania.[14] This changed with the "Education for All" decade declared by UNESCO in the 1970s,[15] where international grants enabled most countries globally to sign up to provide free primary education for all children. Thus, missionary and NGO involvement remained prominent in East Africa, especially where public education funding lagged. In contemporary times, these actors remain instrumental in the donor funding, design, and provision of schools in the region. The Ismaili community, for instance, has played a key role in funding and designing schools in East Africa. The first Aga Khan School in Africa was founded in 1905 in Zanzibar, soon followed in 1918 by a school in Mombasa, Kenya. Aga Khan Schools now operate 200 educational facilities around the Global South. In 2003, the first Aga Khan Academy opened in Mombasa (fig. 5). The academies are high-profile schools that show how modern educational design can be infused with traditional and environmentally appropriate approaches to architecture. The Academy in Mombasa, for example, is influenced by local construction materials, using locally sourced coral stone, and deploys Swahili decorative motifs.[16] It exemplifies the integration of modern educational architecture with traditional and climate-responsive design principles.

Southern Africa had similar structures, yet with the pernicious effect of apartheid, meaning that education was segregated according to skin colour. Schools like Bishops College in Cape Town were reserved for white students, while township schools followed guidelines developed by South Africa's Council for Scientific and Industrial Research (CSIR). At the end of the apartheid era, large donor organisations such as the Urban Foundation funded improved school infrastructure in townships like Port Elizabeth, today Gqeberha. From the late 1960s to the mid-1980s, economic crises and structural adjustment programmes devastated public education funding across Africa. International aid slowed, and many national governments slashed education

Figure 5. The Aga Khan Academy in Mombasa, Kenya. This academy used local construction materials, such as coral stone, and deployed Swahili decorative motifs.

budgets under International Monetary Fund (IMF) and World Bank reforms, leading to the deterioration of school infrastructure and stalled development plans.

By the mid-1990s, in the context of a global economic recovery that included Africa, the "Africa Rising" narrative extended to the emerging architectural practices. South Africa's Wolff Architects gained international acclaim with their Usasazo Secondary School project in Khayelitsha. Francis Kéré's Gando Primary School complex in Burkina Faso pioneered the reintegration of traditional materials and participatory design in rural education infrastructure. Today, there are many Indigenous architectural firms that have achieved international acclaim, including Patrick Waheed Design Consultancy (Nigeria), Design Network's Luyanda Mpahlwa and Wolff Architects (South Africa), Maisha Trust's Tom Vohya and Oku Kanayo (Kenya), and Terrain Architects' Ikko Kobayashi and Fumi Kashimura (Uganda).

The structure and content of educational teaching in Africa has not changed substantially since the reforms of the late 1970s, which introduced the junior and senior secondary school system, along with formalised preschool and kindergarten levels. While senior secondary education included the option for vocational training, the provisions of purpose-built spaces for such training was limited in both design and implementation across African schools. This was largely due to the high costs associated with procuring equipment and training staff, expenses that were rarely met without international assistance. Moreover, vocational education has continued to suffer from a lack of social prestige, with many families and students still placing higher value on more traditional academic pathways. While early childhood education and nutrition programmes have improved through evidence-based initiatives led by the World Bank's Department for International Development (DFID), the infrastructure required to support them – kitchens, dining halls, and school gardens – has been implemented unevenly.[17]

Religion, Health, Education

The raison d'être of Western education has been the liberation of the mind through empirical, neo-religious actions. Arguably, the school, as indicated earlier in this essay, was central to the triumvirate of religion, health, and education. Theories of pedagogy – ranging from early religious proselytism to the liberal educational movements of the 1960s and 1970s – have influenced the trajectory of African education. Thinkers such as Ivan Illich and Paulo Freire, with their critiques of the limitations of Western educational models in the Global South, have provided foundational insights that continue to resonate in policy and academic discourse today.[18]

Yet despite these pedagogical critiques, school *design* has remained relatively untouched. The spatial form of the twenty-first-century African school differs little from the missionary schoolhouse constructed over two centuries ago in coastal towns across the continent. This continuity might be seen as a testament to the durability of the Western education model. But it also reveals the difficulty of synthesising African anthropological understandings of space with inherited colonial design typologies. Earlier pedagogical systems – such as male initiation spaces across many African societies or the fattening ceremonies among the Efik in southeastern Nigeria – were spatially and socially specific. Yet these culturally grounded practices have rarely been reinterpreted or spatially integrated into contemporary educational environments.

A more pressing concern is the mismatch between inherited spatial models and real educational conditions. The standard classroom layout, based on an ideal class size of thirty-five, is often stretched to accommodate over fifty students. Meanwhile, basic considerations like building orientation and environmental performance are frequently ignored. As a result, classrooms are hot, poorly lit, and unusable after dark due to the absence of reliable electricity and sanitation infrastructure. The architectural embodiment of the "African school" remains linked to outdated design norms and standards from the colonial past.

Figure 6. The Green School in Bali is a prominent example of the emerging architectural trend known as "bamboo-tecture". It reflects a broader global movement, seen increasingly across Africa as well, which embraces locally sourced, sustainable materials in building design.

Materials and Methods

As discussed above, the materiality of many contemporary African schools can be traced to the early twentieth-century colonial period's construction practices. This era introduced cement "sandcrete" blocks, tin-metal-asbestos roofing sheets, and glazed aluminium-framed windows. Earlier building forms that had been sourced from local materials like mud or wattle and daub were now being replaced by imported prefabricated structures with steel frames and timber infill panels, and eventually by brick-walled classrooms.

More recently, there has been a tentative return to re-engaging with locally sourced, sustainable materials. Francis Kéré's Gando Primary School complex exemplifies this shift, combining earthen construction with participatory methods.[19] The emerging trend of "bamboo-tecture", inspired by Southeast Asian precedents, is being explored experimentally – for example, the Green School in Bali, featuring The Arc by Elora Hardy, a project shortlisted in 2025 by the Aga Khan Award for Architecture (AKAA) (fig. 6).[20] However, Africa's own full-scale

Figure 7. The Yoruba Heritage Museum in Lagos, Nigeria, is both a cultural landmark and an architectural tribute to Yoruba heritage, one of West Africa's most notable cultures.

"bamboo school" remains elusive. Nonetheless, the exploration of other construction processes began with, again, Kéré's use of traditional material and construction styles in his educational buildings. Mariam Issoufou's mosque conversion, in turn, the Hikma complex in Niger, provides a much-needed example of both building and materials reuse. Importantly, it exemplifies a "community-centred" approach to architecture from conception to construction, uniquely in this case centring on the adaptive reuse of a former mosque to create a library for women, using local workpeople and involving local villagers.[21] Also, Seun Oduwole's storytelling section designed for the Yoruba Heritage Museum powerfully reimagines a traditional educational space within a contemporary architectural language, as an exhibition space for the public, both local and international (fig. 7).[22]

Despite these cases, wide-scale adoption has not occurred. International aid and consultants continue to dominate the discourse around school construction. Bottom-up, community-driven design remains underdeveloped. The intellectual and material autonomy to design educational environments from within – reflecting local knowledge systems and needs – remains a distant dream rather than a reality.

Architectural Inertia

Educational facilities built from the late 1990s through the 2020s reveal an entrenched conservatism in school design across much of Africa. Despite changes in political governance and curriculum reform, school infrastructure has seen minimal innovation. Compared to regions with similar socio-economic challenges – such as Latin America or Southeast Asia – Africa's educational built environment appears largely static.

The curriculum reforms of the 1980s and 1990s, despite promising to reorient pedagogy, did not yield a corresponding transformation in school design. The neoliberal consensus that followed tended to emphasise funding and access, but rarely questioned systems or spatial practices. Although more children now attend school than in previous generations, the spatial and cultural disconnect between education and traditional practices remains significant. Initiation rites and communal forms of learning have largely disappeared, replaced by models that marginalise local forms, materials, and pedagogies. A few innovative projects challenge this norm, but they remain the exception, two exemplars being the AKAA 2025 shortlisted project Startup Lions Campus in Kenya by Kéré and the AKAA-winning Kamanar Secondary School in Senegal by Dawoffice (15th Award Cycle).[23]

The economic crises of the 1980s precipitated the de-nationalisation of school provision. In many countries, this led to the revival of missionary-founded schools – now rebranded as high-status, fee-paying institutions serving the middle and upper classes. While this shift exacerbated educational inequality, it also gave rise to new actors, such as alumni associations, which have played key roles in maintaining older mission schools. In Ghana, for instance, "old students" groups have been crucial in preserving historical coastal schools.

The first decade of the twenty-first century brought renewed interest in community-centred, digitally enabled school models. The "smart school" as an educational hub has gained traction with the spread of mobile computing and internet access. Yet these projects remain largely at the prototype stage and are not widely embedded in national education systems. In Africa, it remains common for architecture studios from the Global North to build schools, but their approaches have evolved. Increasingly, they emphasise collaboration, local materials, and labour. The Rwanda-based MASS Design Group exemplifies this ethos, advocating for community-driven design and sustainable construction practices.[24]

Conclusion

For over two centuries, school design in Africa has undergone significant change, yet a circular logic persists. What began as missionary philanthropy evolved into state-led educational architecture and is now returning to donor-led, often privately run models. In this landscape, it is

Africa's elite who benefit most. While public education is nominally free, the quality of facilities is frequently tied to fees, a circumstance that is deepening socio-economic divides. Elite schools, once limited to colonial flagships like Achimota or King's College, now proliferate in globalised forms with little relation to local culture or climate.

For the majority of African children, public school buildings remain underfunded and unimaginative. They fail to meet the pedagogical and environmental needs of a continent facing enormous educational and ecological challenges. The architects mentioned in this essay show what is possible, but their work is largely one-off and not being replicated on a large scale. Acts of asymmetrical charity alone cannot meet the scale of the task.

The vision of universal, well-designed, and inclusive education articulated in the 1970s remains distant. Yet there is reason for optimism. International networks of architects and educators are engaging with educational design in more thoughtful, culturally grounded ways. Movements like Escuela Nueva in Latin America or the open school models in the United States offer powerful inspiration.[25]

The case studies presented here suggest that young African and global architects – working in contexts of cultural resistance and limited resources – are leading the way in reimagining school design. Their work offers tangible proof that architecture can expand educational possibilities for children across social, economic, religious, and cultural divides. The right to education for all is not only a UN Sustainable Development Goal but a basic human right. Future African schools, if they are to fulfil this promise, must integrate local knowledge, environmental sustainability, and cultural specificity at every level of design and delivery.

---

1   For more on the effect of missionaries in Africa and elsewhere in the Global South, see Michael Twaddle, *Christian Missionaries and the State in the Third World*, ed. Holger Bernt Hansen and Michael Twaddle (London: Boydell and Brewer, 2002).

2   On this, see the Society of Jesus website, https://www.jesuits.africa/jcam-provinces/, and the booklet on the Holy Ghost Mission congregations, *Navrongo Cathedral: The Merge of Two Cultures*, https://craterre.hypotheses.org/files/2017/05/7393_Navrongo_cathedral.pdf.

3   J. F. A. Ajayi, *Christian Missions in Nigeria 1841-1891: The Making of a New Elite* (London: Longmans, 1965); E. A. Ayandele, *The Missionary Impact on Modern Nigeria, 1842-1914: A Political and Social Analysis* (London: Longmans, 1966); A. Babs Fafunwa, *History of Education in Nigeria* (London: Allen and Unwin, 1974); Magnus Bassey, *Mission Rivalry and Educational Expansion in Nigeria, 1885-1945* (New York: Edwin Mellen Press, 1999); Colin Sarah, *How Methodist Missionary Worldwide Brought Education to Nigeria and the Entire Africa* (Summitville, NY: Moonlight Press, 2015).

4   Ola Uduku, *Learning Spaces in Africa: Critical Histories to 21st Century Challenges and Change* (London: Routledge, 2018), p. 53; Hope Masterton Waddell, *Twenty-Nine Years in the West Indies and Central Africa: A Review of Missionary Work and Adventure, 1829-1858* (London: Nelson, 1863); and Ola Uduku, "The Colonial Face of Educational Space", in *White Papers, Black Marks: Architecture, Race, Culture*, ed. Lesley Naa Norle Lokko (London: Athlone Press, 2000).

5   For more on Fry and Drew's school projects in Ghana, see Iain Jackson and Jessica Holland, *The Architecture of Edwin Maxwell Fry and Jane Drew: Twentieth Century Architecture, Pioneer Modernism and the Tropics* (London: Routledge, 2014).

6   For more on the spread of Christian Missions across Africa, see Norman Etherington, "The History of Christian Missions to Africa", *Oxford Research Encyclopaedia of African History*, 30 October 2019, https://oxfordre.com/africanhistory/view/10.1093/acrefore/9780190277734.001.0001/acrefore-9780190277734-e-56.

7   Uduku, *Learning Spaces in Africa*, p. 10.

8   Ola Uduku, "The Nigerian 'Unity Schools' Project: A UNESCO-IDA School Building Program in Africa", in *Designing Schools: Space, Place and Pedagogy*, ed. Kate Darian-Smith and Julie Willis (London: Routledge, 2017).

9   Jackson and Holland, *The Architecture of Edwin Maxwell Fry and Jane Drew*.

10 See Iain Jackson, Ola Uduku, Irene Appeaning Addo, and Rexford Assasie Opong, "The Volta River Project: Planning, Housing and Resettlement in Ghana, 1950-1965", *Journal of Architecture* 24, no. 4 (2019), pp. 512-48.

11 Uduku, *Learning Spaces in Africa*, p. 10.

12 Ibid., p. 8.

13 Ibid., pp. 60-61.

14 Edgar Faure et al., *Learning to Be: The World of Education Today and Tomorrow* (Paris and London: UNESCO Publishing, 1972); UNESCO, "The Right to Primary Education Free of Charge for All: Ensuring Compliance with International Obligations", 2008, https://www.right-to-education.org/sites/right-to-education.org/files/resource-attachments/UNESCO_Right_Primary_Education_Free_2008_en_fr.pdf; and UNESCO, "World Declaration on Education for All and Framework for Action to Meet Basic Learning Needs", 1990, https://unesdoc.unesco.org/ark:/48223/pf0000127583.

15 See Robert W. Strayer, "The Making of Mission Schools in Kenya: A Microcosmic Perspective", *Comparative Education Review* 17, no. 3 (1973), pp. 313-30; on Tanzanian education, see Julius Nyerere, "Education for Self-Reliance", in *Freedom and Socialism: A Selection from Writings and Speeches, 1965-67* (Dar es Salaam: Oxford University Press, 1968); and Thomas Molony, *Nyerere: The Early Years* (London: James Currey, 2015).

16 Farhan Karim, "A Commitment to Excellence: Designing the Aga Khan Academies", *Aga Khan Academies*, https://www.agakhanacademies.org/general/commitment-excellence-designing-aga-khan-academies.

17 See, for example, Ola Uduku, "School Building Design for Feeding Programmes and Community Outreach: Insights for Ghana and South Africa", *International Journal of Educational Development* 31 (2011), pp. 59-66; and Kerina Tull and Róisín Plunkett, "School Feeding Interventions in Humanitarian Responses", 24 August 2018, https://assets.publishing.service.gov.uk/media/5be5b217ed915d6a0d6f6fcf/360_School_Feeding_Interventions_in_Humanitarian_Responses.pdf.

18 See Ivan Illich, *Deschooling Society* (New York: Harper and Row, 1971); Paulo Freire, *Pedagogy of the Oppressed* (New York: Continuum, 1968).

19 Kéré Architecture, "Gando Primary School", https://www.kerearchitecture.com/work/building/gando-primary-school-3.

20 On the Green School, see https://ibuku.com/project/heart-of-school-at-green-school/; and Brigitte Shim, "2010 On Site Review Report", https://escolaecofeliz.wordpress.com/wp-content/uploads/2016/04/green-school-bali.pdf.

21 See "Customs Made: Hikma Religious and Secular Complex in Dandaji, Niger by Atelier Masōmī", *Architectural Review*, 20 March 2020, https://www.architectural-review.com/w-awards/customs-made-hikma-religious-and-secular-complex-in-dandaji-niger-by-atelier-masomi; and Holcim Foundation Awards, "Hikma Complex", 2018, https://awards.holcimfoundation.org/past-winners/hikma-complex.

22 Saeed Kamali Dehghan, "Noisy, Performative and Unapologetically Non-European: Nigeria Welcomes a Museum Like No Other", *The Guardian*, 30 April 2024, https://www.theguardian.com/global-development/2024/apr/30/john-randle-centre-yoruba-culture-lagos-nigeria; and Philip Hughes, *Storytelling Exhibitions: Identity, Truth and Wonder* (London: Bloomsbury, 2021).

23 See "Campus Startup Lions", https://the.akdn/en/how-we-work/our-agencies/aga-khan-trust-culture/akaa/campus-startup-lions; and "Kamanar School", https://the.akdn/en/how-we-work/our-agencies/aga-khan-trust-culture/akaa/kamanar-secondary-school.

24 See, for example, MASS Design Group, "Ilima Primary School", https://massdesigngroup.org/work/design/ilima-primary-school.

25 See Asbel López, "Colombia Exports Its New School Blueprint", *The UNESCO Courier* 52, no. 6 (1999), pp. 14-16, https://unesdoc.unesco.org/ark:/48223/pf0000116246; and Emily Gustafsson-Wright and Eileen McGivney, "Fundación Escuela Nueva: Changing the Way Children Learn from Colombia to Southeast Asia", *Brookings*, 23 April 2014, https://www.brookings.edu/articles/fundacion-escuela-nueva-changing-the-way-children-learn-from-colombia-to-southeast-asia/.

Building Education in Africa

Tubi Otitooluwa, Justicia C. T. Kiconco, Timothy Latim, and Jonathan Kplorla Agbeh

Introduction

Architecture is a powerful force in shaping national identity, educational development, and institutional authority across Africa. The four projects featured in this section – the Senate Building at the University of Lagos (UNILAG) in Lagos, Nigeria, the IWACU Centre in Kigali, Rwanda, the Faculty of Technology at Makerere University in Kampala, Uganda, and the Great Hall at Kwame Nkrumah University of Science and Technology (KNUST) in Kumasi, Ghana – all exemplify how architecture responds to societal needs and cultural contexts, including religion, nationhood, and ethnicity.

UNILAG's Senate Building, conceived in a period of national growth, embodies a commitment to professional development and user-driven design. Similarly, IWACU's transformation from a cooperative hub to an entrepreneurship institute balances functionality with community values. At Makerere University, the Faculty of Technology laid the foundation for training Uganda's first engineers, thus reinforcing architecture's role in advancing national expertise. KNUST's Great Hall, shaped by the intersection of colonial-era planning and post-independence aspirations, serves both as a ceremonial space and as a symbol of institutional growth.

Despite their distinct architectural languages and historical contexts, these buildings share a common theme: they transcend mere function to express national ambition, cultural heritage, and adaptive design. This study examines how these institutions illustrate the shifting role of architecture in African educational and institutional landscapes, analysing their design principles, socio-political influences, and lasting impact on the respective communities.

Senate Building, University of Lagos, Nigeria
Tubi Otitooluwa

Location: Lagos, Nigeria
Date: 1985
Architects: James Cubitt and Partners (now James Cubitt Architects)

Standing at just over 50 metres tall with twelve floors, the Senate Building at the University of Lagos holds the distinction of being Nigeria's tallest occupied university building. Completed in the 1960s, it serves as the administrative nucleus of one of Nigeria's first post-independence universities, born from the recommendations of the 1960 Ashby Commission. This pivotal report assessed Nigeria's educational infrastructure requirements as a newly independent nation, emphasising the urgent role of universities in training a skilled workforce to replace expatriates and drive national development. Before independence, Nigeria's higher education relied on two institutions: Yaba College of Technology (1947) and University College Ibadan (UCI, 1948).

The Senate Building, University of Lagos, designed by James Cubitt and Partners. This striking modernist structure serves as both an administrative hub and an architectural landmark.

While these institutions laid critical groundwork, their limited capacity became glaring after 1960, as Nigeria's population of 45 million increasingly viewed education as a pathway to empowerment.

The Ashby Commission exposed systemic shortcomings, notably the absence of programmes in fields vital to nation-building. In response, the Nigerian government launched four new universities in the 1960s: University of Nigeria Nsukka; University of Ife (now Obafemi Awolowo University); Ahmadu Bello University Zaria; and University of Lagos. Geographically, these institutions were strategically distributed to serve Nigeria's major regions. However, the University of Lagos disrupted this balance, for the southwest already hosted the UCI (now the University of Ibadan). This anomaly reflected Lagos's dual role as administrative and commercial capital.

The development of the University of Lagos came during the oil boom in Nigeria. The then military ruler General Yakubu Gowon (in power from 1966 to 1975) was famously believed to have said: "money is not our problem, but how to spend it."[1] Situated in Lagos, the commercial capital and later the administrative capital of the country, the institution was conceived as both the pride and production centre for the professionals who would participate in the development of the nation.

All of these projects can be seen in the magnitude of investment that went into the first phase of infrastructural development on the campus. Although the Senate Building wasn't a part of the first phase, it followed the same theme. Conceived in the late 1970s, the need arose due to the university's rapid growth. It is one of the structures that benefited from the end-user brief development process and the standard guide for universities, a standard developed by the National University Commission (NUC) in 1977 to guide the design and construction of educational infrastructure. The document localised development in tropical modernism that was propagated by the Architectural Association (AA), emphasising the requirements for thermal comfort and daylighting by natural means, taking the climate, wind, and rainfall context of each location into account. These two factors were to become the anchor for the design.

The designers James Cubitt and Partners (now James Cubitt Architects) were well acquainted with Nigeria and its educational facilities. They had completed their first project in the country in 1954 (Elder Dempster Head Office, Marina) and later developed the master plan for the University of Nigeria Nsukka, as well as several buildings at the University of Ife. Their experience established a familiarity with working alongside local clients. For this project, the client's brief was straightforward: consolidate all administrative functions into one building. The architects had the freedom to choose between a sprawling layout or a tower, but the design had to incorporate the senate chambers. The result – a twelve-storey tower – was an unconventional choice for an educational institution at the time.

The north facade of the Senate Building, University of Lagos. The architects Cubitt and Partners adopted a wrap-around, double-skin facade for the structure.

Relief on the entrance wall by the architects which represents a map of patterns across Nigeria

The structure allows for interactions between buildings thanks to a network of thoroughfares within its double-volume belly, so as to connect existing master plan functions. Access points sit just off these paths, maintaining continuity. Approaching the building, its double-height undercroft and honeycomb slabs create an imposing presence. Yet, its open-access design originally projected a sense of approachability – a "carrot-and-stick" balance for a structure considered to be the seat of power. That changed in 2019 with the addition of an access-controlled lobby at the central stairs and lift, formalising restrictions that had long existed, as three other entrances had been locked for years. While the idea of a zero-barrier administrative building has symbolic appeal, it did not reflect reality. The 1990s and early 2000s saw waves of student unrest, riots, and civil disobedience, often targeting authorities. With campuses as epicentres of protest, an unrestricted administrative building was a soft target. In Nigeria's hierarchical society, a clear division between leadership and those being led remains deeply ingrained.

Additionally, embracing naturally cooled spaces is another area of interest. We can safely say that the idea was not entirely foreign, for it has been adopted in the NUC design standards for university buildings. James Cubitt and Partners adopted a wrap-around, double-skin facade for this structure, made from an external facade of egg-crate hollow concrete measuring 90 by 90 by 60 centimetres and a matching grid storefront steel frame glazing with casement window inserts, both facades separated by a 120-centimetre-wide concrete floor. However, due to security concerns and the need for access restriction to sensitive spaces within the building,

Public space at the foot of the Senate Building

the boundary walkways have been gated at different points on each level, depending on which function is indoors, and air-conditioning lines the space between the two facades.[2] The preference for air-conditioning is not peculiar to this building, sometimes seen as a statement of class, other times just as an absolute necessity due to the low level of indoor comfort.

Finally, I asked a security man who has worked at the Senate Building for over two decades about his opinion of a motif rendered on a feature wall at the entrance. He did not care about a pattern on the wall. As a student at the University of Lagos, I had always wondered about the motif and the patterns represented all over the building through the mosaic tiling of the eggcrate facade. The foreigners' attempt at homage to native patterns and symbols may have been largely ignored here, but this is perhaps a symptom of something deeper, a departure from the appreciation of visual art as an integral part of our traditional expression and storytelling.

In recent years, students and professors from the university's Department of Arts have been installing paintings on the fair-faced concrete of the brutalist architecture within the administrative zone. This exercise elevates the structures and is also well received. We may consider this a slight nod to the motif work on the Senate Building by James Cubitt and Partners and those who came before.

IWACU Centre
Justicia C. T. Kiconco

Location: Kabusunzu Hill, Kigali, Rwanda
Date: 1984
Architects: Unknown

In Kigali's transforming architectural scene, there is a trend of refurbishing older structures or integrating modern technologies to revive historical designs. Among the few enduring buildings from the 1980s, the IWACU Centre stands out for maintaining its original material choices and design, while seamlessly adapting to new functions. The centre exemplifies a modernist approach that harmonises built forms with the natural topography. Its master plan fosters communal learning through interconnected spaces, outdoor pockets, and covered walkways, creating an interactive and inclusive environment.[3] The modular design – characterised by repetitive geometric elements, curved roofs, and expansive openings – achieves a balance between aesthetic appeal and functional adaptability.[4] As Kigali's architectural landscape continues to develop, the IWACU Centre serves as a valuable reference for designing durable and adaptable structures that stand the test of time.

Originally a cooperative training facility, the IWACU Centre has transformed into an entrepreneurship school, demonstrating its capacity to support changing pedagogical models. With self-sustaining facilities, a strong emphasis on passive environmental design, and the integration of local cultural influences, it remains relevant in discussions on adaptive reuse, sustainability, and the role of architecture in shaping educational experiences.[5]

The centre's architecture follows the design principles of tropical educational institutions from the 1980s, which are distinguished by functional planning and modular repetition. Expansive openings seamlessly connect indoor and outdoor spaces, enhancing both ventilation and spatial fluidity.[6] At the same time, the building is rooted in Rwandan topography and culture, adapting to Kabusunzu Hill's natural contours through integrated pathways and communal breakout spaces. Its curved roofs and staggered brick blocks introduce a regional dimension to modernist aesthetics, contrasting with the rectilinear forms typical of similar institutions.

Beyond its architectural merit, the IWACU Centre exemplifies lasting durability, adapting over time while reflecting postcolonial collaboration. Established through a partnership between the Rwandan and Swiss governments, it embodies a commitment to self-reliance through education and cooperation.[7] The name "Iwacu" (meaning "our home") underscores the centre's emphasis on local empowerment and ownership, steering away from colonial architectural impositions.

The IWACU is one of the few educational buildings from the 1980s that still remains, notable for preserving its original material palette and design. It stands as a testament to durable, adaptable architecture.

Originally a cooperative training facility, the IWACU has been transformed into an entrepreneurship school. There is a strong emphasis on the integration of local cultural influences and adaptive reuse.

The master plan is structured around a network of interconnected buildings, strategically positioned to enhance accessibility while preserving the site's natural topography. Winding pathways weave through landscaped courtyards that serve as both circulation routes and social gathering spaces, encouraging interaction among users. These courtyards, punctuated by green spaces and shaded walkways, reinforce the sense of openness and connectivity that defines the centre's spatial organisation. The built environment is characterised by a modular design approach, with repeated geometric elements that create a rhythmic architectural language.[8] Staggered brick blocks, exposed concrete, and curved roof structures contribute to the centre's visual identity and to its environmental responsiveness. Expansive openings and perforated facades promote natural ventilation and daylight penetration, reducing the reliance on artificial systems and enhancing thermal comfort at the same time. The deliberate orientation of the buildings optimises airflow, ensuring passive cooling across different functional areas.[9]

Entrances are carefully integrated into the sloping terrain, with circulation pathways guiding movement between levels in a seamless transition. Covered walkways and open-air corridors link key facilities, including training studios, a multi-purpose hall, lodging accommodations, and a restaurant. These pathways not only facilitate movement but also frame views of the surrounding landscape, reinforcing the centre's relationship with its environment.[10]

The entrances of the IWACU are carefully integrated into the sloping terrain, with circulation pathways that guide movement naturally between different levels.

Internally, the spatial configuration prioritises openness and flexibility. Wide verandas and the breakout spaces give rise to an informal learning atmosphere, encouraging collaboration. Stairs with minimalist handrails provide subtle vertical transitions, maintaining visual continuity between levels. The repetition of modular blocks, interspersed with open spaces, ensures a balanced interplay between built form and nature. The design balances global modernist influences, such as concrete and glass, with local cultural and environmental contexts, incorporating outdoor courtyards and pathways. Although self-sustainable facilities reflect global functionalist trends, they are uniquely tailored to Rwanda's socio-economic realities.

The centre's transition from a cooperative training facility to an entrepreneurship school highlights its shifting pedagogical focus towards business and skill development. Its modular design fosters collaborative learning, with the breakout spaces and courtyards enhancing interaction and engagement.[11]

Faculty of Technology, Makerere University
Timothy Latim

Location: Kampala, Uganda
Date: 1972
Architects: Chudha and Pawa Architects

In 1960, Uganda's Parliament was inaugurated, with its design selected through a Commonwealth-wide architectural competition won by Peatfield & Bodgener Architects.[12] Earlier, in 1954, the Uganda Museum had been completed by Ernst May, and in 1966, Peatfield & Bodgener also designed the National Bank of Uganda. Many of Uganda's iconic architectural landmarks were built at a time when the country had few, if any, locally trained architects. As a result, the narrative of Ugandan architecture was shaped largely by foreign designers. Before 1970, Ugandans wishing to study architecture had to leave the country, with the nearest architecture school located in Nairobi, at what was then the University of East Africa (UEA). The UEA comprised three institutions, one each in Uganda, Kenya, and Tanzania.[13] After the separation of the University of East Africa, its three institutions became Makerere University (Uganda), University of Nairobi (Kenya), and University of Dar-es-salaam (Tanzania). Following the split, each East African nation developed its own universities with programmes in humanities, medicine, and technology to support their growing nations. It wasn't until 1972, with the completion of the Faculty of Technology, that Uganda began training its own architects, marking a pivotal moment in the country's architectural identity.

Construction of the Faculty of Technology at Makerere University, designed by Chudha and Pawa Architects (Joginder Singh Chudha and Harpal Singh Pawa), commenced in 1969. The firm, which operated across Uganda and Kenya during this period, was also responsible for other notable projects, such as Nairobi's Pan African House (now Sanlam House). Historian Douglas Kiereini notes that the Pan African House was designed in a Georgian style to "proclaim the permanence and 'lofty ideals' of British rule in Kenya", reflecting colonial aspirations through classical European aesthetics.[14] This architecture stands in stark contrast to the Faculty of Technology, whose design influences remain unclear. Unlike the Pan African House's overt colonial symbolism, the Makerere project, initiated seven years after Uganda's independence (1962), may have embraced modernist principles suited to the nation's postcolonial identity, though records of the firm's design ethos are ambiguous. Chudha and Pawa Architects dissolved in 1972, shortly after construction of the Faculty of Technology began. Joginder Singh Chudha continued to practise under a new name, Chudha International, as published in the *Kenya Gazette* in 1972.[15]

The design of the Faculty of Technology reveals a functional and pragmatic design philosophy. It is accessed via a reinforced-concrete bridge supported by two columns, which creates

The Faculty of Technology is accessed via a reinforced-concrete bridge supported by two columns.

a sense of detachment from the site. The steep slope beneath the building accentuates its prominence, further emphasised by the contrast between the fair-faced concrete of the main structure and the partially vegetated retaining walls. This enhances the architecture's striking visual presence. The design blurs the distinction between the concrete's structural role and its use as an envelope, lending it the appearance of an active ruin.

The structural grid is peculiar, with four columns spaced a metre apart forming a grid point. The columns are connected by beams a metre deep, spanning 6 metres in total. The envelope of the building alternates between three main materials: a playful honeycomb design, a glass facade that is protected by protruding concrete solar shades, and concrete blocks. The glass is

The Faculty of Technology features a distinctive structural grid, with clusters of four columns spaced a metre apart at each grid point. The columns are connected by metre-deep beams spanning 6 metres in total.

recessed deeply behind the solar shades, creating the illusion of it having few windows or doors, and this adds to the appearance of a monolithic structure. The columns and beams in their rhythmic procession are being used to playfully define the solids and voids through which light and air permeate the building.

The Faculty of Technology project deeply embodies the collaboration between architecture and engineering, with all its main components exposed and forming a part of the spatial experience. It would seem as if the architect were pre-empting future students to consider the importance of the symbiotic relationship between the different construction consultants and how they would interrelate to make a whole, which is interesting because over the years the building has been a popular class assignment, where students are asked to draw and critique different parts of it.

Brutalism has largely faded from prominence at the university, with only one other structure, a 1960s-era building designed by Peatfield & Bodgener, sharing its stark aesthetic. Most newer architectural projects conceal structural elements within their walls, aligning with contemporary design trends seen nationwide. While architects and engineers admire the brutalist structure for its clarity of materiality and construction, public opinion remains divided. A visiting student encapsulated this ambivalence, remarking, "this building has never been completed since the 1970s". Today, it stands as a relic of the past: isolated yet instructive, its lessons in raw materiality and form frozen in time, like a wise teacher without students.

The building envelope alternates between three distinct materials: a playful honeycomb screen, a glass facade shielded by protruding concrete solar shades, and solid concrete blockwork.

External view of the Great Hall at Kwame Nkrumah University of Science and Technology (KNUST), a landmark space for academic ceremonies, cultural events, and public gatherings

The Great Hall, Kwame Nkrumah University of Science and Technology (KNUST): A Landmark at the Intersection of Architectural and Political History

Jonathan Kplorla Agbeh

Location: Kumasi, Ghana
Date: 1967
Architects: Gerlach and Gillies-Reyburn

The Great Hall of Kwame Nkrumah University of Science and Technology (KNUST) stands as an exception in the university's architectural and political history. Unlike many of the institution's other structures, which shifted in design and construction influence due to Ghana's evolving post-independence geopolitical stance, the Great Hall presents an architectural anomaly. The university's master plan was initially developed by the British architects James Cubitt and Kenneth Scott, and then later taken over by Yugoslavian architects associated with the Non-Aligned Movement. However, the Great Hall's design was ultimately commissioned from the Danish architect Max Gerlach and the Englishman David Gillies-Reyburn instead. Their selection raises a key question: Why did architects outside the original British-led master plan design the Great Hall? This essay examines how and why the Great Hall remained an exception in the

Main foyer of the Great Hall, serving as its principal transition space

broader architectural transition of KNUST and what its design reveals about the shifting influences on the university's built environment.

In 1951, the then Kumasi College of Science, Technology, and Arts – now KNUST – was formally established through an ordinance, following recommendations from the Elliott Commission six years earlier.[16] The British colonial administration tasked the English architects James Cubitt and Kenneth Scott with developing a modernist master plan that divided the university's development into five phases, with buildings aligned on a north–south axis to optimise functionality and environmental responsiveness.

However, Ghana's independence in 1957 altered KNUST's development trajectory. Seeking to break colonial ties, President Kwame Nkrumah positioned the country within the Non-Aligned Movement. This political realignment led to the dismissal of Cubitt and Scott by 1958, as Nkrumah looked to other partners for the university's continued growth. It followed that the new phase of KNUST's construction was shaped by the Yugoslav architects Nikša Ciko and

Mira Marasović, who were brought in under Ghana's new ties with socialist Eastern Europe.[17] Their involvement marked a radical shift in the university's architectural direction, with structures taking on a more monumental, function-driven aesthetic reflective of socialist modernism.

Why, then, was the Great Hall commissioned outside this broader transition? Several factors may explain this paradox. First, while the broader architectural shift was motivated by political ideology, practical considerations could have played a role. The Great Hall, as a major public and ceremonial space, may have required expertise that the Yugoslav team lacked at the time. Gerlach and Gillies-Reyburn had prior experience designing institutional and civic spaces, making them suitable candidates for a hall intended to be the centrepiece of university life.

Another explanation could be continuity. Despite the dismissal of Cubitt and Scott, the core principles of their master plan remained in place. The Great Hall was intended to occupy a central, elevated position on campus, forming part of a ceremonial quadrangle alongside the library and parade grounds.[18] Given this continuity, the administration may have sought architects who could work within the existing spatial framework rather than introduce an entirely new aesthetic.

The design proposed by Gerlach and Gillies-Reyburn included a 1,600-seat auditorium, a chapel, a theatre, and an obelisk – although only the multi-purpose hall was ultimately built.[19]

Layout plan showing the central area around the Great Hall

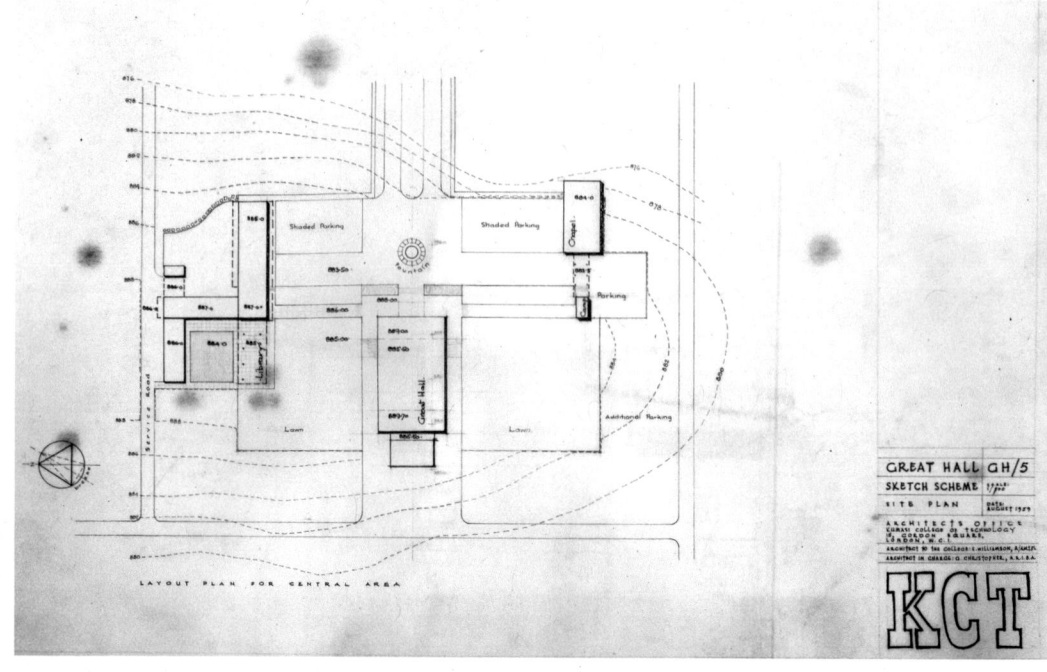

Architecturally, the structure maintains a balance between grandeur and functionality. The hall's neatly defined facade, punctuated by vertical windows, allows ample natural light, while preserving its monumental presence. Its reinforced-concrete frame and cantilevered roof provide both durability and aesthetic refinement, contributing to its distinctive architectural identity.

The Great Hall's role extends beyond its physical form; it is a symbol of resilience and adaptation within KNUST's evolving landscape. Its survival as a project from neither the British nor the Non-Aligned architects reflects the university's ability to navigate political shifts while also maintaining continuity in its built environment. Over the decades, the hall has hosted significant academic, cultural, and political events, solidifying its place as the university's ceremonial heart.

Indeed, the Great Hall of KNUST occupies a unique space in the university's architectural and political history. While most of the university's structures evolved under the shifting influence of British modernism and Yugoslav socialist architecture, the Great Hall emerged as an

Hand-rendered aerial view of the Great Hall, library, chapel, and obelisk quadrangle

exception – designed instead by architects outside both movements. This paradox raises important questions about the intersection of politics, design, and institutional legacy. As KNUST continues to grow, the Great Hall remains not just a physical landmark but a testament to the complexities of architectural continuity amid geopolitical change. Its existence and enduring relevance highlight how architecture, even within politically charged environments, can in fact serve as a bridge between eras, rather than a casualty of ideological shifts.

Comparison and Contrast

Across the Senate Building at the University of Lagos, the IWACU Centre, the Faculty of Technology at Makerere University, and the Great Hall at KNUST, architecture emerges as a tool for societal transformation, reflecting cultural values, historical contexts, and functional demands. Each structure embodies a response to its nation's developmental aspirations, whether through fostering governance and administrative efficiency (UNILAG Senate Building), supporting community-based entrepreneurship (IWACU Centre), shaping engineering and architectural education (Makerere Faculty of Technology), or facilitating political and academic discourse (Great Hall at KNUST). Despite differences in form and scale, all four projects prioritise adaptability, reflecting the evolving needs of their institutions and communities.

However, their architectural expressions and contextual influences vary. The Senate Building and Makerere's Faculty of Technology share a modernist, pragmatic approach, employing reinforced concrete and functionalist design. Yet, while UNILAG's tower symbolises centralised authority and institutional power, Makerere's Faculty of Technology integrates structure and learning, exposing its construction as a teaching tool. In contrast, the IWACU Centre's modular, climate-responsive design merges modernist elements with vernacular influences, creating an open, community-driven environment. Similarly, the Great Hall at KNUST, though modernist in style, incorporates Ghanaian artistic motifs and serves as a cultural landmark, fostering political and social engagement.

Ultimately, these four structures demonstrate how architecture shapes and is shaped by societal needs, cultural identities, and functional imperatives. Whether through the monumental symbolism of the Senate Building, the pedagogical integration of the Faculty of Technology, the community engagement of the IWACU Centre, or the civic and cultural significance of the Great Hall, each case underscores the diverse yet interconnected roles of architecture in Africa's educational and institutional landscapes.

The architectural narratives of these four buildings illustrate the intersection of function, culture, and identity in shaping built environments across Africa. Each structure serves as more than just a physical space; they all embody the aspirations, histories, and evolving needs of their respective societies. Whether through IWACU's integration with its landscape, the Great Hall's role as a centre of discourse, the Makerere Faculty of Technology's cultivation of engineering excellence, or the UNILAG Senate Building's reflection of institutional authority and accessibility, these structures demonstrate how architecture not only adapts to its context but actively influences it. They stand as enduring testaments to the dialogue between tradition and modernity, reflecting how built forms continue to evolve in response to changing cultural and societal landscapes.

1. Colin Legum, "Spending the Oil Money: A Problem, but the Better One to Have", *The New York Times*, 16 March 1975, Section E, p. 3.
2. Tubi Otitooluwa, "Senate House, University of Lagos", in *Modernism in Africa: The Architecture of Angola, Ghana, Mozambique, Nigeria, Rwanda, South Africa, Sudan, Tanzania, Uganda*, ed. Uta Pottgiesser and Ana Tostões (Basel: Birkhäuser, 2024), p. 269.
3. Kim De Raedt, "Between 'True Believers' and Operational Experts: UNESCO Architects and School Building in Post-Colonial Africa", *The Journal of Architecture* 19, no. 1 (2014), pp. 19–42.
4. Emmanuella Ama Codjoe and Justicia Caesaria Tegyeka Kiconco, "Reflections on the Impact of Tropical Modernism on African Primary Schools: A Comparison of Two Schools in Sub-Saharan Africa", *Docomomo Journal* 69 (2023), pp. 52–60.
5. Charl Wolhuter, *Education in East and Central Africa*, vol. 16 (London: Bloomsbury Publishing, 2014).
6. Codjoe and Kiconco, "Reflections on the Impact of Tropical Modernism on African Primary Schools", pp. 52–60.
7. Ola Uduku, *Learning Spaces in Africa: Critical Histories to 21st Century Challenges and Change* (London: Routledge, 2018).
8. Wolhuter, *Education in East and Central Africa*.
9. De Raedt, "Between 'True Believers' and Operational Experts", pp. 19–42.
10. Ibid.
11. Uduku, *Learning Spaces in Africa*.
12. Peatfield and Bodgener Architects, "Registered Chartered Architects", 2025, https://pbarch.org.
13. Mark Olweny, "Foreign and the Local in Architectural Education in Late Colonial and Post-Independence East Africa", *ABE Journal* 22 (2023).
14. Douglas Kiereini, "A Rich History Earns Pan African House Place as National Monument", *Business Daily*, 2 March 2017, https://www.businessdailyafrica.com/bd/lifestyle/society/a-rich-history-earns-pan-african-house-place-as-national-monument-2141862.
15. Republic of Kenya, *Kenya Gazette*, 10 November 1972, 53rd edition.
16. Onassis Lartey and Alexander Boakye Marful, "Campus Planning and Architecture: A Comparative Study of Kwame Nkrumah University of Science and Technology (KNUST) and University of Ghana (LEGON)", *Preprints* (June 2021).
17. Mojca Smode Cvitanović, "Tracing the Non-Aligned Architecture: Environments of Technical Cooperation and the Work of Croatian Architects in Kumasi, Ghana (1961–1970)", *Histories of Postwar Architecture* 3, no. 6 (2020), pp. 34–67.
18. Lartey and Marful, "Campus Planning and Architecture".
19. Timothy Latim and Jonathan Kplorla Agbeh, "Rukurato Hall, Banyoro, Uganda and the Great Hall, KNUST, Ghana: Two Case Studies from Africa", *Docomomo Journal* 69 (2023), pp. 61–69.

Hybrid Rhythms: Alioune Diop University Teaching and Research Unit

Deen Sharp

Figure 1. Designed by IDOM, the Alioune Diop University Teaching and Research Unit in Bambey, Senegal, features a generous canopy that offers vital shade in a notoriously hot region.

The Alioune Diop University Teaching and Research Unit in Bambey, Senegal, invites its users into the building with the offer of shade (fig. 1). Inspired by the practice of locals waiting and socialising under trees, thin metal trunks with irregular V-shaped branches support a large external roof that provides protection from the unforgiving sun. Temperatures can reach over 40 degrees centigrade in this arid region of the country. Students socialise as they wait for their classes in the building's cool embrace. The welcoming northern facade of the building is juxtaposed with a formidable solar barrier on its southern face. Triangular perforations puncture the wall to ensure that the sun is blocked, while the air is encouraged to pass through the building, creating natural ventilation. This massive yet delicate wall, with the constant repetition of its hollow concrete pieces, embodies the late Senegalese President Léopold Sédar Senghor's poetic vision of an architectural style rooted in "asymmetrical parallelism", emphasising "a diversified repetition of rhythm in time and space", as a guiding design principle.[1] The imposing southern wall faces an area planted with local fauna and flora that the building's rainwater and filtered wastewater flow into. It results in a vegetated space that dramatically transforms the building with the seasons, creating a dense green area in the rainy season that turns gradually brown, only to once again bloom anew (fig. 2).

Figure 2. Students playing basketball beside the southern wall of the Alioune Diop University Teaching and Research Unit

"For us what was important was to develop a building that responded to the challenges of the site, and above all, [was] an adaptation to the local context," explained the architect Federico Pardos Auber.[2] The Spanish architectural firm IDOM designed the Alioune Diop University Teaching and Research Unit to capture the bold aspirations of a young, fast-growing institution and region. Through its design, the structure builds on the legacy of post-independence universities in Senegal, while pushing forward global approaches to architecture that are responsive to both climate and context in a resource-constrained setting. IDOM sought to create a building that makes a bold architectural statement, serving as an aspirational symbol for a nationally significant university. To achieve this, the architects unified diverse elements that are organised into five subunits – the 500-seat lecture hall, thirteen classrooms, three laboratories, ten lecturers' offices, and two meeting rooms – to create a single, cohesive whole (fig. 3). This singular form is not a solid block but rather a carefully orchestrated composition of spatial connections with porous boundaries. The design establishes an intricate, environmentally responsive set of relationships, creating a dynamic interplay between the building's in-between spaces, interiors and exteriors, and solids and voids. This responsiveness is evident in how the structure manages solar exposure, promotes natural ventilation, incorporates shading, and optimises water use, allowing it to distinguish itself while coexisting harmoniously with the environmental and social ecology of its surroundings (fig. 4).

Hybrid Space: Bambey and the Diourbel Region
The university is set in the Diourbel Region of Senegal, 5 kilometres from the town of Bambey, which lies about 120 kilometres east of the capital, Dakar, along the historic Dakar–Bamako railway line. Home to approximately 40,000 inhabitants, Bambey serves as a hybrid space where Senegal's rural hinterlands meet the urbanised coastal areas. Diourbel, positioned at the intersection of pastoral traditions and rapid urbanisation, has experienced a shifting socio-economic landscape driven by the growing presence of university students, professionals, and small business owners. This establishment of Alioune Diop University in 2007, building on existing institutions, has accelerated this transformation, attracting a dynamic mix of intellectuals, scientists, political and social activists, and entrepreneurs, from urban centres into the heart of the hinterlands. Bambey, and its environs, is now a hybrid rural-urban space, where the rhythms of agricultural life harmonise with the energy of political discourse and academic pursuits, fostering a rich coexistence and interplay of diverse and professional identities.

Bambey's position as a hybrid space has unsurprisingly made it a focal point for important debates on the tension between the particular and the universal, tradition and transformation, and sustainability and growth. Fama Diagne Sène, director of the library at Alioune Diop

Figure 3. Lecture hall at the Alioune Diop University Teaching and Research Unit

University and a renowned author, has actively engaged these themes. In her novel *La Momie d'Almamya* (The Mummy of Almamya), Sène explores the complex interplay of rites and traditions, immersing readers in a narrative that bridges historical consciousness with contemporary renewal.[3] She challenges traditional norms and advocates for a balance between respecting tradition and embracing necessary social change.

This debate resonates with, and is rooted in, the broader Négritude movement, a literary and philosophical initiative that emerged in the 1930s and 1940s, led by the former President of Senegal Léopold Sédar Senghor.[4] Négritude was a response to European colonialism and aimed to reclaim African identity, heritage, and culture. Importantly, considerable effort by members of the Négritude movement was spent on trying to resolve the tension among the particularities of the Black African experience and on integrating this knowledge in a universal framework that celebrated their contributions to world civilisation that colonialism otherwise had erased.

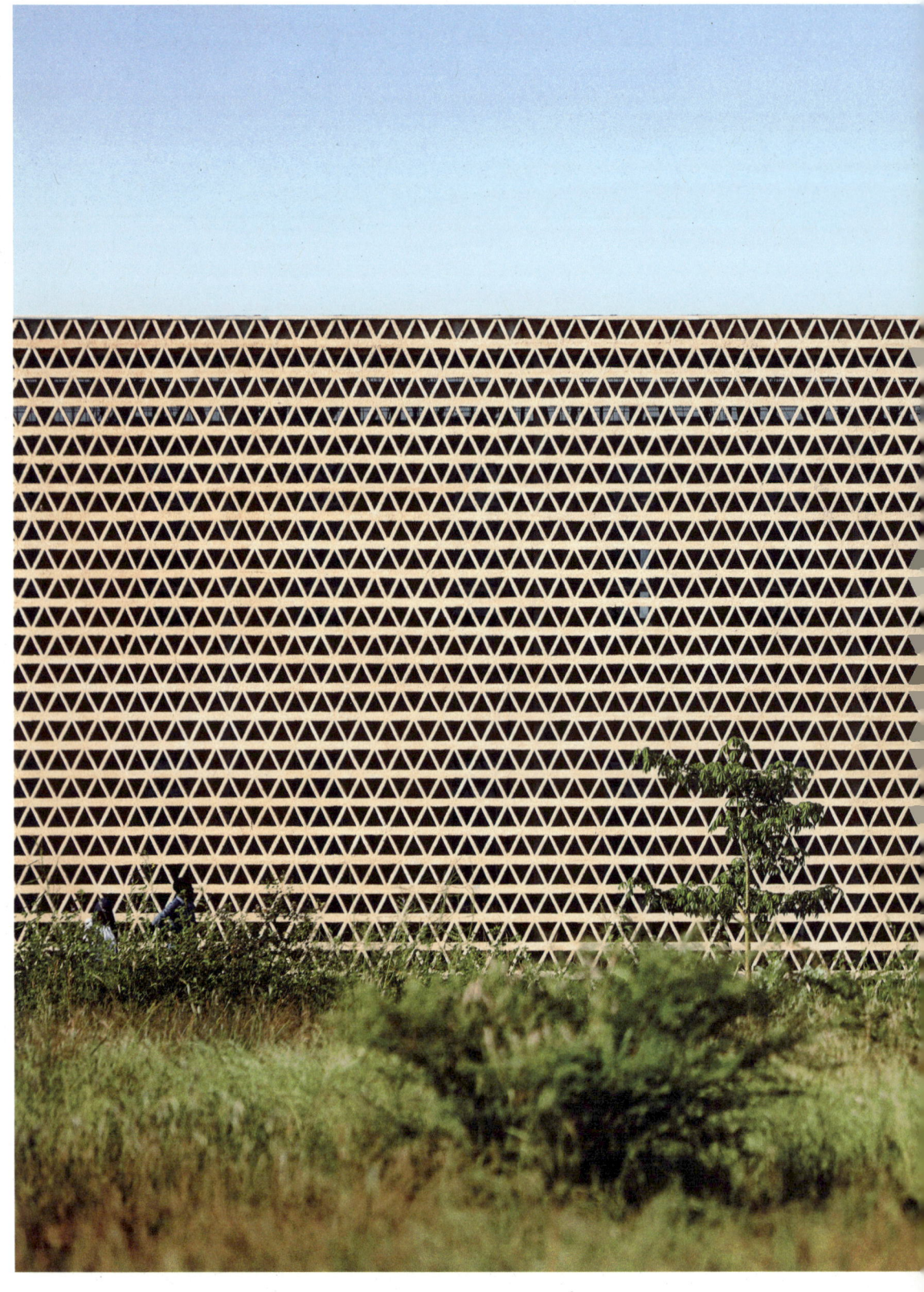

Figure 4. The southern lattice wall, made up of 20,000 triangular concrete pieces, provides passive cooling by allowing sunlight and air to pass through the intricate facade.

Figure 5. A bird's eye view of the site before construction. Bambey lies about 120 kilometres east of the capital, Dakar. Here, Senegal's rural hinterlands meet the urbanised coastal areas.

Figure 6. The town of Bambey has experienced rapid urbanisation in recent years, and the establishment of Alioune Diop University in 2007 accelerated this transformation.

Senegalese philosopher Souleymane Bachir Diagne elaborates that the universal for the Négritude movement is anchored in the notion of the "civilisation of the universal", which sets out the idea of a civilisation born from the encounter of all particular human cultures meeting in the "rendezvous of give and take".[5] Négritude, he argues, is focused on the in-between spaces, where hybridity thrives. As Diagne notes, the continued power of Négritude is its anchoring in hybridity, particularly evident in "the arts that come alive through the multiplication of encounters and crossroads".[6] In the crossroads and hybrid spaces of Bambey, the rhythms of rural life and traditions coexist with the intellectual energy and aspirations brought about by its growing urban population. This coexistence does not merely juxtapose old and new, the rural and the urban, but it enriches both, creating a space that is simultaneously rooted in local identity and practice and open to global influences – a hybrid rhythm that is at once urban and rural, local and global.

Constrained Space: The "Peanut Basin"

Along with these pulsating hybrid rhythms, however, more ominous tones are reverberating through this region. The Senegalese government's desire to establish a major university here was a direct response to the growing economic and environmental pressures the Diourbel Region is experiencing (figs. 5 and 6). This area is part of Senegal's "Peanut Basin" that has historically been a major centre for groundnut (peanut) production, a critical export crop and source of income for Senegal, reflecting how the region is an important part of the national economy and economic growth. However, weaknesses are apparent as well, such as higher levels of poverty and illiteracy in the Diourbel Region than the national average, and it is also an area that is highly vulnerable to the impacts of climate change. Soil degradation, erratic rainfall, and extreme temperatures are already negatively impacting agricultural productivity in this region.[7]

The declining opportunities in agriculture are resulting in an increasing number of youths leaving Bambey and its environs for the capital and other urban centres in search of non-farm-based incomes. Families in the Bambey region have long sent younger members of the family to Thies or Dakar in the dry season for urban jobs – working in, for instance, domestic occupations, informal street trade, or as bus driver assistants – to send money back home.[8] As a long-established practice, seasonal migrations are expanding deeper into the central "Peanut Basin" and for prolonged periods, as rainfall continues to be deficient and production lower.[9] There is an expectation that as agriculture continues to become less efficient and competitive, the labour force engaged in agriculture will continue to de-agrarianise and thus migrate to urban centres.[10] It is in the context of these challenges that the Senegalese government, with support from the World Bank, founded Alioune Diop University and commissioned the expansion of the university, as part of an effort to encourage youth to stay in rural areas and also to provide educational programmes appropriate to these contexts.

The educational and training activities at the university reflect and are purposefully responsive to the ecological factors facing this region and the country. A central part of the offering of the university is the Higher Institute for Agricultural and Rural Training (ISFAR), which trains students in agronomic sciences and agricultural and rural development. A major aim of the university is to contribute to training Senegal's next generation, so as to help the country achieve food security and sustainable development, equipping students with skills in agroforestry and regenerative agriculture to achieve greater climate resilience for the region and country. Improved education and training will be increasingly important so that farmers are able to implement the required climate-smart management strategies and technologies, enabling them to modify crop operations during the growing season.[11]

Knowledge Space: Alioune Diop and the Postcolonial

The university's mission extends beyond addressing the agricultural and climate-resilient needs of the region. While recognising the integral importance of agriculture and rural livelihoods, the Senegalese government envisioned a broader purpose when establishing Alioune Diop University in the hinterland of Bambey – one that transcends agriculture to foster diverse forms of knowledge and development. The university is named not after an agronomist but after the prominent Senegalese intellectual Alioune Diop, who is best known for establishing the journal *Présence Africaine* in 1947, and who was (along with former President Senghor and poet Aimé Césaire) an integral member of the Négritude movement (figs. 7 and 8). Central to Diop's philosophy and the Négritude philosophy both was the assertion of Africa's cultural and intellectual agency, challenging colonial narratives that had long dismissed African epistemologies.[12] A fundamental aspect of Diop's vision was the creation of educational and cultural institutions that serve as both custodians and incubators of African knowledge. He saw scientific research and rigorous intellectual inquiry as indispensable to Africa's rapid development, but he also argued that these aspects must be integrated into frameworks rooted in African socio-cultural realities.[13]

Geography has always been of fundamental importance to the production and consumption of scientific knowledge.[14] Science is all too often thought of as placeless, but on its never-ceasing travels, it always has a site, a venue, a place where it is confirmed, debated, or rejected. These are the learning ecologies of science. Alioune Diop University is forging forward with the task of establishing a knowledge base that does not merely adopt global models but critically adapts them to local contexts and needs as well. It is a site of scientific *production* and also consumption. This principle is applied from regenerative farming techniques to the political economy, where global theories and methods can only be effective when embedded in the lived experiences and practices of Senegalese communities. This local application is in turn a key part

Figures 7 and 8. The Senegalese intellectual Alioune Diop, who is best known for founding the journal *Présence Africaine* in 1947 (top); and the entrance to Alioune Diop University

of how new global scientific insights can be produced. The university's mission reflects this ethos, fostering an intellectual environment where scientific advancement is not detached from local realities but actively informs and is informed by them.

This commitment to contextual knowledge production extends beyond the pedagogy into the physical spaces where education takes place. The design of educational institutions has long played a role in signalling agency and intellectual sovereignty in postcolonial Africa. The Senegalese government, in line with many postcolonial states, has repeatedly turned to education as a means of addressing regional or national challenges; and universities, in turn, have played a vital role in contributing to the architectural landscape of the country.

British-Nigerian architect Ola Uduku and Ghanaian architect and researcher Kuukuwa Manful argue that, in postcolonial Africa, the building and design of educational institutions denoted freedom from colonisation and a pathway to self-rule.[15] These institutions have profoundly influenced the history and practice of architecture across the continent. As Uduku and Manful observe: "More than half a century later, these edifices borne of hope and expectation have generally stood the test of time and remain recognisable features in many African cities and landscape settings."[16] This is certainly true in Senegal, where university buildings past and present continue to play a defining role in establishing a national and regional architectural language. A notable example is the library and lecture theatres at Cheikh Anta Diop University in Dakar, which embody post-independence architectural aspirations. These are buildings that sought to blend international standards, practices, and techniques, while remaining rooted in the cultures and needs of the local and national contexts.

Sustainable Space: Climate-Responsive Architecture

The Alioune Dioup University Teaching and Research Unit exemplifies how international sustainability principles can be adapted to a specific, and challenging, socio-economic and environmental context. Its intelligent yet straightforward approach integrates local materials and craftsmanship, strategic spacing between buildings, and appropriate technological interventions, resulting in a design that is both environmentally conscious and functionally responsive. The Master Jury of the Aga Khan Award for Architecture stressed in their citation of the building how the construction technology allows for repetition and the possibility of local uptake in other buildings, thus serving as a model for implementing environmentally conscious design.

In such a heat- and water-stressed context, considerations of heat and shade, ventilation and water use, are central. As the architect Federico Pardos Auber explains, a crucial inspiration for the project was taken from the way trees provide shelter. The aim was to use shade and cross-ventilation to facilitate cooling and breeze with minimal energy consumption. A large double roof that runs across the five subunits ensures that direct solar radiation is avoided, while ventilation is fostered through the Venturi effect (where airflow is accelerated as it passes through a narrow space, creating a cooling effect). The heat-reflecting metal outer roof, supported by steel lattice beams, establishes a layer between the lecture rooms on the upper floor, allowing for ventilation between them (fig. 9). The roof extends to form a 10-metre-long canopy on the north side of the building that runs along its whole length and draws hot air up and away. The double roof helps to reduce the interior temperature by up to 15 degrees centigrade. This covered space is supported by thin metal columns of a varying two-branched shape that articulate the influence of trees in the design of the building. This shaded area forms a place for

Figure 9. Colonnade supporting the upper gallery. Considerations of heat and shade, as well as ventilation and water use, were central to the building's design.

Figure 10. View of the access ramp and the southern lattice wall. The ramp both enables accessible access and acts as a public space for users.

Figure 11. The triangular perforations that comprise the southern wall. The facade is made up of simple blocks with triangular perforations that were prefabricated in situ by a workforce drawn from the local town of Bambey.

students to socialise at the start or end of classes, and – a user innovation established independently of the architects – for cars to be parked in the shade.

The remote site of the university meant that there were no sewage or rainwater networks. To address this circumstance, the architects created infiltration rafts with vegetation that collects rainwater and filtered wastewater by means of different-sized, basalt-lined exterior canals that retain sediments and slow the speed of the incoming water. An elongated ramp not only provides accessibility to the upper floor on the western side of the building but also creates a public space that overlooks the stone-lined basin and its native vegetation (fig. 10).

This structure is distinguished by the southern facade made up of 20,000 triangular concrete pieces, creating an intricate lattice wall that blocks direct sunlight but allows air through. It took over a hundred workers six months to construct the latticework, which was built manually on site by means of a stainless-steel mould and then air-dried. It echoes smaller features seen on local buildings (fig. 11). The facade is made up of simple blocks with triangular perforations that were prefabricated in situ by a workforce drawn from the local town of Bambey. This intricate wall creates not only a contextually influenced aesthetic that is also crafted on site (both in terms of being constructed there and by local labor) but one that contributes to the strategies for passive cooling.

The Alioune Diop University Teaching and Reseach Unit is a building that both defines and is shaped by its context – a hybrid object. Through its engagement with the social and environmental ecology of its site, it delivers impactful, affordable, and low-maintenance solutions. It navigates the in-between spaces of inside and outside, light and shade, present and absent. The university must be understood within this broader learning ecology that informs its design and purpose. While deeply rooted in the particularities of its context, it also embodies a bold universalist architectural vision. By remaining grounded, following the social and ecological actors of this site, IDOM has created a work of global significance, achieving what Senghor described as "the deepening and coexistence of all particulars".[17]

---

1 Jean Francois Lamoureux, Jean-Louis Marin, and Fernand Bonamy, "The International Fair of Dakar", *Architectuul*, https://architectuul.com/architecture/the-international-fair-of-dakar.

2 *2019 Award Recipient – Alioune Diop University Teaching and Research Centre*, YouTube video, posted by the Aga Khan Development Network, 14 August 2019, https://www.youtube.com/watch?v=qv4RX5_K4n4.

3 Fama Diagne Sène, *La Momie d'Almamya* (Dakar: Les Nouvelles Éditions Africaines du Sénégal, 1996).

4 Souleymane Bachir Diagne, *African Art as Philosophy: Senghor, Bergson, and the Idea of Negritude*, trans. Chike Jeffers (New York: Seagull Books, 2011).

5 Souleymane Bachir Diagne, "In Praise of the Post-Racial: Negritude Beyond Negritude", *Third Text* 24, no. 2 (2010), pp. 241–48, esp. pp. 245–46.

6 Ibid., p. 247.

7 Nadège Garambois, Ulysse Le Goff, and Lucie Thibaudeau, "Agrarian Dynamics and Climate Change in the Senegalese Sahelian Peanut Basin", in *Agrarian Systems and Climate Change: Journeys of Adaptation in the Global South*, ed. Hubert Cochet, Olivier Ducourtieux, and Nadège Garambois (Wallingford: CABI, 2024), pp. 15–37.

8 Ibid., p. 28.

9 Ibid.

10 Askar Mukashov, Christian Henning, Richard Robertson, and Manfred Wiebelt, *The Role of Global Climate Change in Structural Transformation of Sub-Saharan Africa: Case Study of Senegal*, Kiel Working Paper no. 2187 (Kiel: Kiel Institute for the World Economy, 2021), p. 20.

11 Inoussa Zagre et al., "Climate Change Adaptation Strategies among Smallholder Farmers in Senegal's Semi-Arid Zone: Role of Socio-Economic Factors and Institutional Supports", *Frontiers in Climate* 6 (2024), p. 8.

12 Alioune Diop, "Editorial: For an African Modernity", *Présence Africaine*, Nouvelle série no. 116 (Fourth Quarter 1980), pp. 12–19.

13 Ibid., pp. 14–15.

14 David N. Livingstone, *Putting Science in Its Place: Geographies of Scientific Knowledge* (Chicago: University of Chicago Press, 2003).

15 Ola Uduku and Kuukuwa Manful, "Buildings for Higher Education in Africa", *Docomomo Journal*, Special Issue 69 (2023), https://docomomojournal.com/index.php/journal/issue/view/44.

16 Ibid., p. 4.

17 Cited in Diagne, "In Praise of the Post-Racial: Negritude Beyond Negritude", p. 241.

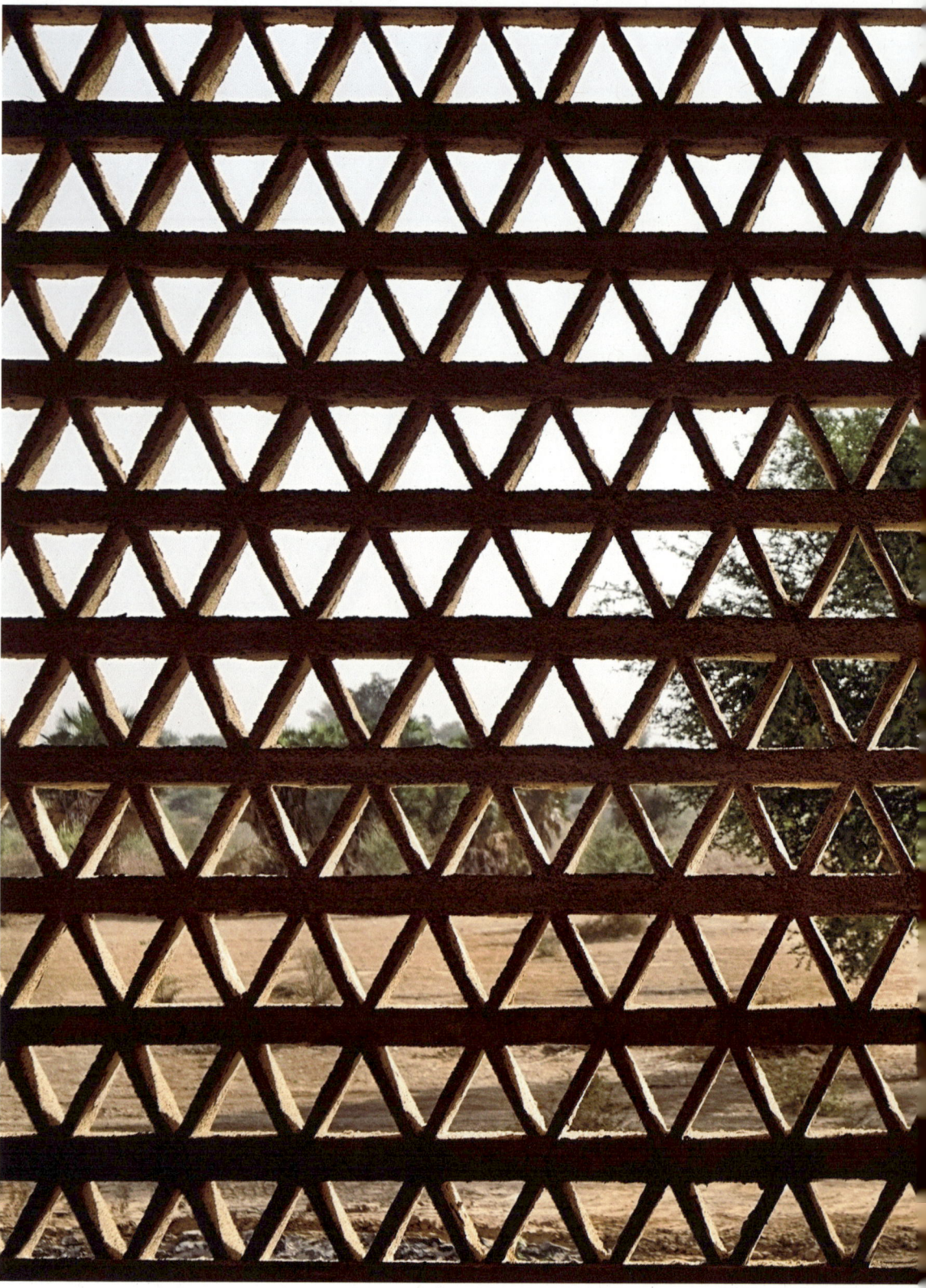

The participatory latticework forming the southern facade of Alioune Diop University demonstrates how architecture can integrate local materials, social relations, and ecological intelligence into educational practice.

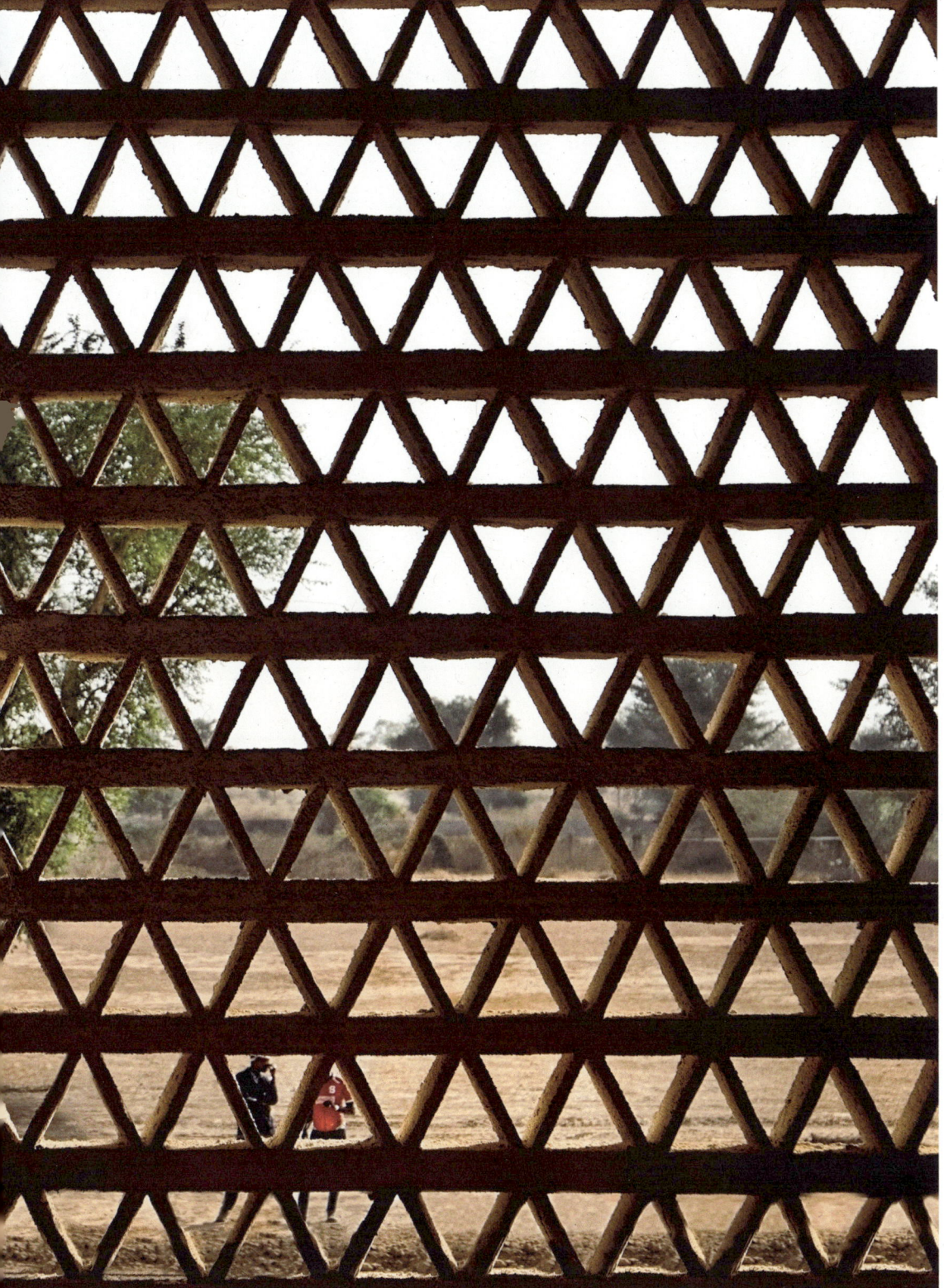

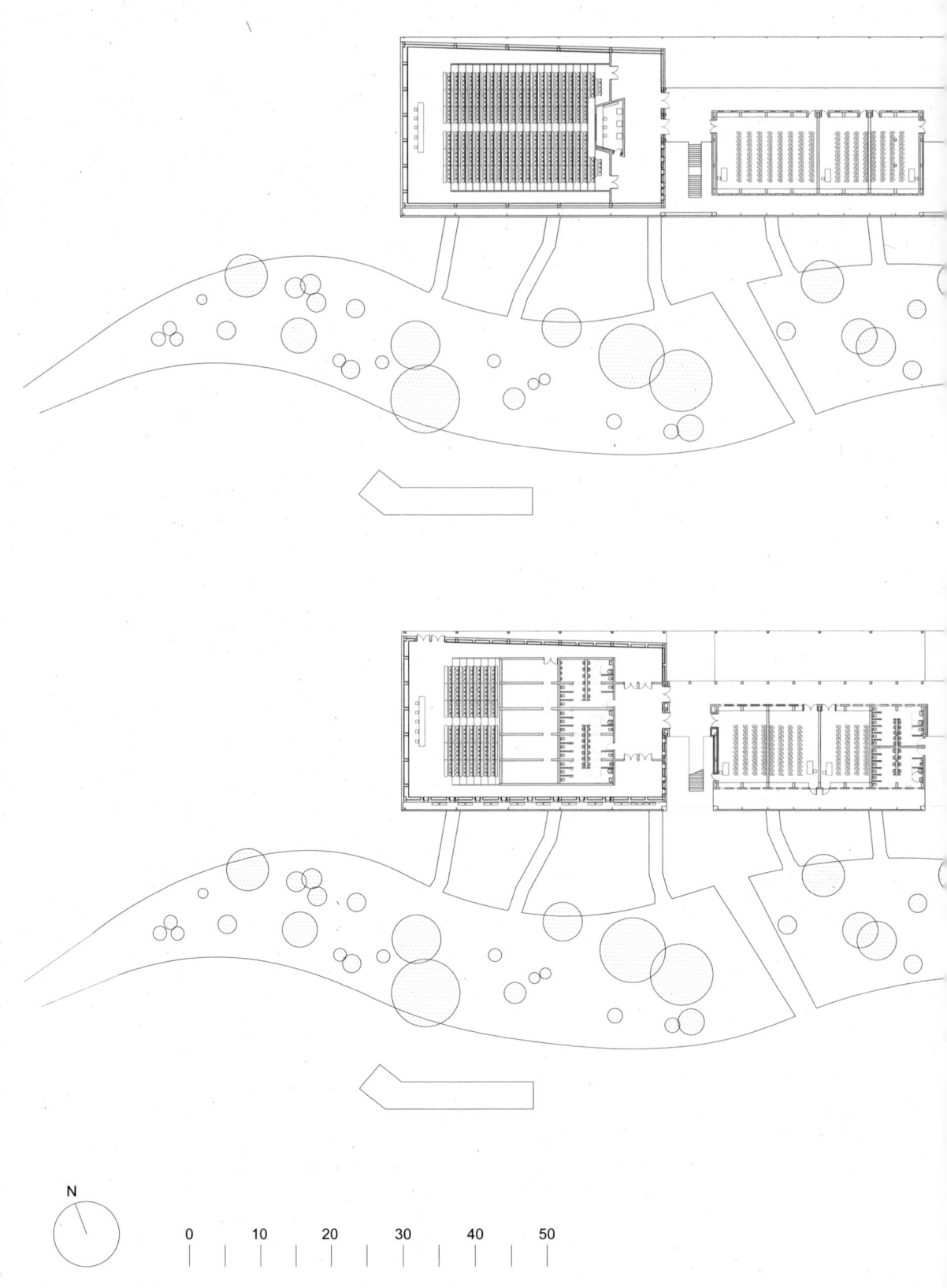

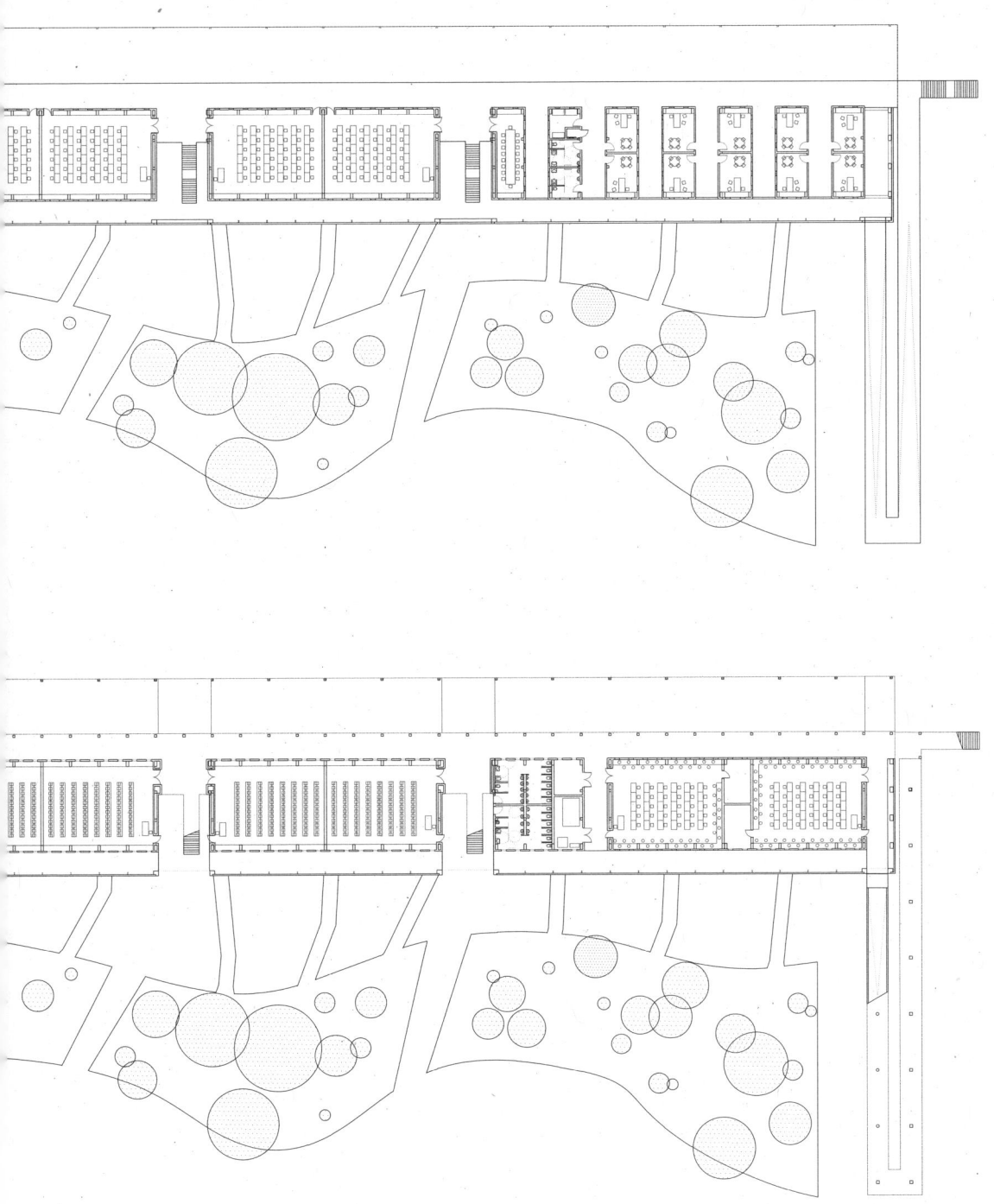

Site plan of the Alioune Diop University Teaching and Research Unit, designed by the Spanish architectural firm IDOM

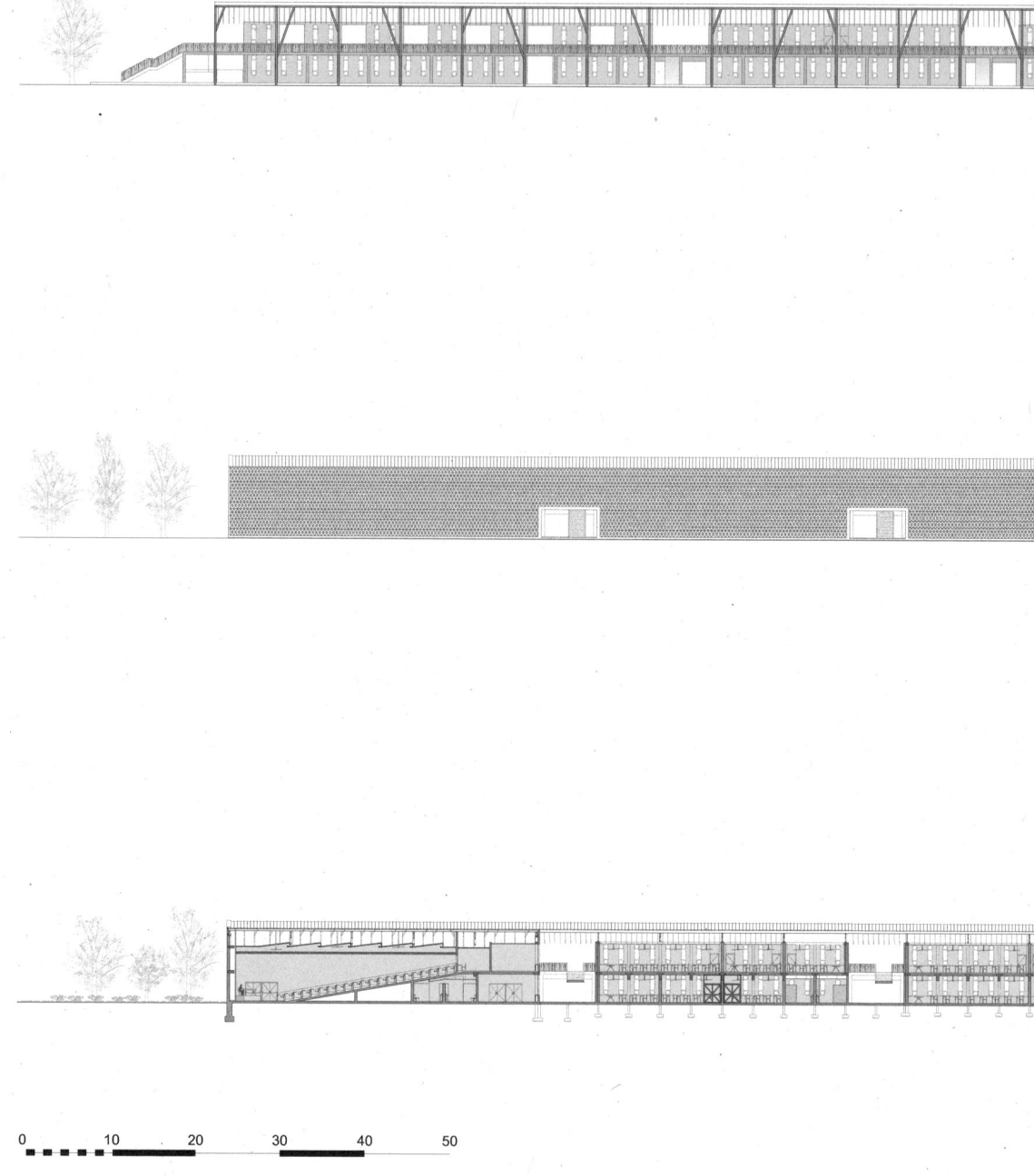

Section of the Alioune Diop University Teaching and Research Unit in Bambey, Senegal, showing the deep canopy structure and passive ventilation strategies that help protect the building from the region's intense heat

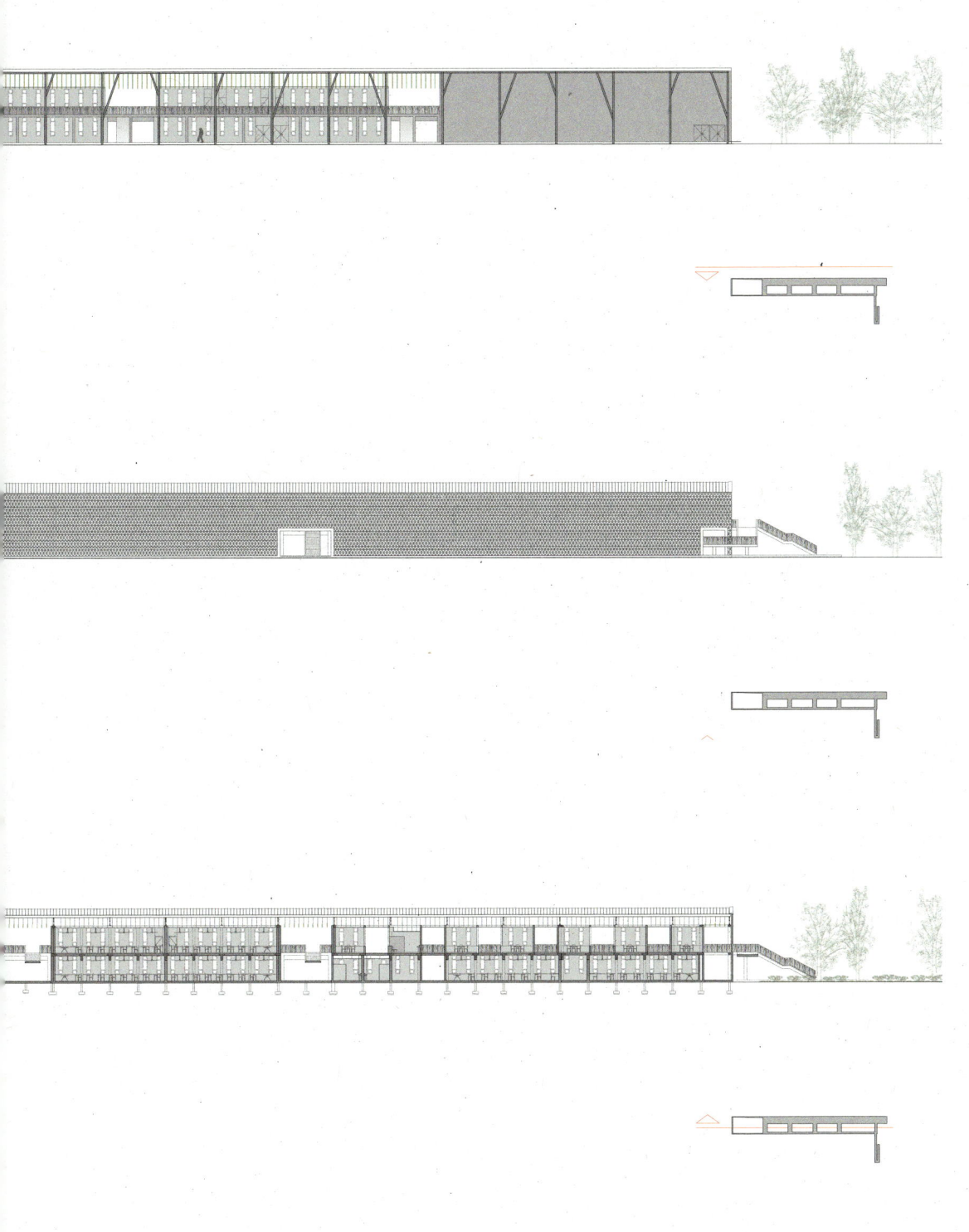

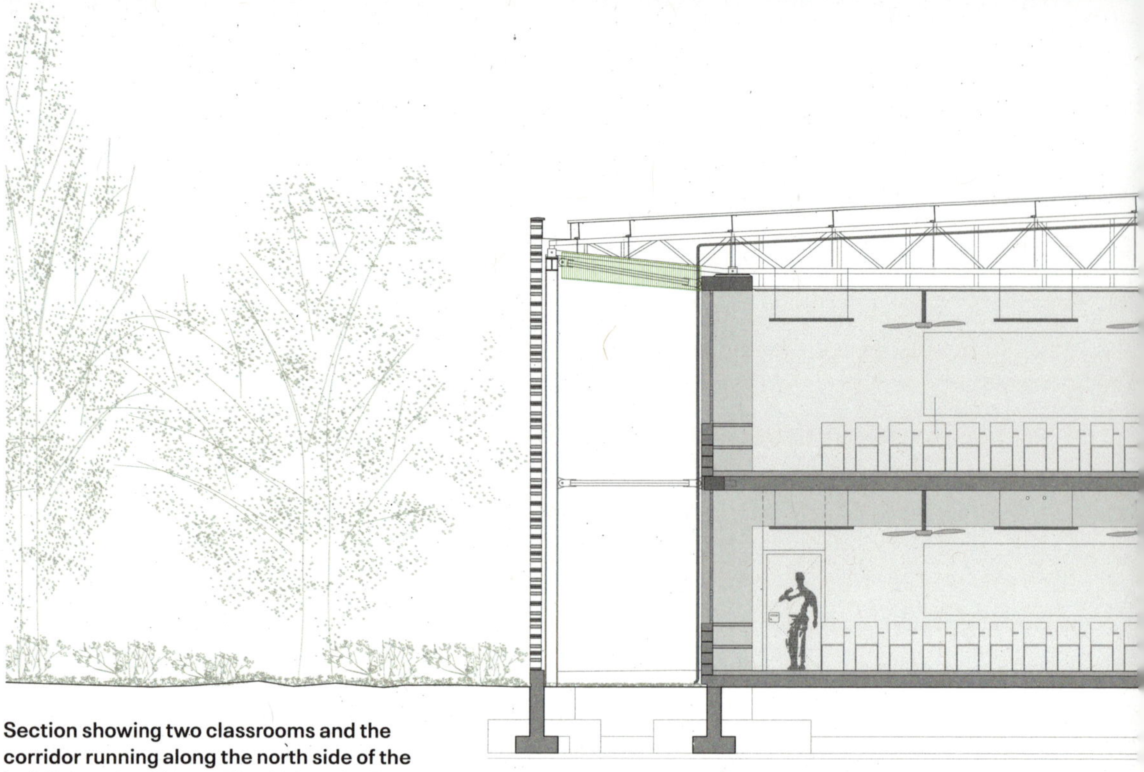

Section showing two classrooms and the corridor running along the north side of the building at the Alioune Diop University Teaching and Research Unit. The corridor provides circulation while also helping to shade the classrooms from direct sunlight.

Section illustrating the entrances to the main conference hall and the external staircase, which connects different levels of the Alioune Diop University Teaching and Research Unit

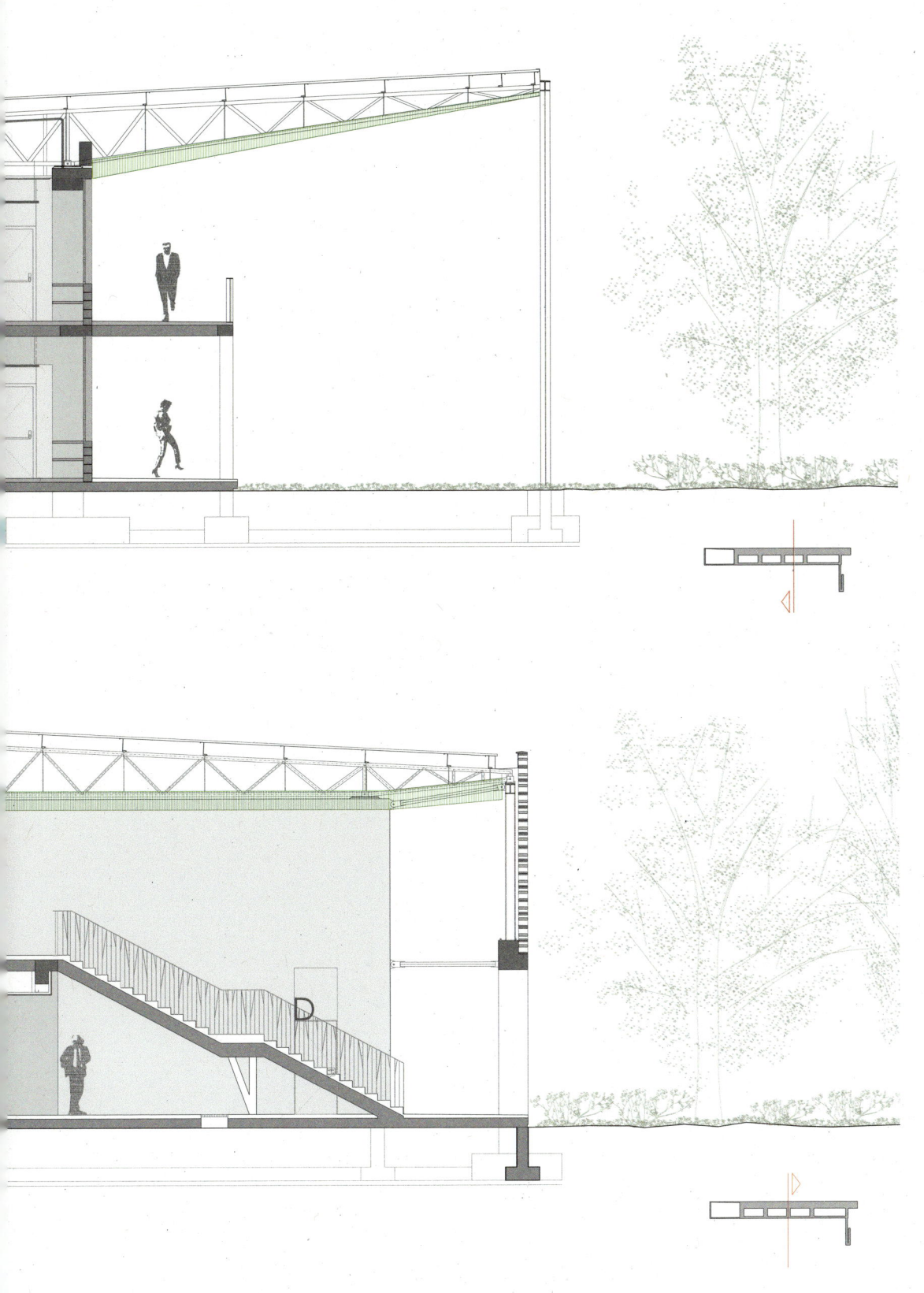

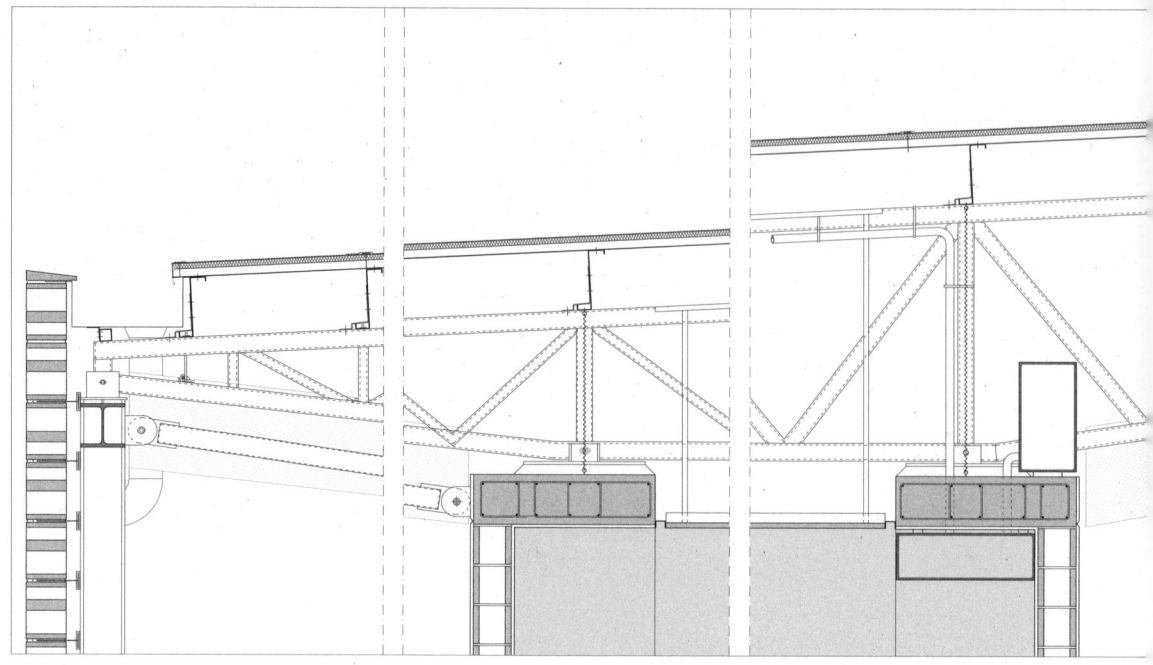

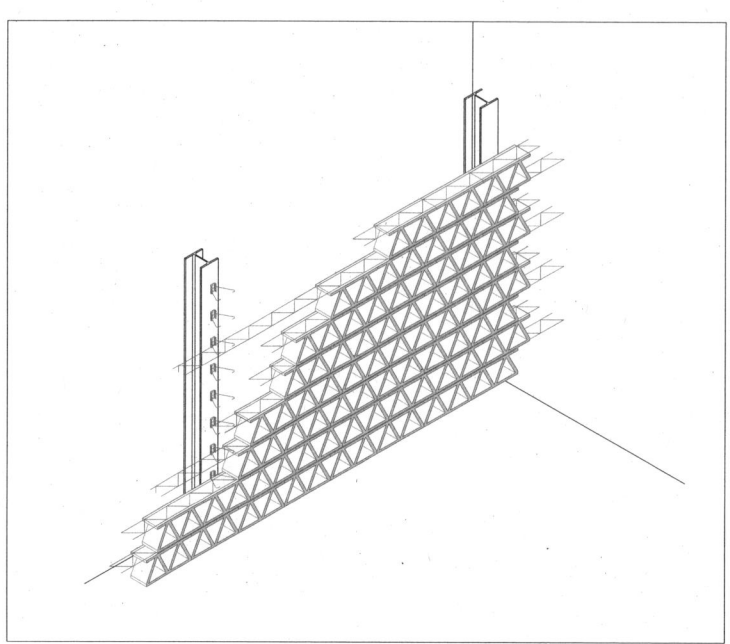

Detail illustrating how the individual concrete pieces fit together to create the distinctive lattice wall, combining structural logic with environmental performance

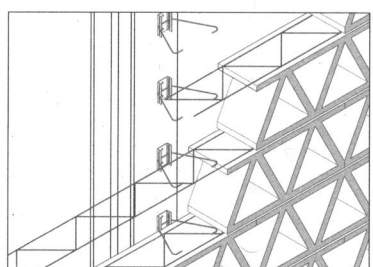

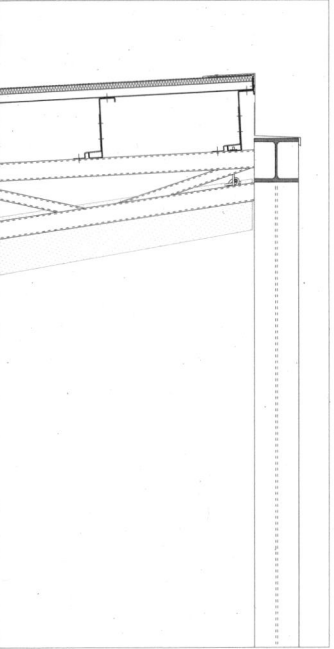

Detail of the roof at the Alioune Diop University Teaching and Research Unit, showing the double-skin construction designed to enhance thermal performance and provide additional shading

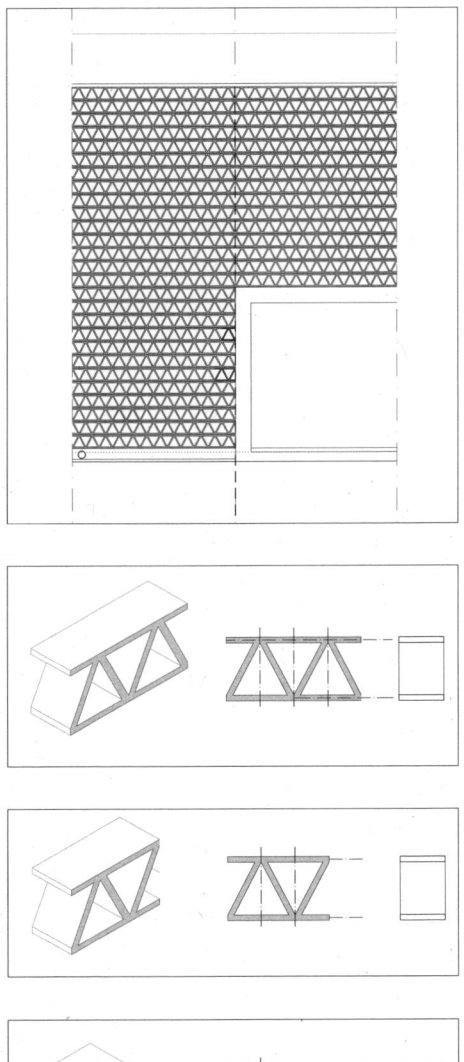

Detail of the precast concrete pieces that form the large lattice wall, combining structural function with shading and ventilation

Technical detail of the drainage and infiltration system designed for the Alioune Diop University Teaching and Research Unit. The drawing illustrates how water is distributed through a network of perforated pipes and modular drainage structures, surrounded by gravel to promote infiltration and reduce surface run-off.

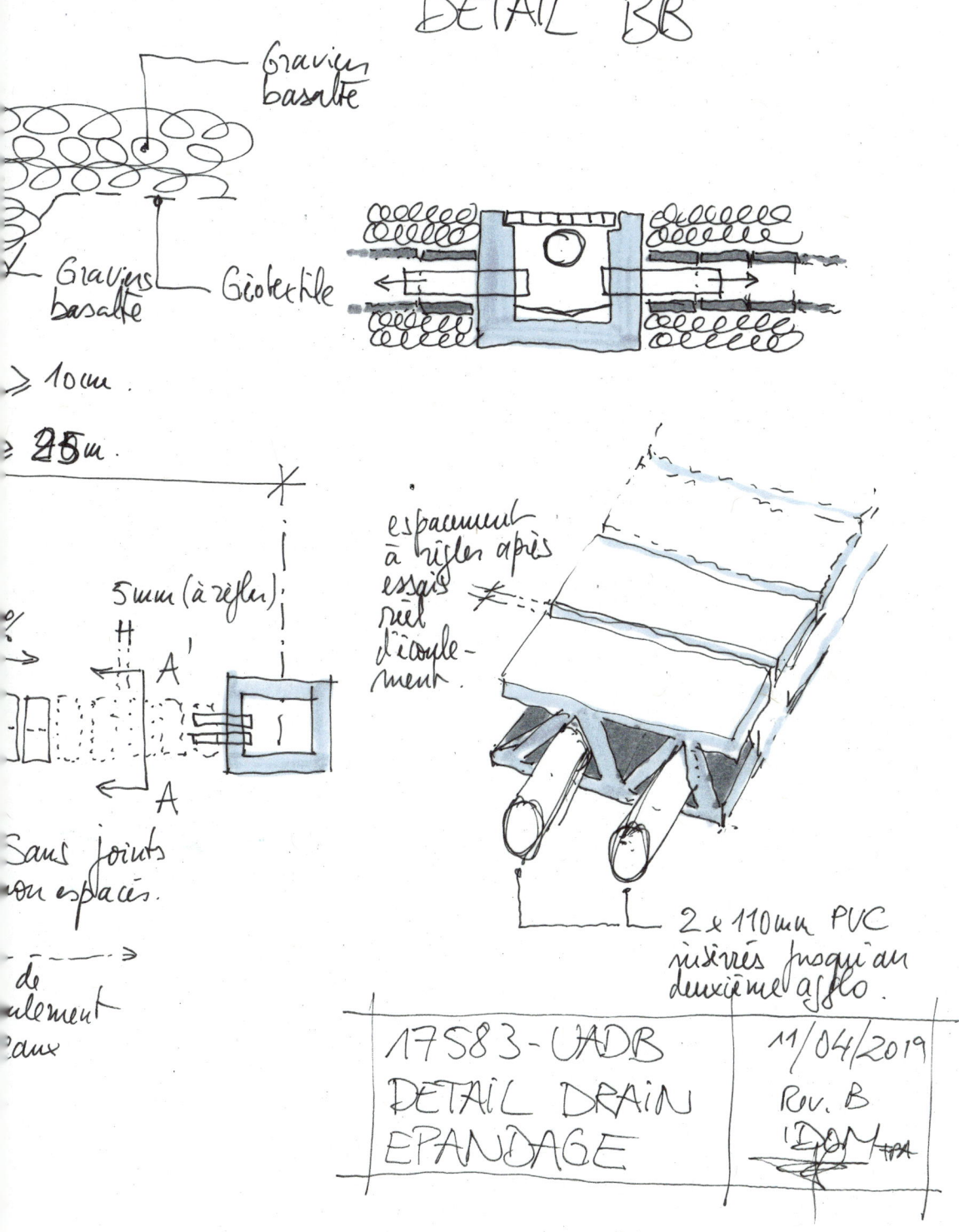

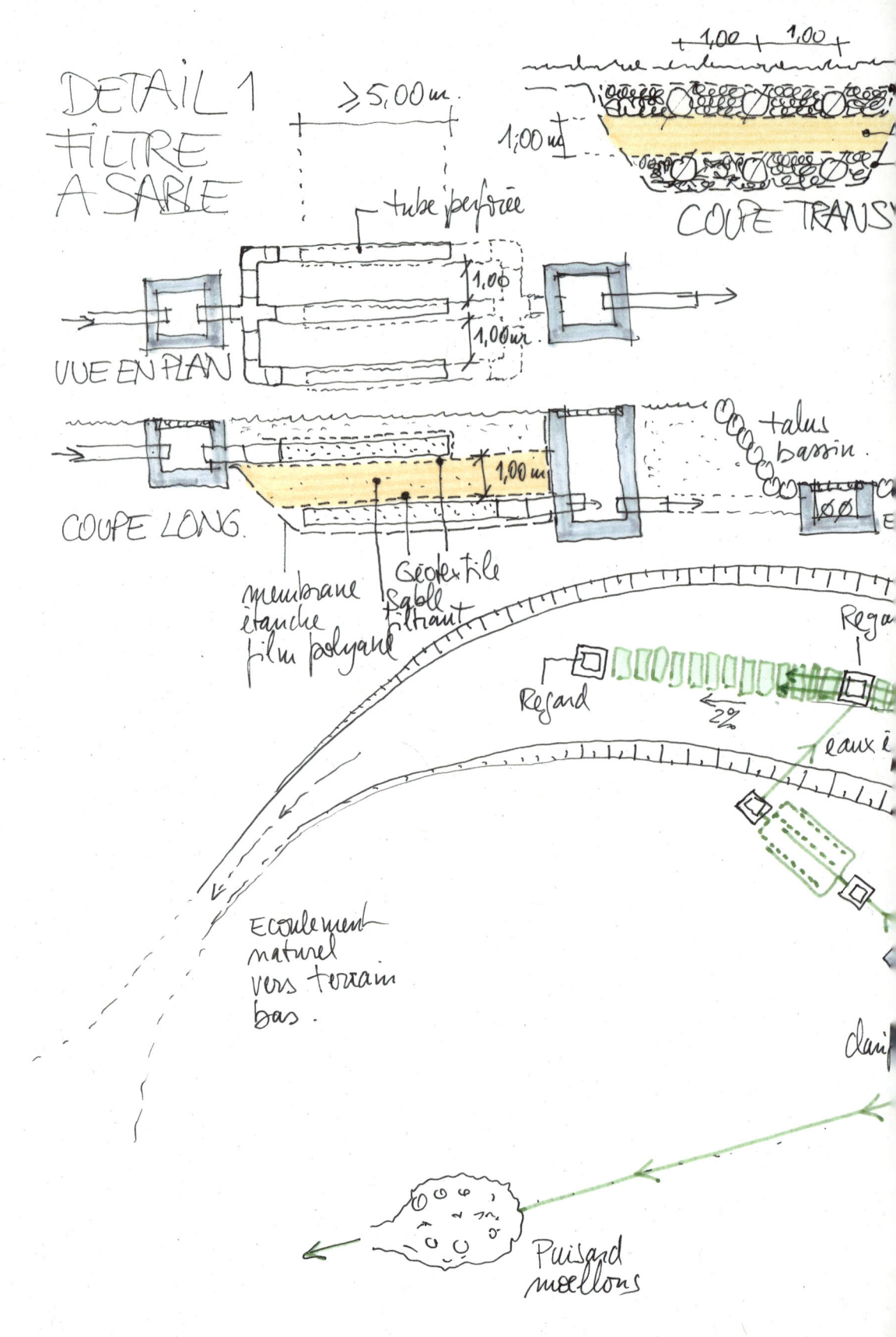

Site plan and technical details of the wastewater and rainwater management system for the Alioune Diop University Teaching and Research Unit. The drawing shows how treated wastewater is filtered through sand-beds and distributed via infiltration trenches, while rainwater is directed to basins and soakaways. This integrated system reduces environmental impact and reflects the project's sustainable approach to water management in an arid climate.

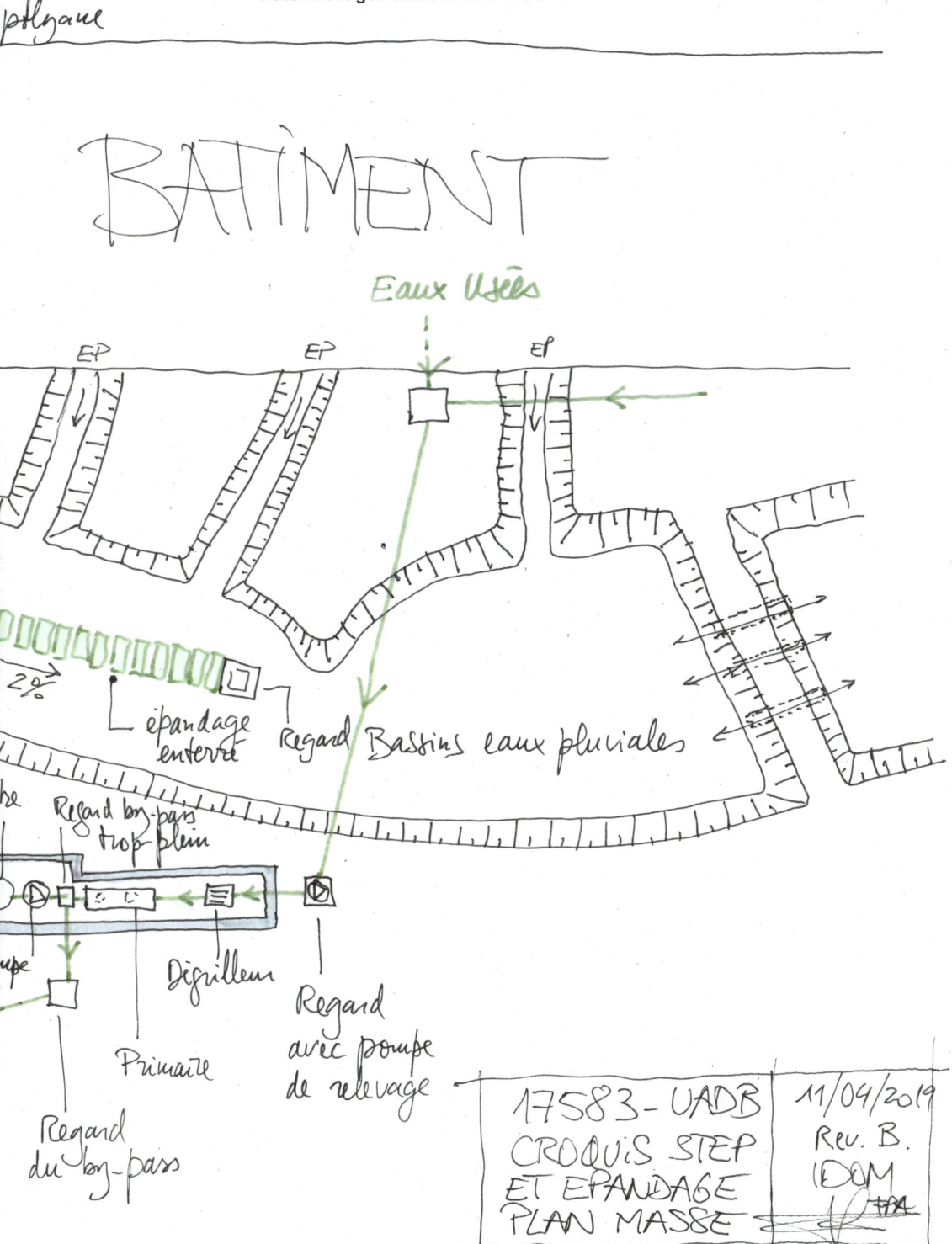

ARCHITECTURE AND THE MATERIALS

OF SOCIAL
ENGAGEMENT

Connecting Every Curve: The Architecture of Community at Kamanar Secondary School

Deen Sharp

Figure 1. Three of the modular vaulted *awlas* (classrooms) at Kamanar Secondary School (CEM) in Thionck Essyl, Senegal. Designed by the Spanish architects Dawoffice, the distinctive vaulted structures use locally sourced materials and modular construction techniques to create durable, climate-responsive learning spaces.

The repetitive rhythm of undulating clay vaults shapes the Kamanar Secondary School (Collège d'Enseignement Moyen, CEM) (fig. 1). Each of these modular vaulted structures is called an *awla* in the local Diola (Jola) vernacular. The distinct catenary design, according to the architects at Dawoffice, emerged from a principle of "common sense." Their commitment to using local materials, labour, and design shaped a structure that responds to the constraints and possibilities of its ecology. Stabilised earth bricks form structurally sound vaults that minimise material stress, resulting in a durable, low-maintenance construction. The earth sourced on site, being structurally weak, necessitated this vaulted form to distribute weight efficiently and ensure stability. While these *awlas* differ architecturally from the region's vernacular forms, the construction techniques used are deeply rooted in local materials and craftsmanship. At every single point – designing, digging, constructing, and ultimately utilising these spaces – the community played an active role. This was not just a school built for them but a future built by them (fig. 2).

Figure 2. Two CEM students sit in front of an *awla*. The vaulted classroom structures provide well-ventilated, durable learning spaces designed to respond to the region's climate, while using locally sourced materials and labour.

Casamance: Fragments, Links, and Continuities

The Kamanar Secondary School is in Thionck Essyl, a town located in Senegal's southern region of Casamance. Situated between Anglophone Gambia to the north and Lusophone Guinea-Bissau to the south, Casamance is physically separated, for the most part, from northern Senegal. Notably, the Spanish architects of Dawoffice often travelled from their office in Barcelona, flying into The Gambia before driving to Casamance to reach the school site. Casamance stands in contrast to the Sahelian character of northern Senegal, with its landscape defined by rivers, forests, and mangrove swamps. While the north is shaped by the cultivation of groundnuts and herding cattle, the south is distinguished by rice farming and fishing.

The Casamance region has experienced one of Africa's longest running conflicts, lasting over forty years. A low-intensity secessionist war that has ebbed and spiked over the decades has killed more than 5,000 people, displaced over 60,000 (now split between Senegal, The Gambia, and Guinea-Bissau), and left 800,000 living in a state of uncertainty.[1] The four-decade-long conflict has turned large tracts of territory into no-go zones due to land mines that have ravaged agricultural areas and the tourist economy.[2]

The region's long-standing conflict has been difficult to resolve, in part due to the splintering of the secessionist movement into factions across Senegal, Guinea-Bissau, and The Gambia.[3] This broader theme of fragmentation, both physical and political, has shaped Casamance's struggles. Its geographical separation from the rest of Senegal has reinforced its political and social disconnection from the rest of the country. These challenges highlight the spatial dimension of poverty in Senegal, with Casamance specifically affected.[4] Poverty levels in Casamance are higher than the national average, driven in part by limited market access and poor transport connectivity.

While the war has heavily impacted livelihoods in Casamance, education has been less affected, relatively speaking. Historically, the region has been one of the most educated areas outside of Dakar, with some of the highest recorded literacy levels in the country.[5] The importance of education in Casamance may also be explained by it becoming a site of political struggle between nationalists and secessionists. The Casamance population places a high value on formal education and often sends their children far outside their villages to areas with public schools.[6] In the absence of sufficient state funding, many communities have at times self-funded the construction of schools and collaborated with the state to assign teachers. To support the expansion of formal education, there continues to be a series of innovative funding models involving communities, national and foreign donors, non-governmental organisations, and the state. The challenge of inadequate state funding for formal schooling is by no means unique to Casamance or Senegal. As Ola Uduku has noted, school policy and provision across Africa has turned full circle now that private and missionary organisations – which were fundamental to establishing Western education systems in Africa – have returned to this role.[7] She adds: "Few of today's governments in the emerging world have the financial resources, political strength or will to deliver the quality or level of education that the continent requires."[8]

Dawoffice: Architect, Funder, Contractor, Connector

The trend of community and non-state actors stepping in to support education is exemplified by the work of the Spanish architectural practice Dawoffice and the CEM project specifically. In constructing the Kamanar Secondary School, Dawoffice was not only the architect but also the project catalyst, fundraiser, donor, manager, trainer, and community organiser.

The origins of this project began in between Barcelona and Casamance. For several years, Aina Tugores, a member of the Dawoffice firm, had initiated several different collaborative projects around the world, and had established a strong relationship with the community in Thionck Essyl. In 2014, the chief architect and founder of Dawoffice, David García, joined Tugores in Casamance to help with a model of the project she was working on. This first trip to Thionck Essyl left a deep impression on García, who fomented a strong connection with the welcoming local community. Following the initial trip, García decided that a project should be developed to support the community.

Long before construction began or a new school project was even agreed upon, David and Aina made multiple visits from their Barcelona office to Thionck Essyl – a journey of approximately twelve hours each way, including flights and overland travel if going through The Gambia, although the travel time could be up to twenty-four hours if routing through Dakar. Travelling between Barcelona and Thionck Essyl became a regular practice for many Dawoffice staff members throughout the project. The early visits enabled Dawoffice to conduct a self-initiated study on local schooling needs, which confirmed serious overcrowding issues in classrooms, and led to a proposal for a new school. At the time, Thionck Essyl had only one secondary school.[9] A dialogue was established between residents and local administration officials to understand the community's needs and to define an appropriate architectural programme. Dawoffice not only involved the local government but also engaged with neighbourhood chiefs, women from the village, and the broader community.

In cooperation with the architects, the community selected a publicly owned plot of land that is 2 hectares in size and close to the Casamance River to build the school, while taking various issues into consideration, such as how far the children would have to travel. Mangroves extend from the mouth of the Casamance River, resulting in an area that lies in between land and sea, populated with large boababs, bougainvillea, and mango trees. The planning team took

Figure 3. One of the first *awla* (classroom) structures to be built at the Kamanar Secondary School

Figure 4. A worker clearing the site in preparation for the construction of the Kamanar Secondary School. Dawoffice took great care in responding to the local ecology.

great care in responding to this ecology and shaping the school in relation to it. Existing trees became organising elements for the school, and the shade they provide was maximised throughout the design (fig. 3). More fruits trees have been planted along with the construction of the school buildings to provide further shade, but also income through selling the fruit. This adaptability and responsiveness to local needs and contexts became a defining feature of Dawoffice's approach. The very design of the school – built in modular units – and the hands-on training provided to the community ensured that further expansion of the school could be done by the community independently (fig. 4).

Although CEM is a government-run and owned public school, Dawoffice raised the construction funds in Spain. To facilitate legal processes and streamline funding transfers, they established the non-profit Foundawtion in 2014. This foundation formalised Dawoffice's commitment to provide high-quality architectural design to communities that typically lack access to such

Figure 5. Craftspeople lift the wooden framework used to form the catenary arches of the *awla* classrooms at the Kamanar Secondary School. This temporary structure guided the construction of the distinctive vaulted design.

resources.[10] CEM became Foundawtion's first project. Initially, fundraising was conducted on a small scale, through community-driven initiatives in Spain, such as jazz concerts, photography, drawing exhibitions, an illustrated book, and auctions, which financed the construction of the first modular structure, or *awla*. The completion of this initial phase helped to attract larger donors, notably the multinational group Teknia that manufactures metal and plastic components. Over the course of three years (2017–19), Dawoffice through its foundation was able to raise 468,000 euros for the project. Teknia's substantial donation, which covered nearly 50 per cent of the costs for the entire project, enabled the completion of the school and the development of additional projects.

Even after the school's completion in 2020, Foundawtion has remained actively engaged with CEM, offering support while deliberately avoiding fostering dependency. Each month, it funds electricity, cleaning services, security, and maintenance. While the government covers most of the teachers' salaries, Foundawtion pays directly for the librarian and informatics

Figure 6. A completed arch forming part of the *awla* structure at the Kamanar Secondary School. The distinctive catenary-shaped vault provides both structural strength and improved thermal performance.

teacher. The modular design enables ongoing expansion, with buildings added as needs arise and funding is secured. In 2021, for example, following guidance by the director of the school, a new building was constructed for a separate office. Rather than creating reliance, Dawoffice and its foundation have taken on a role of reinforcement – if the foundation were to disappear tomorrow, CEM would continue to thrive. This enduring partnership is built not on necessity, but on mutual respect and a shared commitment to elevating Thionck Essyl towards greater prosperity and sustainability (figs. 5 and 6).

Designing For and With Community

At the core of this project is the idea that architecture can be a key organising tool through which community is both utilised and uplifted. From its inception, CEM was designed not just for students but for the broader community, considering both its environmental and social ecology. From the start of the design process, the mayor, his technical team, local teachers, and the broader community were all actively engaged in assessing whether the architectural plans for CEM met their needs. This consultation process led to substantive revisions. At the request of local women who sell homemade snacks to the children, the entrance gates were deliberately set back from the site's perimeter, creating a public space. Additionally, a dialogue between the architects and the president of the local Women's Association, Oumy Sagna, ensured that the bathroom design appropriately addressed both cultural and gender-specific needs (see page 130).

A large part of the town was directly or indirectly involved in the formation of the school and still today continues to be associated with it. Over the five-year CEM construction project, 164 people drawn directly from the school and its environs participated. For example, the use of clay to create the catenary vaults provided an opportunity to revive traditional building techniques. To construct the vaults, Dawoffice worked closely with local masons, merging materials from the area with construction methods from Catalonia. This was not a didactic process but rather one of mutual learning, where architects, builders, and the community exchanged knowledge and expertise. García explained that this was also Dawoffice's first experience working with earth and constructing vaults, making it a project defined by experimentation and research, not just for the local masons but for the architects as well. Following the completion of the first vault, Dawoffice invited local masons in the area to provide a critical assessment. Many, though impressed by the interior space, doubted that the clay vaults would survive the first rainy season, an uncertainty García himself shared, albeit to a far lesser extent. Concrete had been seen as the only material capable of withstanding the rains, not a structure built quite literally from the earth beneath it. Yet, the vaults endured, and soon local masons were discussing how to adapt the form and material for their own homes.

The use of stabilised rammed earth for the construction of each of the modules provided environmental and economic benefits, offering optimal thermal performance while utilising materials directly from the site (figs. 7 and 8). Excavation for the earth also served a dual purpose, for the quarry was subsequently transformed into a sunken sports field. Each clay vault is closed by wooden lattices that allow enough light and air into the rooms. The clay and lattices act as an evaporating cooler, ensuring that no air-conditioning is needed (figs. 9 and 10). The vault is covered with a metal sheet to prevent rain on the clay and to provide an air chamber sheltered from direct sunlight, so that the sun's heat is dissipated before it radiates into the *alwa*. Advocates

Figures 7 and 8. Workers excavating soil on site for the production of stabilised earth bricks used in the construction of the Kamanar Secondary School

of rammed earth have long highlighted its advantages, not only as an environmentally sustainable and cost-effective material, but also for its ability to mobilise collective labour and self-help.[11] CEM is a compelling example of these principles in action.

It was not just the clay that facilitated community and training opportunities. The school furniture was conceived by the Spanish furniture designer Marc Morro and made by locally based Lamine Sambou (see page 128) and his team of carpenters. Morro designed the furniture

Figure 9. A student walking in front of the *awla*

Figure 10. The clay vault with wooden lattices that allow enough light and air into the rooms for passive cooling

Figure 11. Spanish furniture designer Marc Morro and local carpenter Lamine Sambou collaborate on making a chair for the school.

and acted as a tutor to the carpenters (fig. 11). Following the completion of the first classroom, students were invited to sit in the chairs and provide feedback on the design. As part of the construction of the school, Foundawtion also financed and built a carpentry workshop for Sambou. The carpentry workshop now continues to supply the school with furniture and provide maintenance services. The school also acted as a catalyst for Sambou to establish what is a thriving private carpentry business supplying furniture.

The success of Sambou's carpentry workshop and the process of training the many people engaged in the construction of CEM spurred Dawoffice to build on this potential to promote circular economics and provide more training opportunities for the young.[12] It is not only the school that is designed in a way that can easily expand; the management structures that created it were expanded as well. Using the same principles as CEM, another agreement was established with the government to build a vocational training centre at a nearby site. The Professional Training Centre Bajankusoor is now under construction.[13] The training centre includes workshops for individual training lines that include electromechanics and accounting.

The expanded work of Dawoffice in Thionck Essyl is an articulation of the strong bond that has been created not just with the school but with the local community and government as well. At CEM, the architects established a deep working relationship with the local community in the construction of the school, and not just with the local masons and carpenters who helped with the structures (fig. 12). Dawoffice also established a volunteer scheme that was supported by the local community. The volunteers were predominately recently qualified architects from Spain or final-year architecture students. They would spend three months at a time at CEM helping with the design, management, and construction. A total of sixty-two volunteers assisted in the construction of CEM in total (fig. 13). These volunteers were hosted by two elders from the

Figure 12. Craftspeople build the arch of an *awla*. At the Kamanar Secondary School, the architects established a deep working relationship with the local community and craftspeople while building the school.

Figure 13. Volunteers were hosted by Gaston and Tanta in the local village. Communal dinners provided space for design conversations and relationship-building.

local village, Gaston and Tanta (see page 132). The volunteers, in turn, helped Gaston and Tanta with repairs to their home, including the construction of a well and the installation of solar panels. The foundation paid for a local woman to cook lunch and dinner for the volunteers and, importantly, dinners would be collective events; it was an opportunity for village residents to discuss the project with the architects. García explained that these regular dinner dialogues created a space to discuss not only the design but also how the architects and volunteers engaged with the workers on site in particular. It provided an opportunity to talk about translation, expression, training, and manners, elements that all contributed to improving both the design process and the working environment.

A vibrant, fully functioning learning ecology has been established at the Kamanar Secondary School. Classrooms are now filled with the energy of Senegal's next generation learning the critical analytical skills and tools they need to survive in a digitalised and information-saturated world (fig. 14). The sports field is enlivened by children training hard to be the next Sadio Mané. The design, construction, and operations of Kamanar Secondary School were, and continue to be, defined by the project's various connections and associations, such as between the Catalonian-based architectural studio Dawoffice with its non-profit Foundawtion and the small Senegalese town of Thionck Essyl. Also, the individual connections – among the architect David García, his team, the teachers, the municipality, Tanta and Gaston, the broader community, and the flora and fauna – all provide the foundations and ecology for this built environment.

Figure 14. The school is now a thriving centre of learning.

1 Mark W. Deets, *A Country of Defiance: Mapping the Casamance in Senegal* (Athens, OH: Ohio University Press, 2023), p. 6.

2 Eromo Egbejule, "Senegal's Troubled Casamance Region Hopes for Peace with Rise of Local Boy to PM", *The Guardian*, 28 August 2024, https://www.theguardian.com/world/article/2024/aug/28/senegal-casamance-region-peace-ousmane-sonko-prime-minister.

3 Chris Simpson and Mamadou Alpha Diallo, "Between War and Peace: Forgotten Conflicts – Casamance", *The New Humanitarian*, 3 August 2015, https://www.thenewhumanitarian.org/2015/08/03/between-war-and-peace.

4 Agence Nationale de la Statistique et de la Démographie (ANSD), *Senegal Poverty Mapping Report*, 2016, p. 19, https://www.ansd.sn/sites/default/files/2022-11/SEN_PovMap_160512_rapport%20Version%20Anglaise.pdf.

5 Deets, *A Country of Defiance*, p. 127.

6 Réseau des Îles de Casamance / Lower Casamance Islands Network, "Éducation en milieu enclavé / Education in a Landlocked Environment", https://reseau-iles-casamance.org/?page_id=1153.

7 Ola Uduku, *Learning Spaces in Africa: Critical Histories to 21st Century Challenges and Change* (London: Routledge, 2018), p. 71.

8 Ibid, p. 72.

9 Foundawtion, "CEM Kamanar School", https://foundawtion.org/en/archivos/4604.

10 Ibid.

11 Farhan Karim, "Reinventing Earth Architecture in the Age of Development", in *The Routledge Companion to Architecture and Social Engagement*, ed. Farhan Karim (London: Routledge, 2018), pp. 241–52.

12 Foundawtion, "Professional Training Centre Bajankusoor", https://foundawtion.org/en/archivos/4636.

13 Bajankusoor is the name that traditionally denotes the place where the local wise men of the areas of southern Senegal sit down to think, discuss, and make decisions that structure the course of society. See Foundawtion, "Professional Training Centre Bajankusoor" (ibid.).

LAMINE SAMBOU
CARPENTER

I began working with Foundawtion in 2014. After a year, they told me, "We want to keep working with you," but at the time, I had no equipment and not even a workshop. Foundawtion offered to help if I could find a piece of land. They built me a workshop and provided equipment so I could work with them. That's when my life really changed. I started earning a living and supporting my family. But the workshop isn't just for me – it benefits the whole community. People come to work with me, and together we've built a livelihood. I'm very grateful to the foundation for what we've achieved.

Another big change came with the construction of the CEM school. It motivated the children to study harder and dream bigger. CEM Kamanar is a beautiful, welcoming school like we've never had before. Even the teachers love working there, and the children feel proud to study there.

My own son once told me, "Dad, one day I'll succeed so I can go study at CEM." Now, he's in his second year there. He sees me working at the CEM school and has asked, "Dad, is it really you who did all this?" I told him, "Yes, it's me," and he thanked me. That moment made me proud.

Today, I'm respected in my village and community, but I always say this isn't only because of me; it's thanks to the foundation and what we've built together.

We share this success as a team.

OUMY SAGNA
PRESIDENT OF THE WOMEN'S ASSOCIATION

I was involved from the beginning of the school's construction, working closely with the women in our community. Women are the ones who assess the situation and take action. When we engaged with the Spanish team, we spoke up so that our priorities would be understood.

From the women's side, we were deeply involved. The old school was too small to accommodate all of the students, so expanding it became necessary. With the approval of the town hall and the support of the municipal council, we made land available for construction. We couldn't act alone – community and institutional support were essential.

Our contribution wasn't financial, but we ensured that our voices were heard. We worked to integrate the school into the community, reduce overcrowding, and make education more accessible. When the foundation called on us, we responded. Education is our first priority. We encourage the children to study hard, to aim for excellence, and this school became a step in that direction.

It wasn't an easy process, but communication and awareness-building helped us move forward. We continue to meet and assess the conditions, because the work isn't finished. More still needs to be done to meet the needs of the students.

As women, we manage households, raise children, and make sure that they grow strong and capable. This school is part of that larger responsibility. It's through activity, intelligence, and perseverance that things move forward – not through wealth alone.

The project involved everyone – men and women alike – because we share a common responsibility for the well-being of our children. The land we chose for the school is part of that commitment. It's part of what we could do, and we did it. But our work continues, and there are still more needs we are preparing to bring forward.

Gaston and Tanta hosted the foreign volunteers who came to work with Dawoffice and Foundawtion in constructing the school. Here Gaston explains their experience in hosting the volunteers and the impact of the school on the community.

GASTON AND TANTA

I remember when the first volunteers came to our village in 2016. My son, Mohamed, was still in high school at the time. He had connected with them and invited them to spend weekends with us. Eventually, they asked if they could stay more permanently, and we welcomed them into our home. We had two rooms that were normally used for storing food and equipment, and we cleared them out so the volunteers could live there. We even moved the contents into the kitchen to make space. The volunteers handled everything – installing cement floors, fitting doors – without asking for anything in return.

They offered to pay rent, and even the town hall sent someone to ask what we would charge. But I refused. I told them we don't do that. I had been hosted myself when I was younger and living in Dakar. I never paid rent or for food. It would have been wrong of me to do otherwise now. Hosting the volunteers felt right, and it was done out of friendship and solidarity, not money.

From the moment they moved in, a strong bond grew between us. We shared everything – meals, stories, responsibilities. They respected us, and we treated them like family. All the volunteers who passed through here became like sons to me. That experience of cultural exchange was meaningful. I still remember how deeply they engaged with the community, and how naturally they became part of our lives.

The CEM (Kamanar Secondary School) they helped build truly transformed our village. It's not like anything else I've seen in Senegal – or even in Africa. The design, the facilities, the environment – it's modern, well maintained, and thoughtfully built. Students now have proper spaces to sit during breaks, ventilated classrooms, and even showers. It's a far cry from the overcrowded classrooms we had before, with fifty or more students packed into a single room. Now, they have space, comfort, and dignity in their learning.

What makes me most proud is how the CEM is maintained. The foundation and its partners continue to take care of it. I've seen it myself – small repairs, improvements, regular upkeep. That kind of commitment is rare. Visitors from Dakar, Saint-Louis, and even international delegations come to see the CEM because it has become a model. They're always impressed by its quality and the welcome they receive from the staff and community.

We've also benefited from the workshop and other initiatives linked to the CEM. And just recently, volunteers organised an event to award certificates to those involved in the construction – recognising not just the physical work, but the collaboration that made it all possible.

In every sense, this experience has shown me the power of community, hospitality, and cultural exchange. We've gained much more than a building. We've gained friendships, opportunities, and a future for our children. That's something I'll always carry with me.

The entrance to the Kamanar Secondary School is more than just a gateway; it functions as a small social space that connects the school to the daily life of the surrounding community.

The *awla* is built as a modular unit, and the hands-on training provided to the community is aimed to ensure that further expansion of the school can be done independently.

Stairs leading to the water tower

A tin roof protects the clay arches of the *alwa* from the rain.

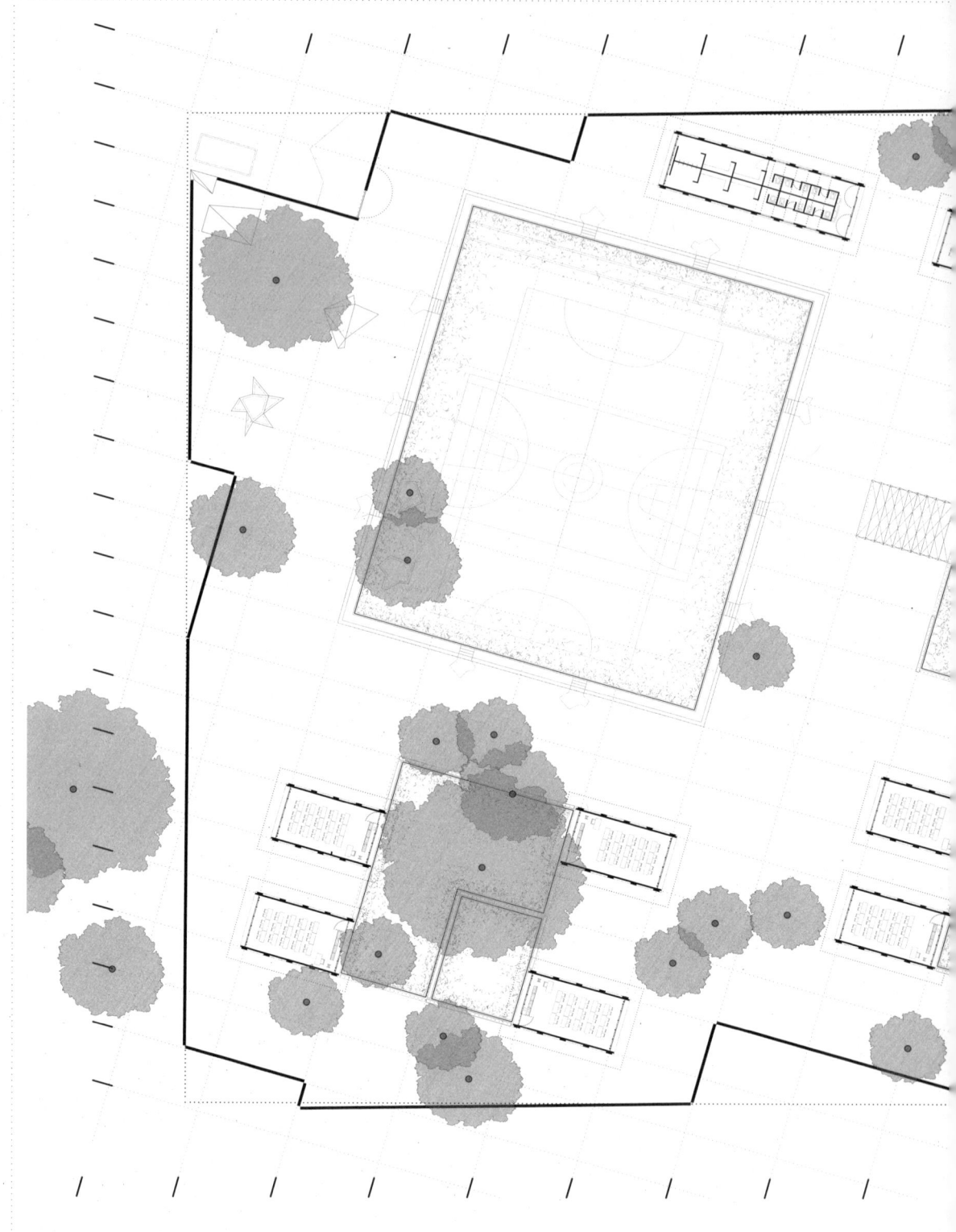

Site plan of the Kamanar Secondary School (CEM)

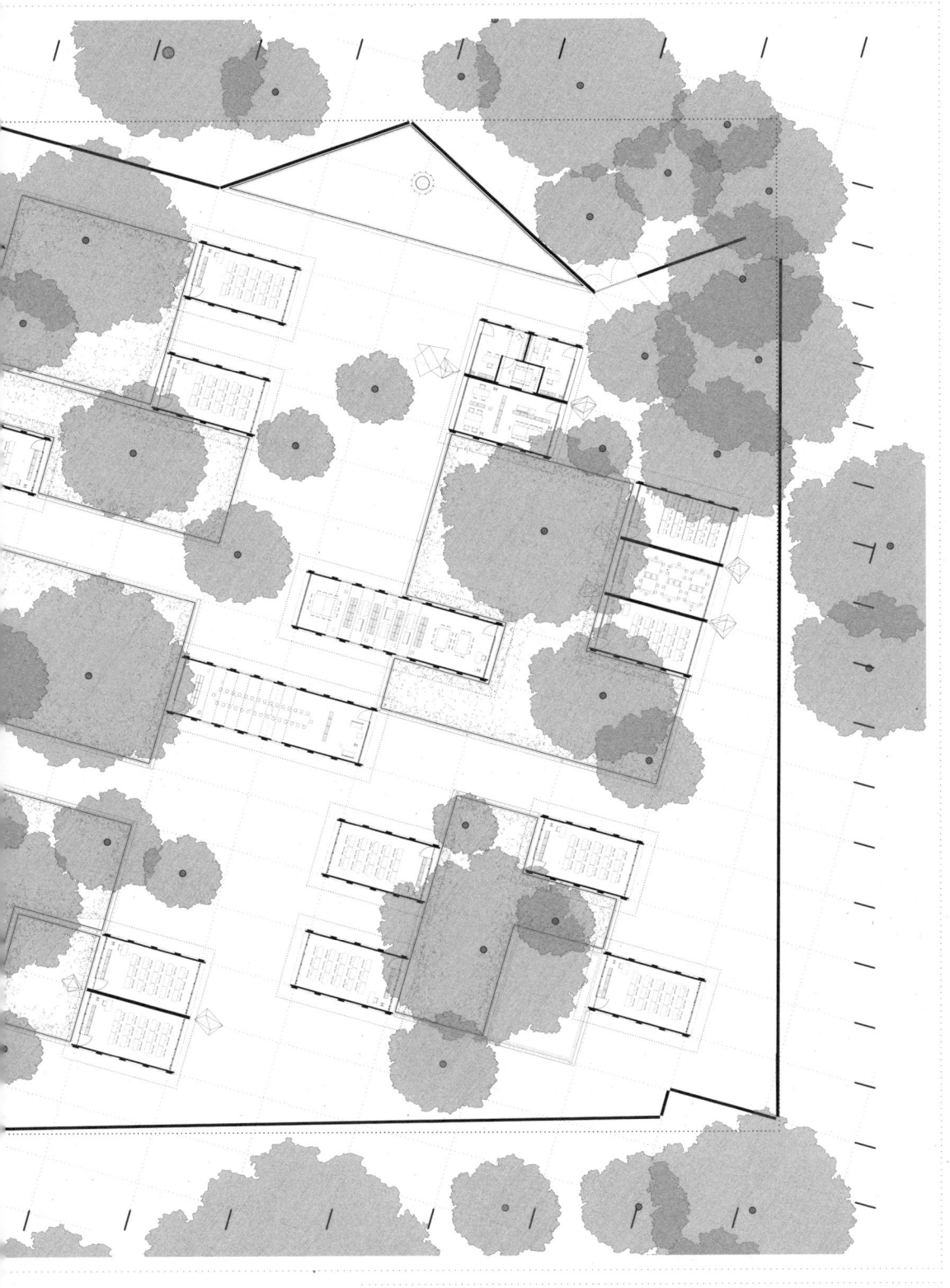
CEM KAMANAR | DAWOFFICE
Títol del plànol

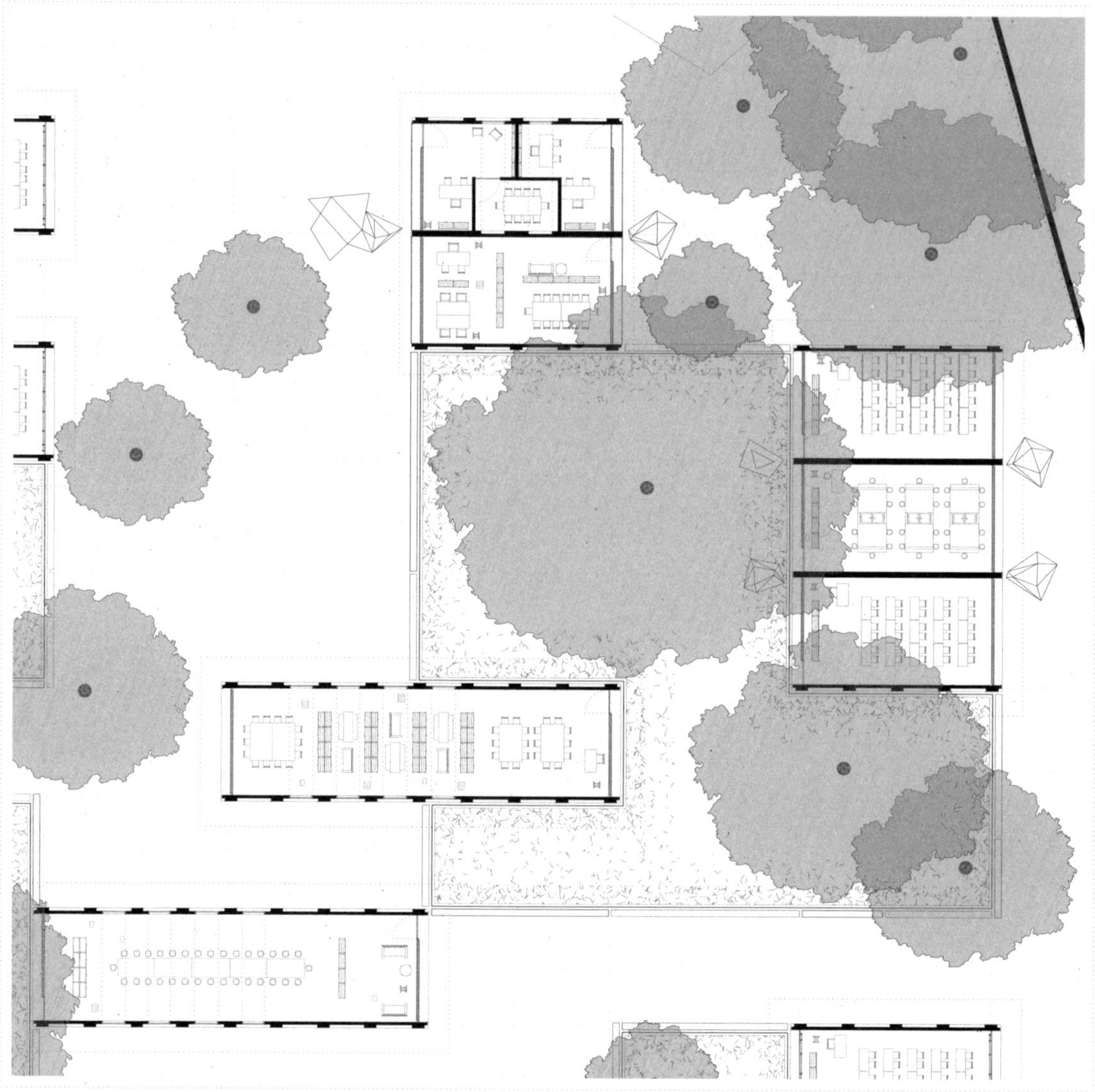

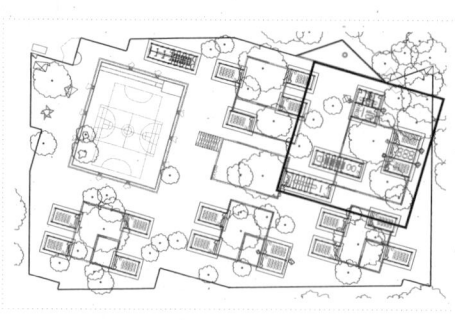

CEM KAMANAR | DAWOFFICE
Titol del plànol

02

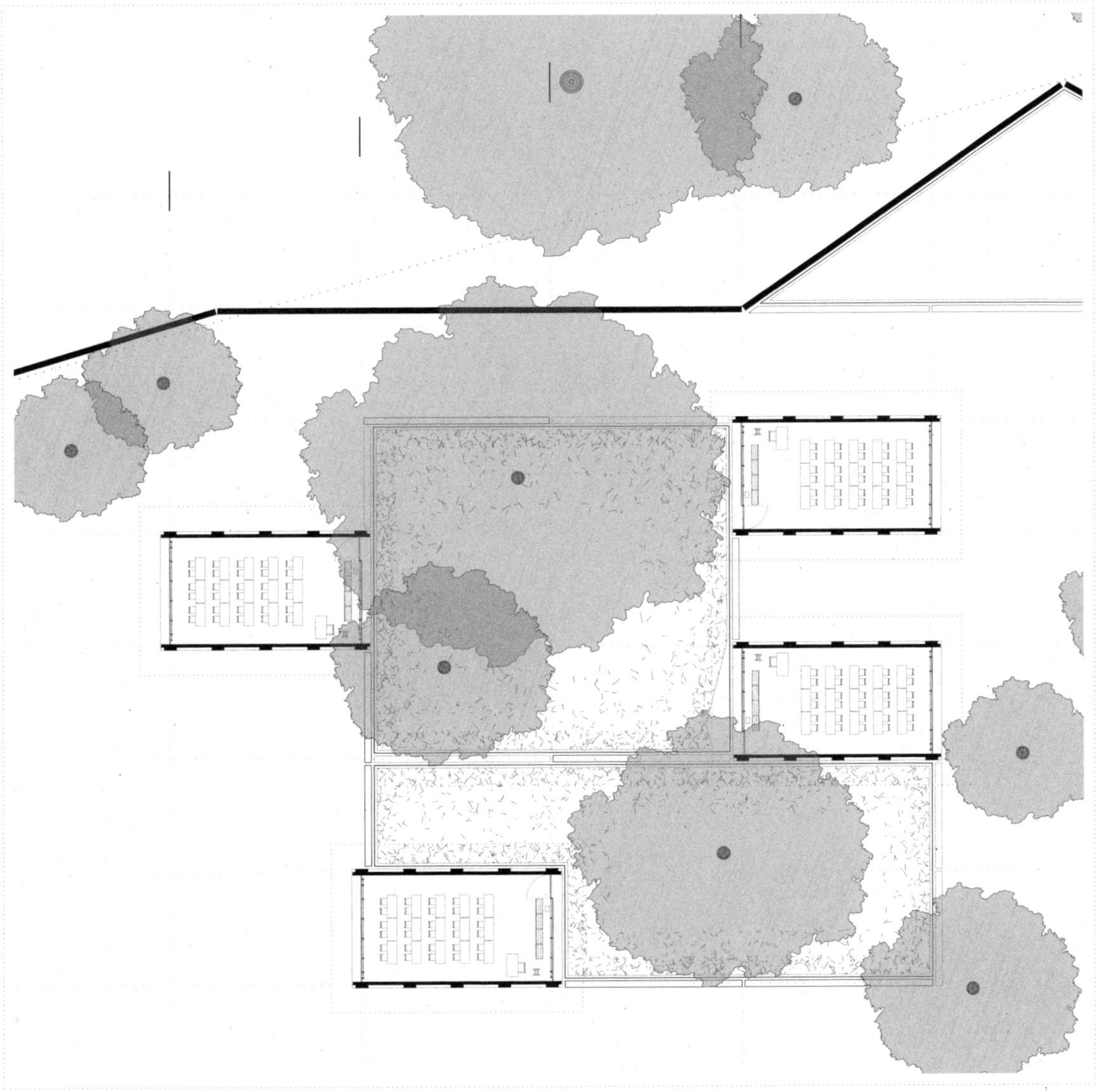

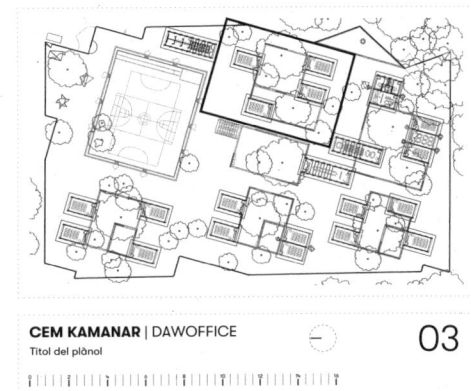

CEM KAMANAR | DAWOFFICE
Titol del plànol

03

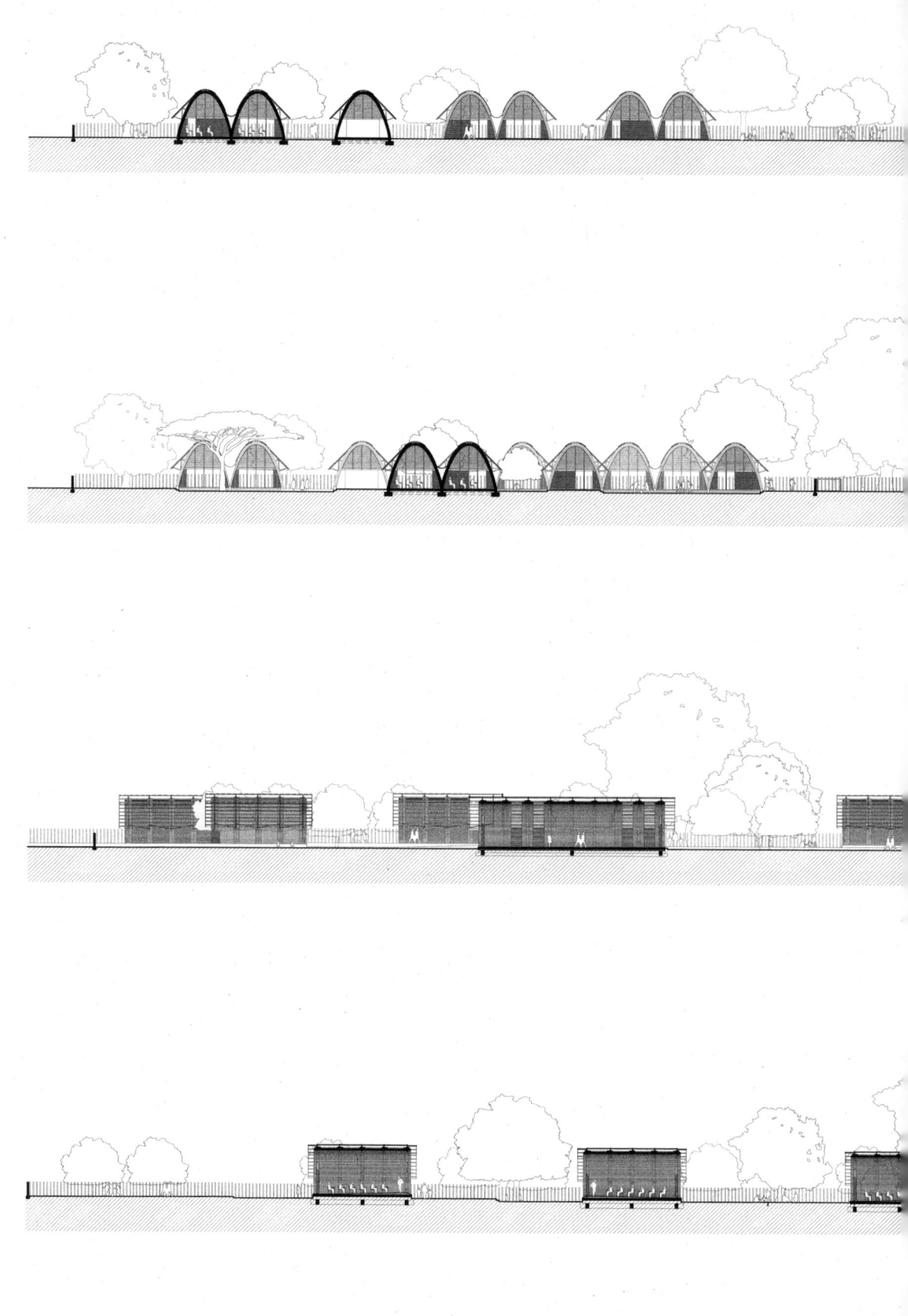

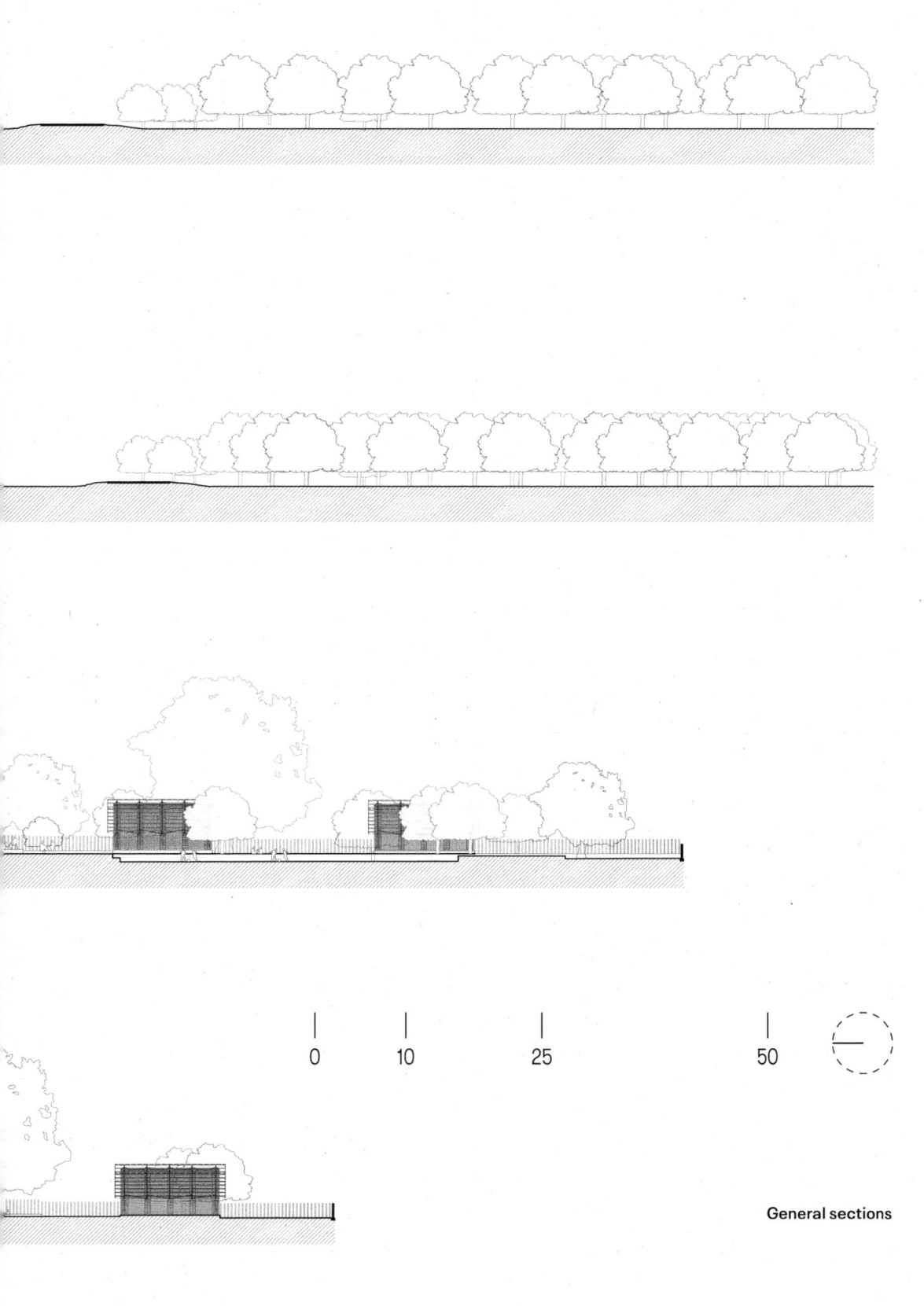

General sections

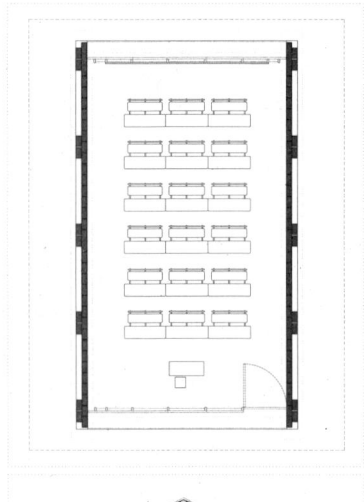
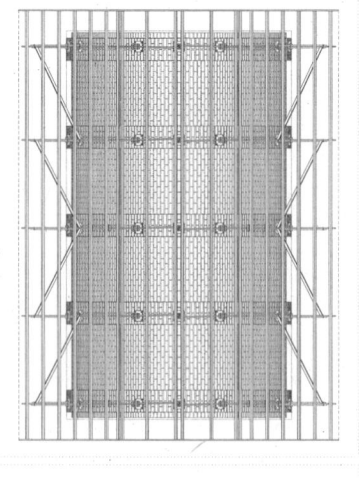
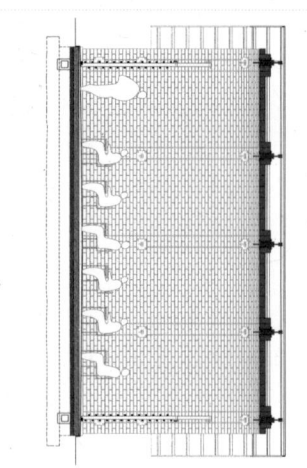
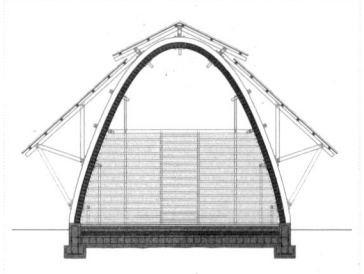
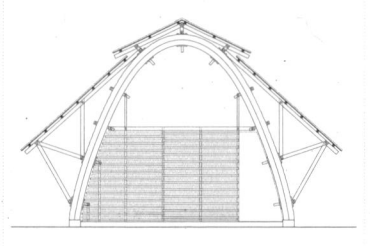
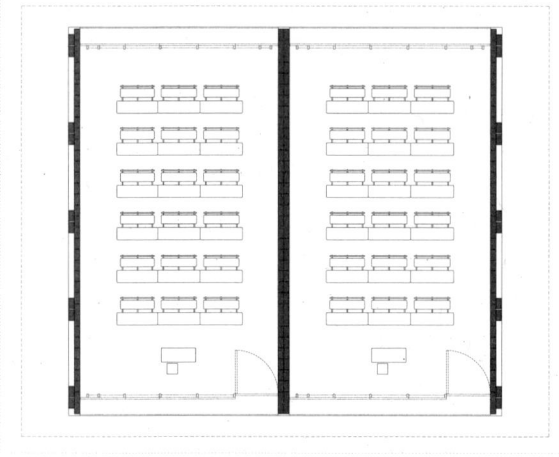
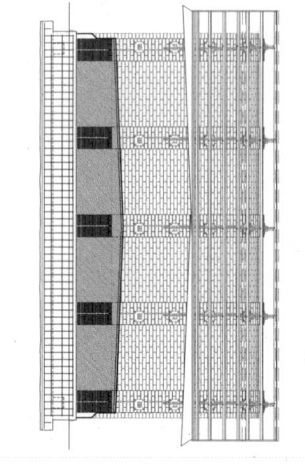
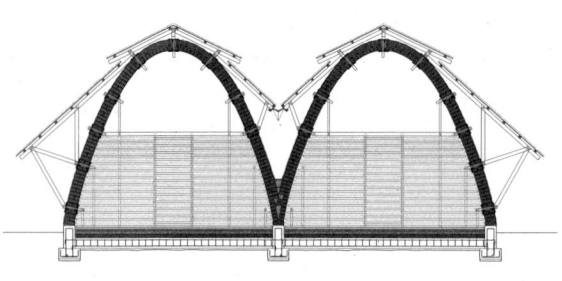

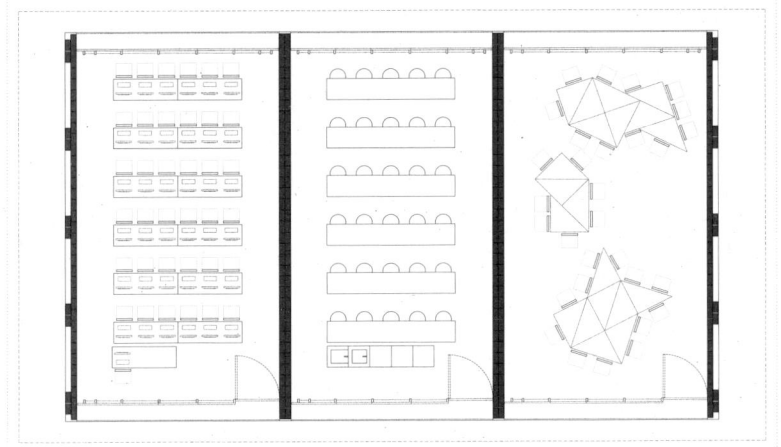
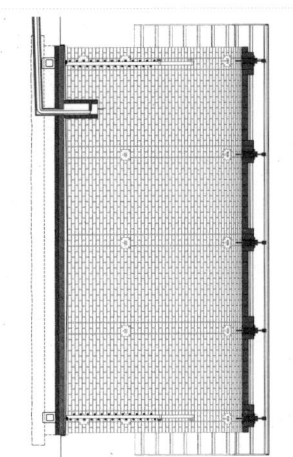
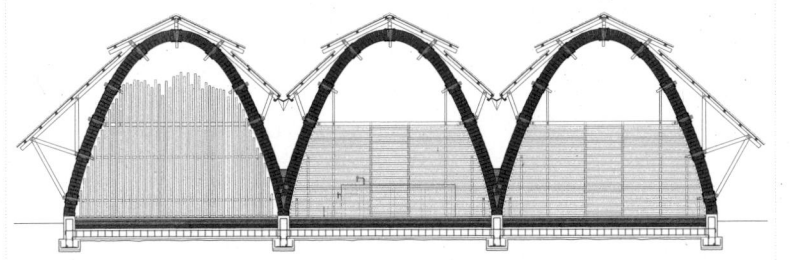

detall 05

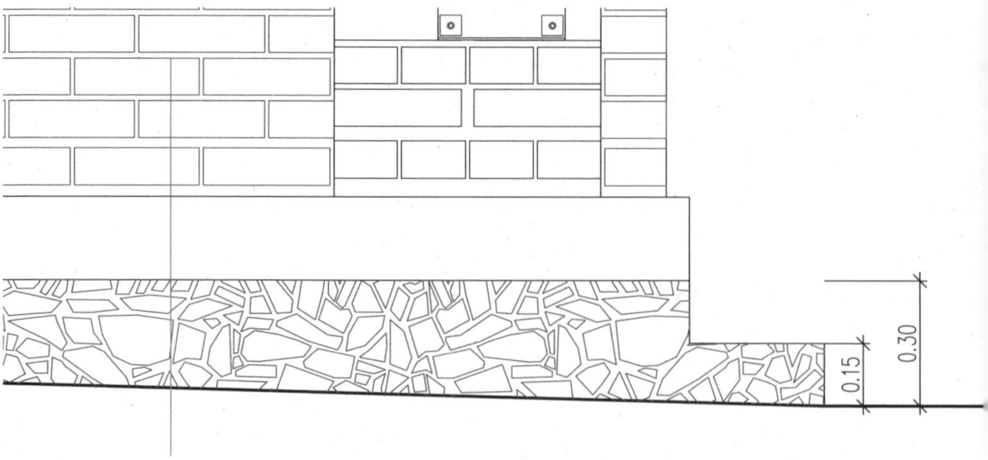

0.30
0.15

Detail of the wall finished with reused ceramics

detall 02

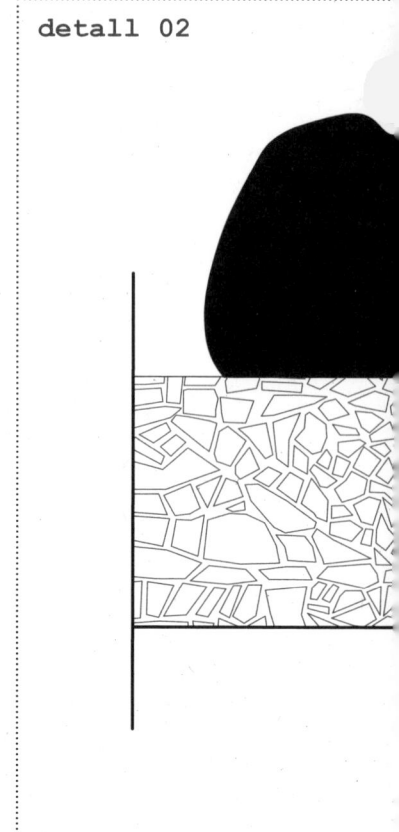

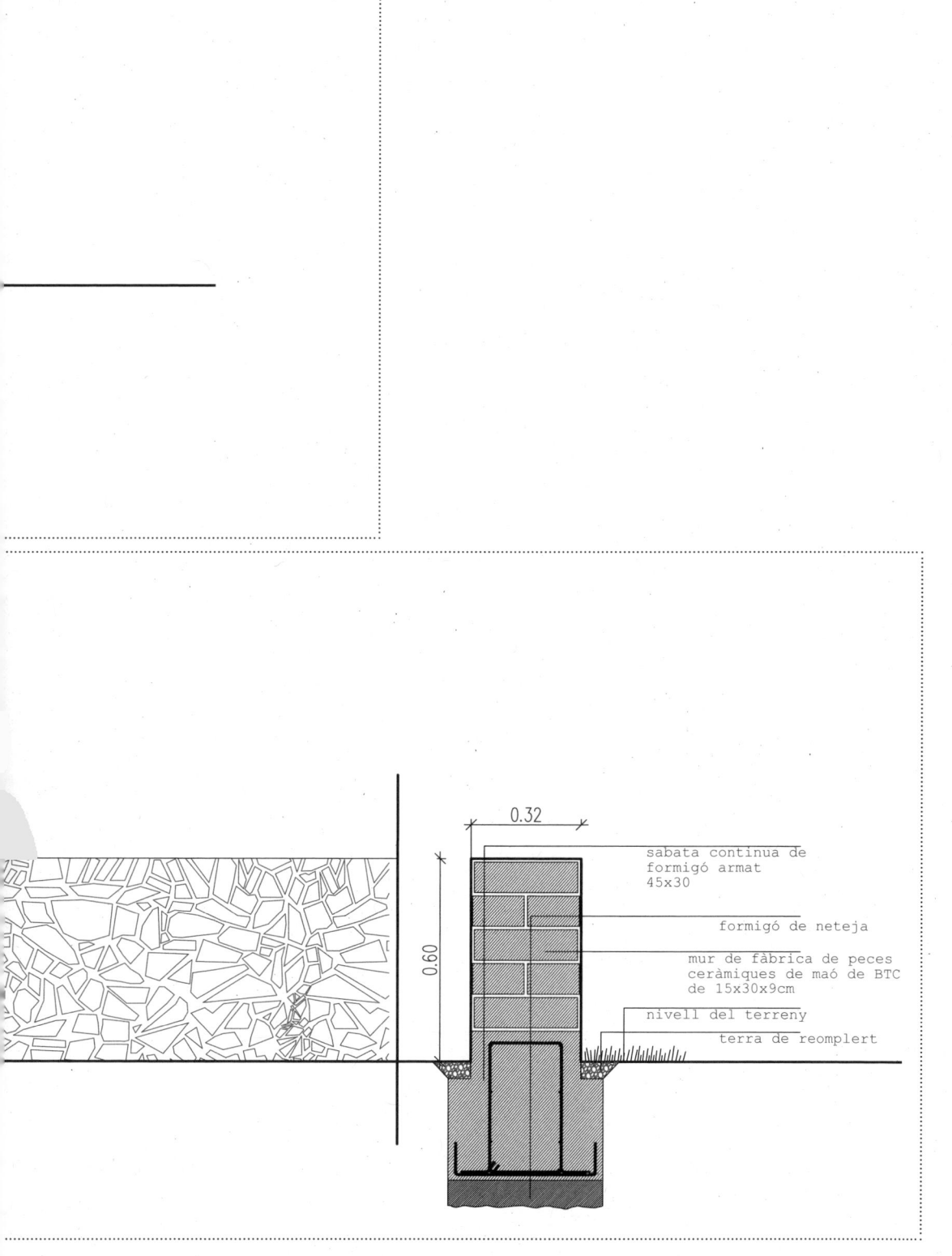

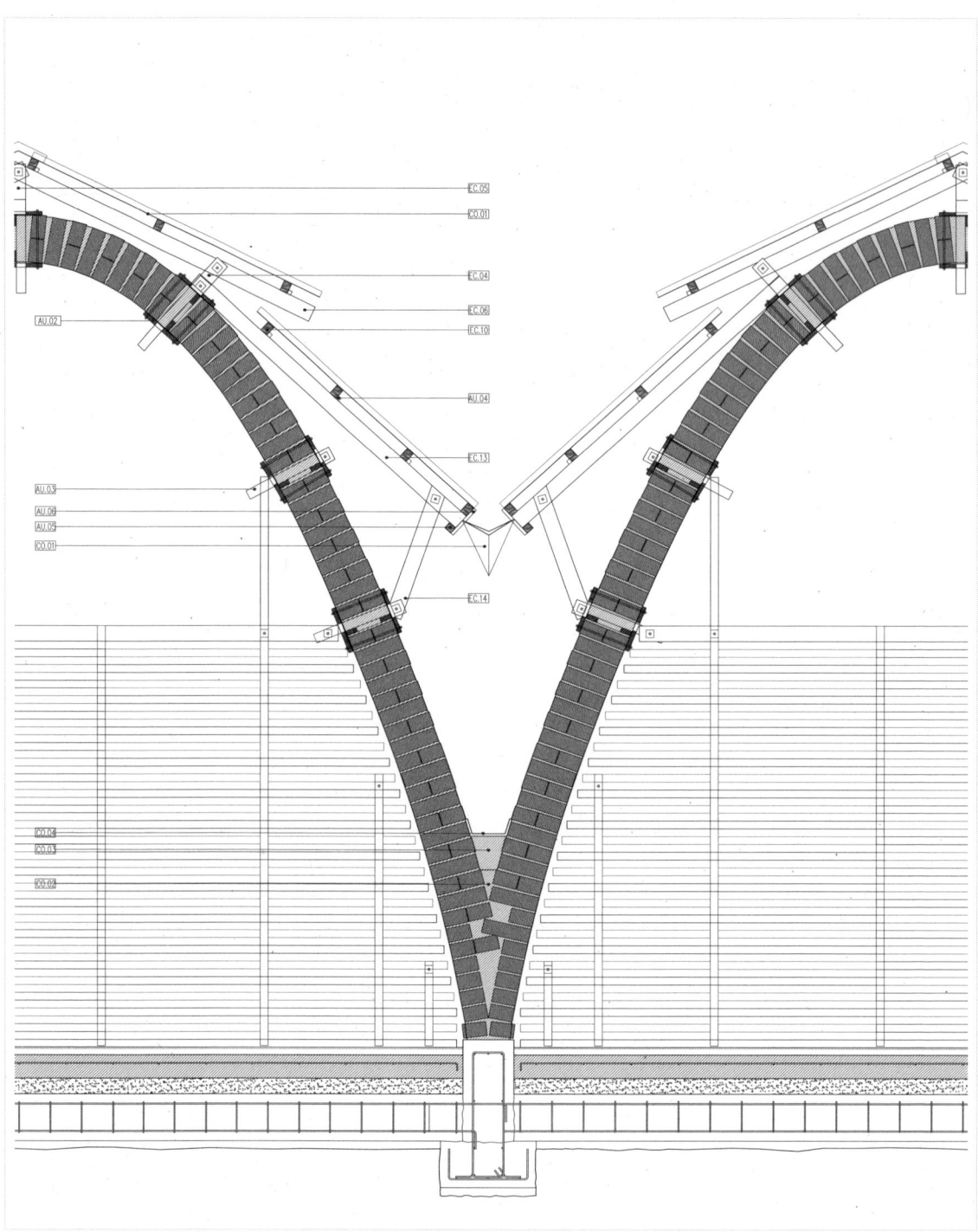

Detail of the catenary arches of the *awlas*

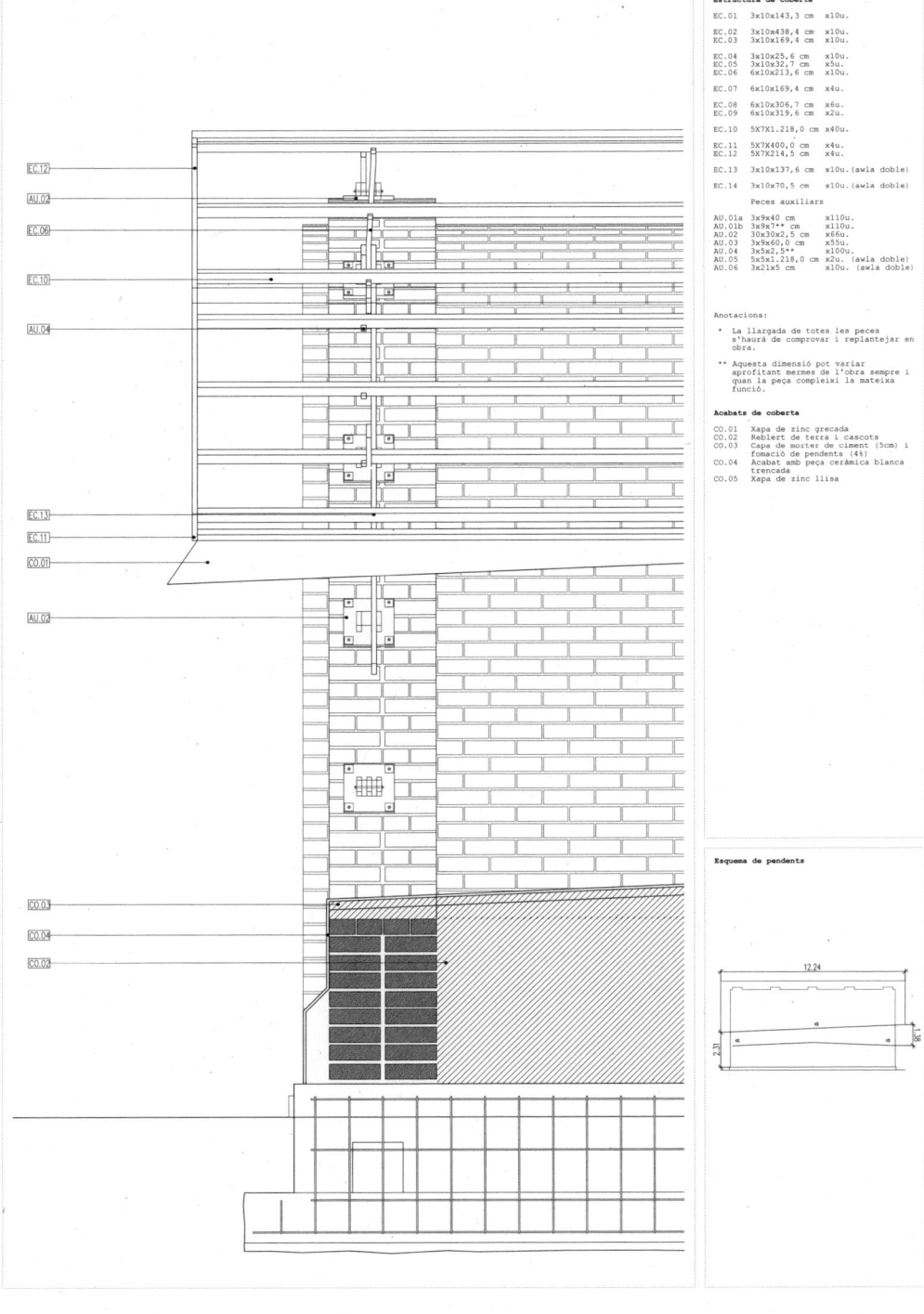

Estructura de coberta*

EC.01	3x10x143,3 cm	x10u.
EC.02	3x10x438,4 cm	x10u.
EC.03	3x10x169,4 cm	x10u.
EC.04	3x10x25,6 cm	x10u.
EC.05	3x10x32,7 cm	x5u.
EC.06	6x10x213,6 cm	x10u.
EC.07	6x10x169,4 cm	x4u.
EC.08	6x10x306,7 cm	x6u.
EC.09	6x10x319,6 cm	x2u.
EC.10	5X7X1.218,0 cm	x40u.
EC.11	5X7X400,0 cm	x4u.
EC.12	5X7X214,5 cm	x4u.
EC.13	3x10x137,6 cm	x10u. (awla doble)
EC.14	3x10x70,5 cm	x10u. (awla doble)

Peces auxiliars

AU.01a	3x9x40 cm	x110u.
AU.01b	3x9x7** cm	x110u.
AU.02	30x30x2,5 cm	x66u.
AU.03	3x9x60,0 cm	x55u.
AU.04	3x5x2,5**	x100u.
AU.05	5x5x1.218,0 cm	x2u. (awla doble)
AU.06	3x21x5 cm	x10u. (awla doble)

Anotacions:

* La llargada de totes les peces s'haurà de comprovar i replantejar en obra.

** Aquesta dimensió pot variar aprofitant mermes de l'obra sempre i quan la peça compleixi la mateixa funció.

Acabats de coberta

CO.01 Xapa de zinc grecada
CO.02 Reblert de terra i cascots
CO.03 Capa de morter de ciment (5cm) i fomació de pendents (4%)
CO.04 Acabat amb peça ceràmica blanca trencada
CO.05 Xapa de zinc llisa

Esquema de pendents

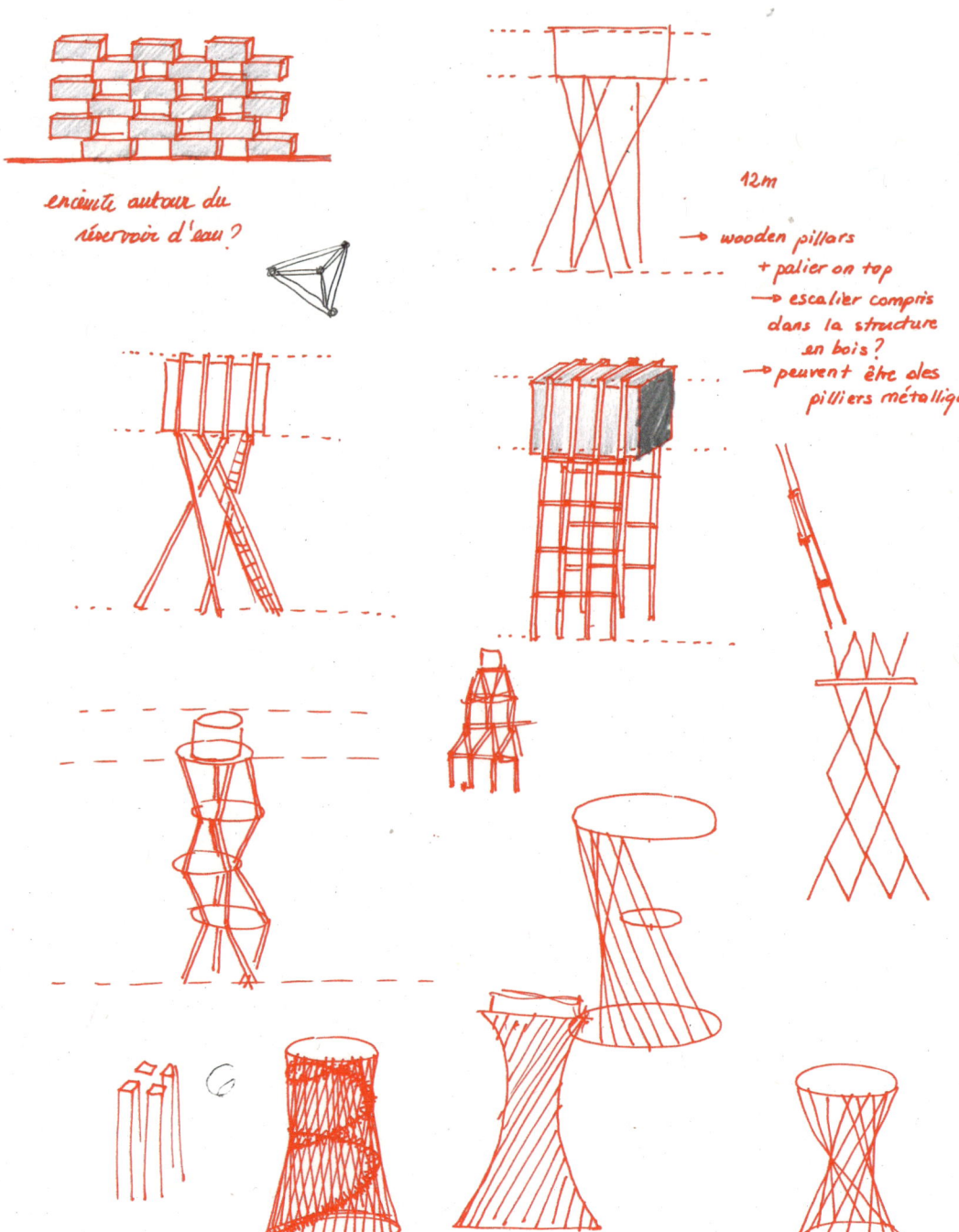

Dawoffice architectural reference sketches

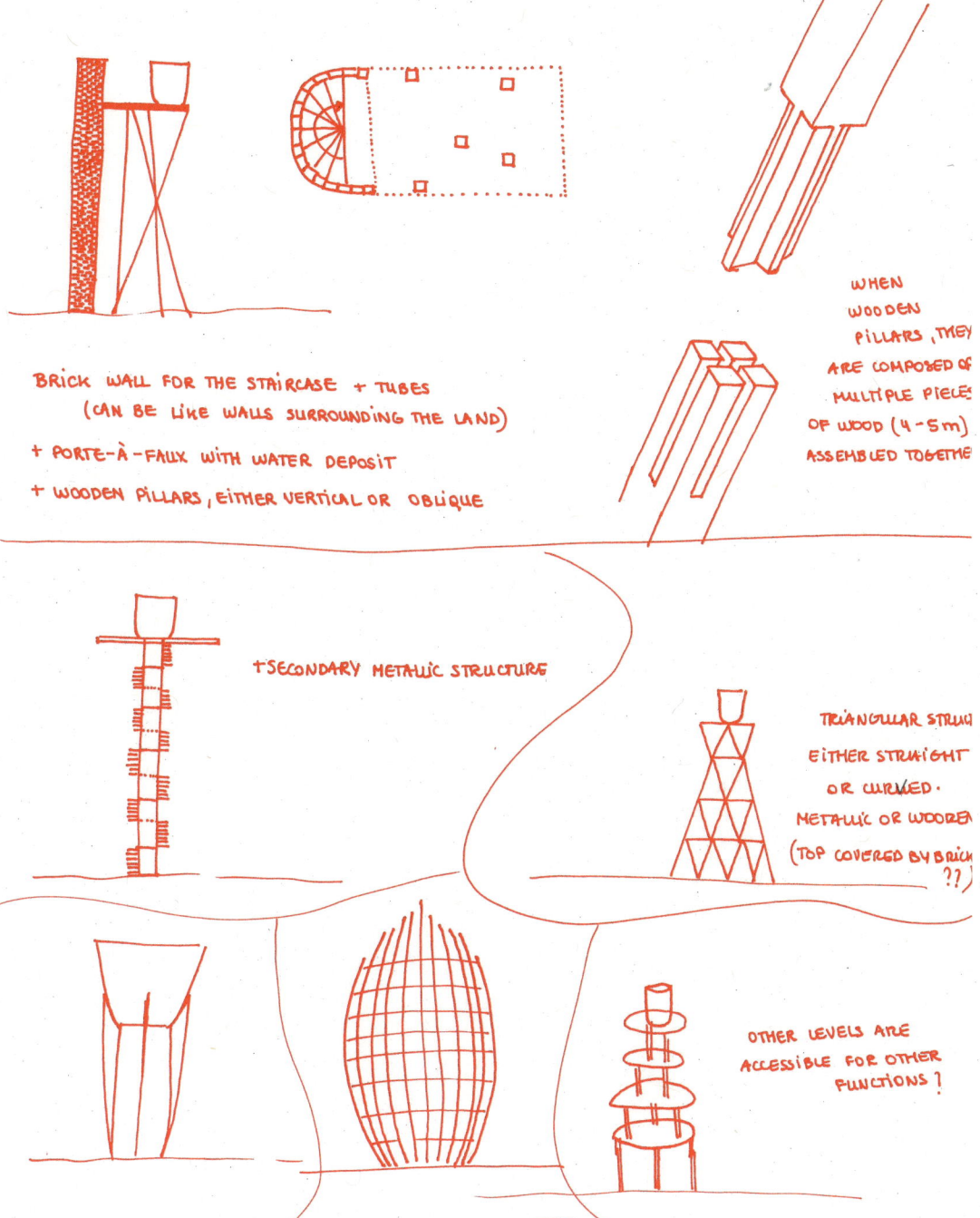

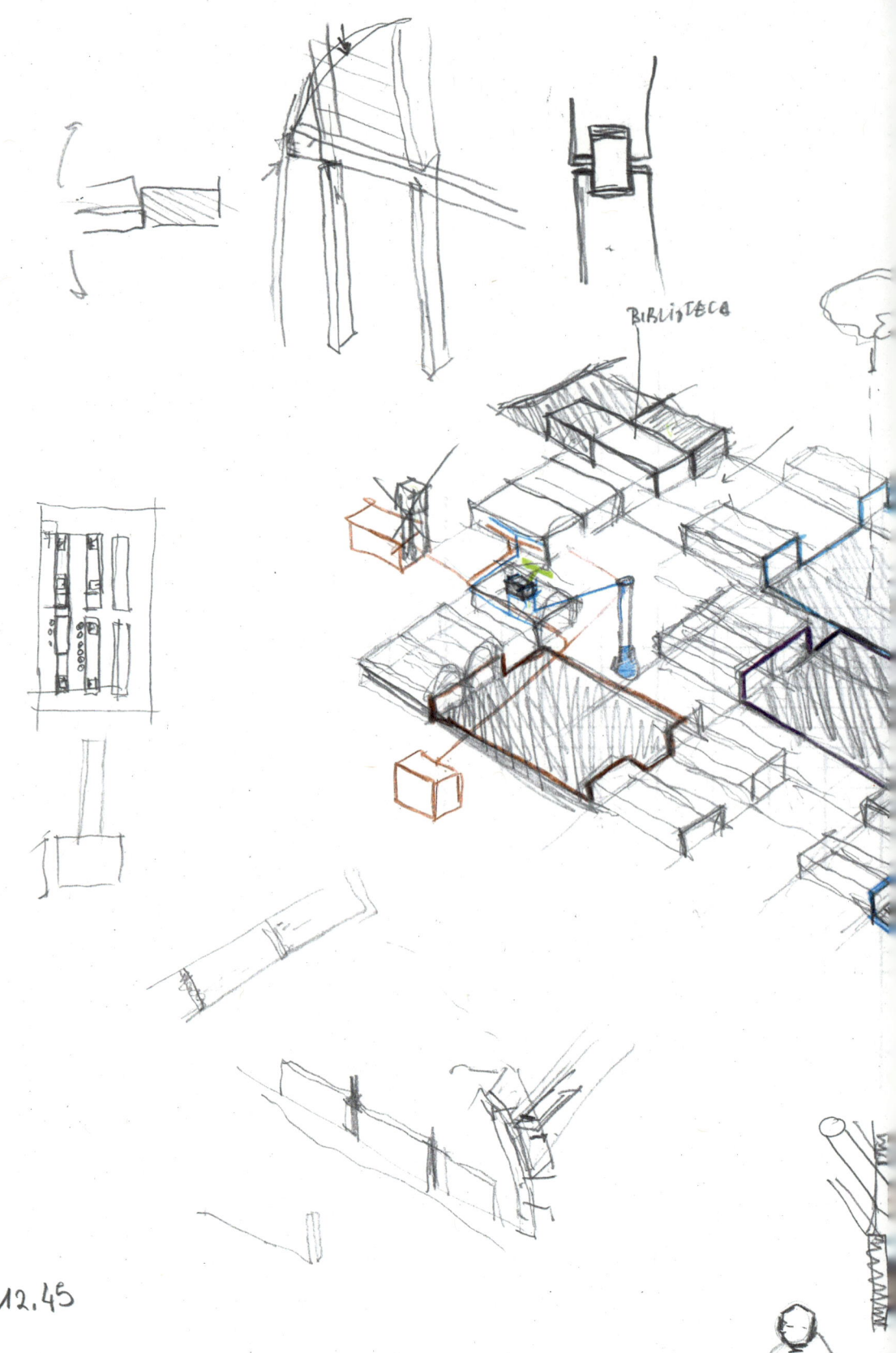

12.45

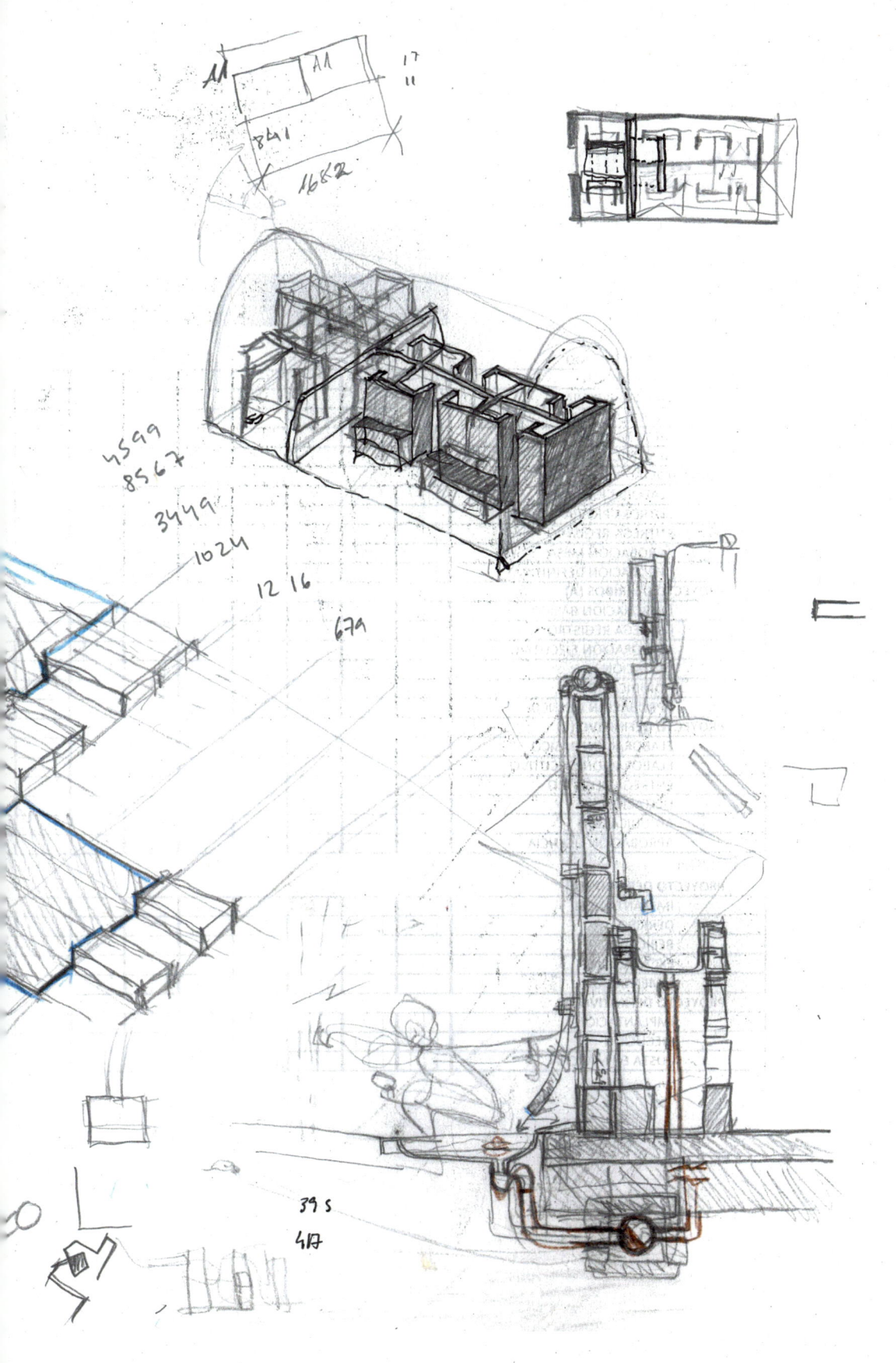

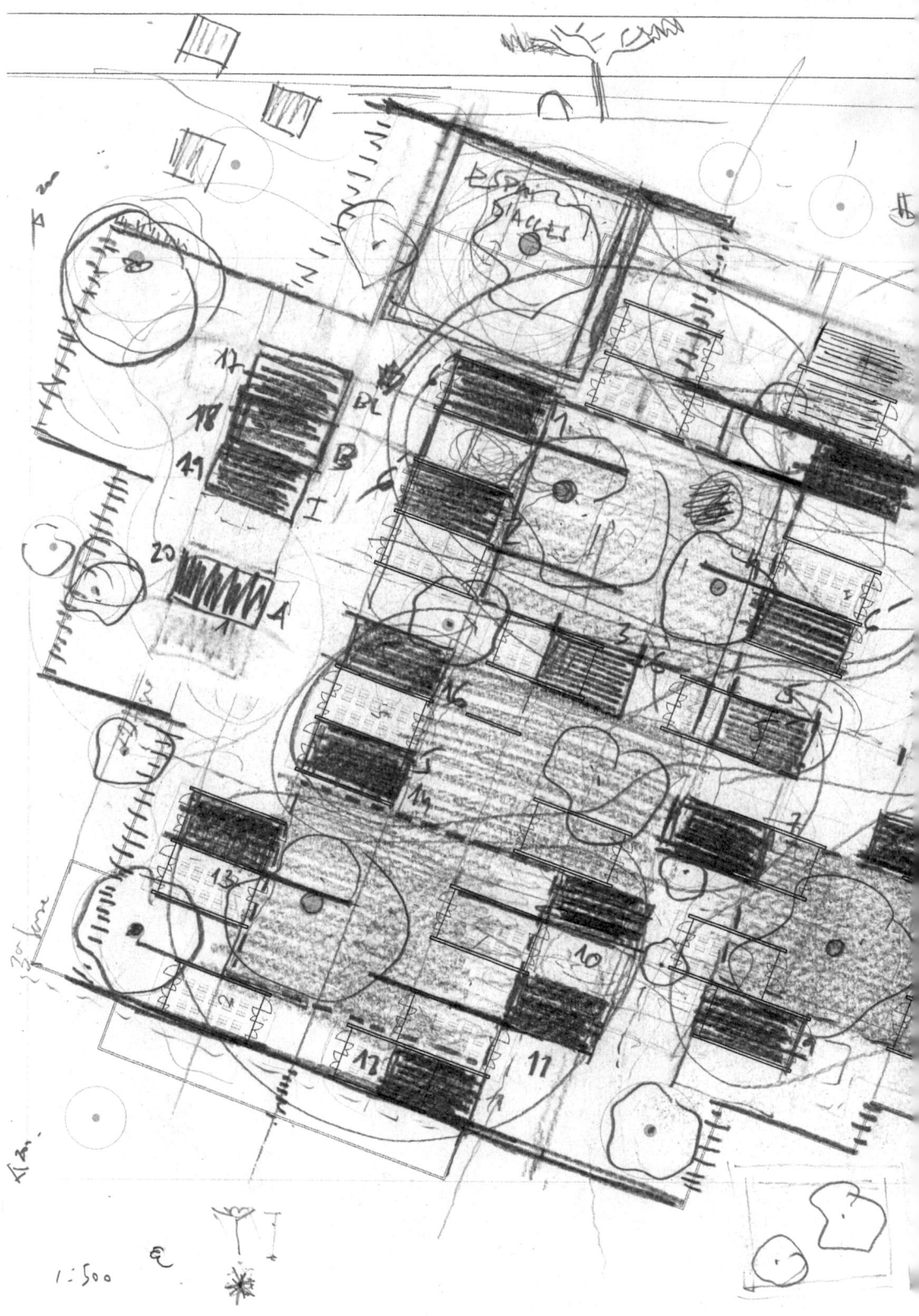

A sketch of the site

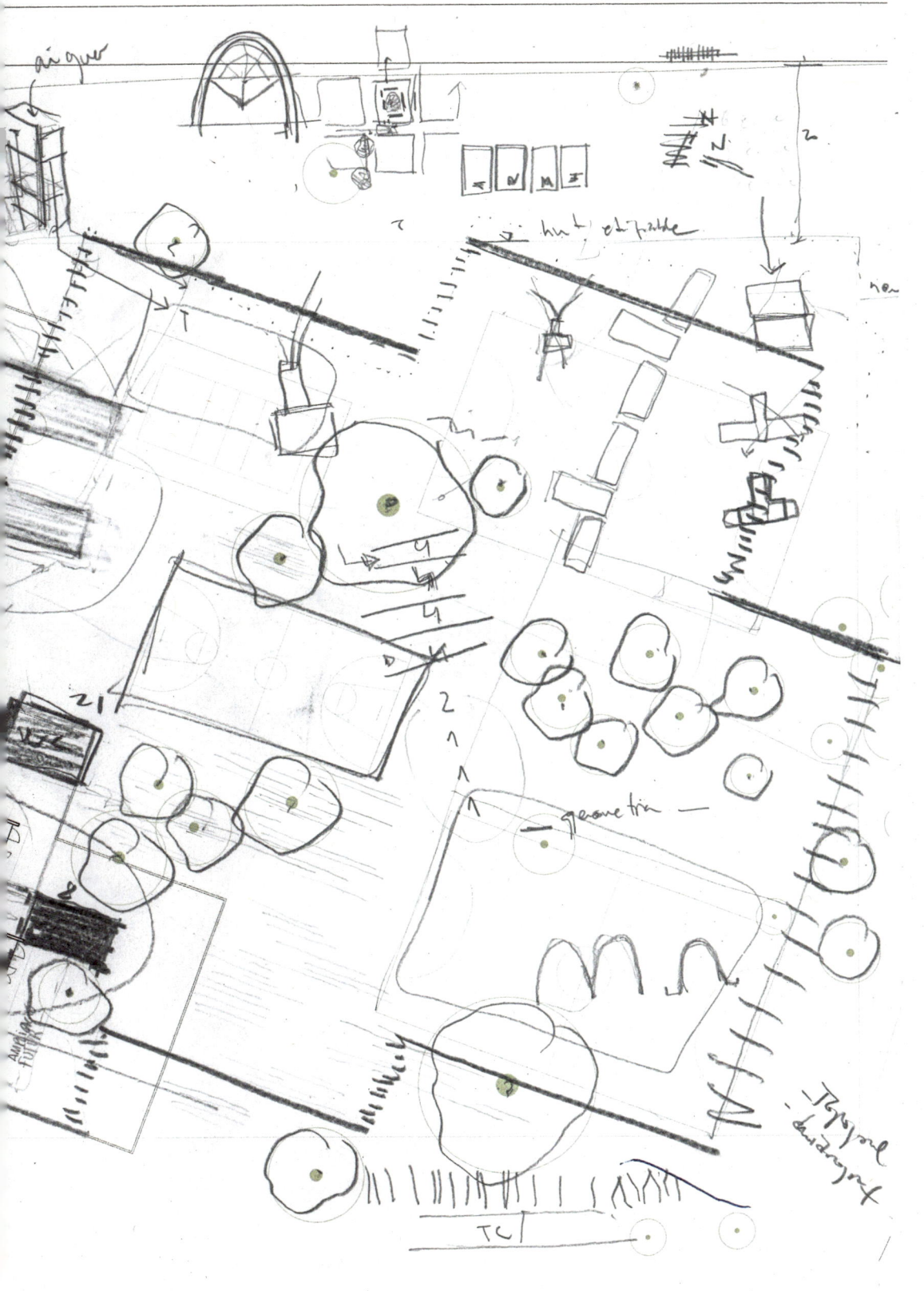

Socially Engaged Architecture as a Pedagogical Practice

Farhan S. Karim

Introduction

Education and its built environment have long been battlegrounds in anti-colonial movements throughout the Global South, shaping visions of liberation while often entrenching colonial legacies.[1] The reform of education remains a central concern for postcolonial nations, yet paradoxically, these efforts often reproduce the very logic of what Gayatri Chakravorty Spivak has called the colonial "teaching machine", embedded within postcolonial "development" narratives.[2] In *Outside in the Teaching Machine*, Spivak describes the "teaching machine" as a pedagogical system that perpetuates coloniality in the name of modernity, compelling postcolonial subjects to adopt hegemonic knowledge and values.[3] In order to disrupt or to *unlearn* this system, Spivak suggests, new kinds of pedagogical practices are imperative.[4] Building on this idea, I argue that the architectural design of educational buildings can potentially disrupt the "teaching machine" by introducing critical learning environments that honour diverse ways of knowing and experiencing.

While Gayatri Spivak's pedagogical programme calls for a fundamental restructuring of knowledge institutions, Lisa Rosén Rasmussen highlights how spatial arrangements – such as classroom layouts modified by teachers[5] – are deeply intertwined with pedagogical ideas. Extending this view, we can argue that architectural space itself can actively shape and support the kinds of transformative pedagogical practices that Spivak advocates. In this sense, space is not just a backdrop for education but a critical participant in how learning and empowerment unfold. This essay examines three architectural projects in Bangladesh that critically reconsider the role of education and educational buildings in fostering a more equitable society, both economically and epistemologically. Each of these projects – the Modern Education and Training Institute (METI) School in Rudrapur (2007), the Arcadia Education Project in South Kanarchor (2019), and the Community Spaces in Rohingya Refugee Response (2022) – received the Aga Khan Award for Architecture and employed *social engagement* as a core design strategy to create critical learning environments.[6] Their significance lies in three key aspects. First, all three projects challenge the hierarchy between architectural form and process, instead adopting a non-hierarchical approach that treats both as mutually constitutive. Second, they extend community involvement beyond the initial design phase, embedding participation into the ongoing life of the building. And third, they demonstrate how care, as a strategy of social engagement, can shape architectural practice and process.

Making and Caring as Social Engagement

Designed by the German architect Anna Heringer, and commissioned by Dipshikha, a non-governmental organisation (NGO), the METI School was the third project built in post-independence Bangladesh to win an Aga Khan Award. Located in the village of Rudrapur, the school

Figure 1. The METI School designed by the German architect Anna Heringer replaces the disciplinary spaces of the public school with a playful atmosphere that facilitates "learning with joy".

provides education for children and young people up to age fourteen, as well as workshops for trade-related skills.[7] Dipshikha adapted aspects of the Montessori method to the local context, referring to their approach as "formational and life-oriented learning".[8]

One of the key architectural strategies for expressing this "life-oriented" approach was to replace the pervasive disciplinary spaces of the public schools with a playful atmosphere resonating with the rural environment, one that facilitates "learning with joy". Nevertheless, the initial decision to use "mud" in combination with local materials such as bamboo, along with the unconventional use of long, colourful fabrics as curtains, was initially met with scepticism by local stakeholders (fig. 1).[9] The school's first headmaster, Prodip Tigga, voiced concerns that the image of a mud-built school might clash with parents' aspirations, stating: "A mud school would symbolise to most of them that they cannot afford anything better."[10] Despite these concerns, the construction process – a combination of donated labour from the school community and the paid labour of the architect and the NGO administrators – fostered a growing appreciation for this alternative vision.[11]

Although there was limited aesthetic input on the design from community members, Anna Heringer worked with local builders and artisans to refine traditional construction techniques for the project, but also to record the process for future use by craftspeople. Community engagement was conceived as an ongoing exchange of knowledge between the local experts who had an understanding of available materials, the architect, and the commissioner.

Figure 2. The METI School is devoid of traditional furniture and features unusual circular openings made of bamboo and mud. Children play in soft "caves", which encourages us to reimagine the familiar archetype of a good school.

Devoid of conventional furniture, marked by circular openings, and constructed from bamboo and mud, the METI school challenges the prevailing notion of a "good school" in Bangladesh, typically associated with *paka* (brick) buildings where strict discipline and even corporal punishment are seen as necessary for producing financially successful individuals.[12] In contrast, widely circulated images of METI show children playing in soft, caved spaces at the rear of the building (fig. 2). This invites a reimagining of what a school can be. Its "soft" interiors offer a compelling critique of the rigid, disciplinarian environments that dominate Bangladesh's educational landscape.

The Arcadia Education Project in South Kanarchor, in turn, is a school that was completed in 2016 by the Dhaka-based architectural firm Saif Ul Haque Sthapati. It was commissioned by the Maleka Welfare Trust, a family-run foundation established by Razia Alam, a retired schoolteacher who returned to Bangladesh after living in the United Kingdom. Upon her return, Alam initiated a pilot preschool programme on the outskirts of Dhaka, operating from a rented property. When the lease ended, the trust planned to establish a permanent school on its own land, aiming to offer educational services to the rural community.[13] Due to budget constraints, the

Figure 3. The Arcadia Education Project by the architectural practice Saif Ul Haque Sthapati was designed to float over the monsoon water and settle on land during the dry season.

trust purchased an inexpensive plot of land that floods, with up to 3 metres of water for four to five months each year during the monsoon season (fig. 3). In response, an "amphibious" school was constructed: a building designed to float during the floods and rest on solid ground during the dry season. Serving as a preschool for nearby villages, the project addresses a critical gap in early childhood education for the rural community, as Bangladesh's public education system does not include this segment.

As it turned out, the school did not survive beyond its fifth monsoon, sparking debate about the value of low-tech, eco-conscious architecture.[14] The building's short lifespan and its destruction by natural forces suggest that architecture must exist, transform, or disappear in conjunction with the community it is a part of. From the outset, Saif Ul Haque and Razia Alam were aware that the project would require ongoing care and upkeep from the community. This inevitability of being *cared for* was seen not as insufficiency, but as an a priori fact that conditions architectural existence. While the design process – particularly the spatial and aesthetic decisions – was largely directed by the architects, the continued existence of the building depended on the care of the community. This stands in contrast to the logic of monumental architecture, which is designed to endure for centuries, even in ruin, and theoretically demands minimal upkeep from the society it serves.[15] The initial carbon-intensive investment in monumental structures is justified by their long-term durability and low maintenance requirements. On the other hand, the Arcadia School – what we might call low-carbon yet perishable architecture – can only endure so long as the humans it serves remain actively engaged in its preservation.[16] While these two models – monumental and perishable – are not necessarily mutually exclusive, the latter could not be more relevant in the contemporary age.

Care across all three projects considered in this chapter is a strategy of social engagement. It is important to distinguish *care* from *maintenance*. Maintenance typically implies a transactional service – provided by professionals and valued through monetary exchange. In contrast, care refers to a sustained, non-exchangeable commitment from the community that the building serves. Giorgio Agamben's analysis of *use*, as discussed in *The Use of Bodies*, the final volume of his *Homo Sacer* series, is particularly relevant for our discussion.[17] Extending Marxist analysis on *use*, Agamben argues that human existentiality lies in its capacity to become *useful* by transforming the natural world into a *useful* system. However, this notion of *use* does not imply the commodification of natural resources. Instead, it suggests an existential awareness that arises from engagement with the material and natural world, while eschewing the exchange value that an object might produce.

According to Agamben, a social system that can decouple exchange value from use value opens up the possibility of care in which society sustains the material and natural world through prolonged engagement. This concept is especially relevant in understanding the life and eventual demise of the Arcadia project. With the low-cost, unstable land and the concomitant low-cost materials, the exchange value of the school building as a product receded into the background. The residual use value of education could only be sustained through the community's continued care and engagement with the building – not as a commodity, but as a living space. From this perspective, the Arcadia School, along with the other two projects, poses a bigger question: Are we willing to care?

One of the architects of the project Community Spaces in Rohingya Refugee Response, Rizvi Hassan, observed: "An architect can be three things: useless, an enhancer, or a dictator."[18] For Hassan, architects are only able to contribute real *use value* to a building if the project, through its creation, enhances the collective potential of a community by fostering ongoing engagement. Khwaja Fatmi, Saad Ben Mostafa, and Rizvi Hassan designed a range of structures across thirty-two camp sites in Ukhiya, Cox's Bazar. These spaces provided essential support for Rohingya refugees – Myanmar nationals who, in one of the largest waves of displacement in 2017, fled to Bangladesh to escape ethnic and religious persecution. Six of the thirty-two structures, including a central community centre, were distinguished by the Aga Khan Award for Architecture in 2022.

At the outset of the project, social engagement was not a priority, as the main objective was to create shelters for the refugees on the newly cleared forestland as quickly as possible. However, the architects soon recognised the importance of incorporating the perspectives of the refugee community, and, with the support of the Bangladeshi international development organisation BRAC, resources were eventually allocated to facilitate community involvement through workshops. Colourful patterns and motifs, drawn from Rohingya cultural traditions, were integrated into the designs to evoke fragments of memory from their displaced homeland.[19] While the architects employed a strategy of "bare minimum" architecture, it did not, to borrow Agamben's term, produce "bare life".[20] Unlike the historical development of refugee housing in Bangladesh and elsewhere, these spaces reflect dignity, care, and cultural identity – even in their most stripped-down form (fig. 4).

The learning spaces in the Rohingya refugee camps differ significantly from the previous two examples, as these centres serve multiple functions – ranging from training programmes for women to workshops where skilled artisans from the refugee community share their knowledge with fellow camp residents and members of the Bengali host community. The primary objective was not to provide conventional vocational training or formal education; rather, *learning and making* were conceived as processes through which the community could find healing, regain agency, and reclaim dignity (fig. 5).

Figure 4. The architects Khwaja Fatmi, Saad Ben Mostafa, and Rizvi Hassan designed a range of structures across thirty-two camp sites in Cox's Bazar, Ukhiya, offering vital spaces and infrastructure.

Figure 5. Learning spaces in the Rohingya refugee camps serve multiple functions, from workshops for artisans to training for women. They were designed as spaces for healing and empowerment.

Figure 6. The building features a convoluted U-shaped roof and plinth, enclosing a series of free-form rooms in varied geometric shapes that host multi-purpose learning activities.

The building features a convoluted U-shaped roof and plinth with a series of distinct, free-form rooms: four Corbusian bean-shaped spaces, one octagonal room, one hexagonal room, a rectangular room, and two irregularly shaped spaces, hosting a range of multi-purpose learning activities (fig. 6). The Corbusian floating organic shapes are juxtaposed with lightweight, natural materials like thatched roofing and bamboo walls. Due to the Government of Bangladesh's restrictions on using durable materials in Rohingya refugee camps, building regulations limit masonry walls to a maximum height of 3 feet (91 centimetres). In response, the architects elevated a lightweight metal framework on a row of low concrete blocks and incorporated a continuous "ribbon window" composed of folding wooden shutters.

    Portions of the ceiling are covered with colourful patterned fabric sourced locally, and the refugee community actively participated in decorating the interiors with hand-painted patterns and motifs. The result is a warm, vibrant, and welcoming space – one that subverts the prevailing image of refugees living in a state of "bare life" and challenges the austere architecture often associated with displacement.

Social Engagement as a Pedagogical Tactic

Socially engaged architectural practices are relatively recent developments in architectural thought. Influential early generation architects like Muzharul Islam (1923–2012, member of the AKAA Master Jury in the 1978–80 cycle) and Bashirul Haq (1942–2020) believed in the positivist power of architecture as a creative and liberating form of political expression.[21] Their generation trusted that the newly independent country – following the Bangladesh Liberation War in 1971 – would succeed in empowering society and its architects. Their works reflected this optimism, featuring economically and climatically optimised construction details and formal articulations.[22] Yet, as hopes for a stronger democratic state gradually faded, the concepts of private sector involvement and citizen participation began to take greater prominence in architectural thinking.[23]

We can trace the concept of social engagement in Bangladeshi architecture from two major influences: Hassan Fathy's idea of *amāna*,[24] a sense of responsibility, and Balkrishna Doshi's concept of *sangath*, meaning "to accompany", which is also the name of his architectural practice. Fathy's architecture and philosophy have been commonly studied in architectural schools in Bangladesh, while Doshi maintained direct relations with Bangladesh's architectural circle. Fathy viewed architecture as a collective creative activity that requires careful deliberation and choice. Within this process, individuals and communities exercise their *amāna* – responsibility – where every decision impacts both the builders and the surrounding environment. Fathy emphasised the importance of individual engagement in the building process.[25] For him, architecture becomes a deeply personal and communal act, where every choice reflects a profound sense of responsibility towards both people and the environment.

The term *sangath* was used by Balkrishna Doshi to describe a collaborative approach to design, where the architect's vision not only shapes architecture but also responds to the project's environmental, social, and human context.[26] Doshi's landmark project – Aranya Community Housing – exemplifies this approach. It was a recipient of the Aga Khan Award for Architecture in the 1993–95 cycle.[27] In this project, Doshi conceived the housing as a flexible framework designed to evolve and transform according to its inhabitants' desires, economic conditions, and cultural preferences. While Doshi did not intend for the residents to be directly involved in the design process as co-designers – recognising the challenges in predicting the needs of future residents – *sangath* provided an open-ended framework. Doshi believed that this framework would empower inhabitants to take ownership of the structure and adapt, develop, and transform it as their needs evolve. This concept can also be situated within the broader philosophy of participatory architecture by Giancarlo De Carlo, who invited Doshi to curate the 1987 issue of *Spazio e Società* that De Carlo edited.[28]

Hassan Fathy and Balkrishna Doshi continue to serve as key points of reference in the evolution of socially engaged architectural practice in Bangladesh. Notably, Fathy's concept of *amāna* emphasises that while craftspeople and builders operate within a predefined design framework provided by the architect, they retain the agency to introduce subtle modifications during construction. In this sense, *amāna* can be meaningfully compared to how art historians distinguish between "art" and "craft". While every piece of craft is unique due to its handmade nature, the artisan, by the norm, follows a fixed prototype or pre-existing design. Although artisans may introduce minor variations, they remain fundamentally loyal to the original form. In contrast, artists are expected to depart from the prototype – whether formal or historical – to incorporate more radical, personal expressions, resulting in entirely distinct works.

In the Rudrapur and Arcadia school projects, the carpenters and builders had limited involvement in the initial design ideation. Yet, through their material engagement and hands-on contributions, they left distinct personal imprints on the final structures. In this sense, architecture becomes a collective artefact – one that bears individual traces within a cohesive formal and historical framework. It is no surprise that the Rudrapur school is often referred to as a "handmade school", a term that highlights its artisanal spirit and collective authorship – qualities that directly echo Fathy's notion of *amāna*.

The Rohingya project also incorporates the spirit of *amāna*, but it further draws on Doshi's idea of *sangath* – a term implying collaboration and unity. This school project empowered refugee users with broader control over the design process, allowing them to make significant decisions both aesthetically and programmatically. Across these three examples, the principles of *amāna* and *sangath* were not only philosophical references but also employed as deliberate design strategies. Together, they advanced the architects' mission of deepening social engagement through built form.

Performing Social Engagement

Architects engaging with the disenfranchised communities have expanded the boundaries of their profession, taking on roles as public service providers and political activists.[29] In this sense, socially engaged architecture has intersected with ideas of cultural anarchism, where architects seek to subvert institutional norms by embedding communities within the architectural process. Anarchist theories have played a key role in the evolution of participatory architectural theory, both in Europe and in the United States. For example, Giancarlo De Carlo's connections to the Italian anarchist movement shaped his participatory architectural approach.[30] In the context of Bangladesh, the concepts of citizen agency and social engagement were never explicitly discussed in terms of cultural anarchism. Nevertheless, in the face of a weak and decaying state, distrust in the state and government became a productive area for creative practices.

Unlike the visionary utopias of European anarchism, socially engaged projects in Bangladesh are less invested in grand narratives of progress and systemic transformation. Instead, they

Figure 7. The Arcadia School uses three types of locally sourced bamboo and repurposed steel drums for buoyancy, assembled with traditional rope-tie techniques and waterproofed with boiled gaab fruit. Each joint reflects the craftsmanship of the local artisans.

focus on pragmatic alliances that are more interested in uniting the community and various stakeholders through the design and construction process – often on a temporary or one-time basis.[31] The three buildings in Bangladesh considered here can be seen as micro exhibition spaces that host a coordinated social engagement performance without placing undue hope on the future, thus evading any utopian zeal.[32]

The performative aspect of these three buildings is further strengthened by the commissioning agencies. All three projects are commissioned by non-governmental organisations or private welfare trusts to serve marginalised rural populations or refugees, addressing the gaps left by the respective state's limited educational and welfare services.[33] The state's delay in providing adequate primary education prompted NGOs to step in, serving as a shadow governance.[34] While national educational initiatives traditionally sought to implement structural

Figure 8. Children play in the courtyard of the Learning Spaces in the Rohingya refugee camp.

changes, these contemporary NGO interventions are exemplary, recognising from the outset that they lack the capacity to initiate lasting structural change.[35] These three projects are illustrations of what can emerge from the margins when the state underperforms its responsibilities.[36] Architecture embodies this shadow existence – emerging at the crevices of public sectors, provoking an alternative model, and offering examples through performance.

The performative dimension of social engagement breaks the hierarchical master-slave relationship between *form* and *process*.[37] In general, architectural thinking – for practical purposes – prioritises *form* over *process*. As a result, this creates a hierarchical cognitive structure in architectural thought, where *form* is considered more important than the *process*. Concurrently, other thinkers reverse this model by prioritising *process* over *form*. While we can continue to debate which should take precedence, it is important to recognise that this game of prioritisation – whether of process or form – is limited by the theoretical presupposition that one concept must dominate the other or that the two concepts are naturally bounded by a master-slave relationship. Social engagement projects present a possibility where all elements involved in architecture – whether living or non-living – can exist and operate in a non-hierarchical way.[38]

The three buildings share a common methodology: architects sought to mediate between form, space, fabrication, material sourcing, and transport, and the intentions of the communities they served. In the case of the Arcadian School project, the architect Saif Ul Haque rethinks the conventional binary between form and process by actively involving the community of builders in material selection, fabrication, and transportation.[39] While the school's final form may appear as a carefully controlled geometric structure, its construction reveals a distinctive aesthetic shaped by collaborative making. The design incorporates three types of bamboo, chosen for its lightweight durability, with the structure's buoyancy supported by repurposed 30 gallon steel drums encased in bamboo frameworks. These materials were sourced from nearby villages and transported to the site by river. To protect the structure from water damage, local artisans treated key elements with a traditional waterproofing method using boiled gaab fruit. Rather than using conventional metal fasteners, rope-tying methods were employed to secure joints, ensuring the building's structural integrity while preventing rust. Each knot and bamboo joint carries the personal mark of the artisan who crafted it. In this way, the building's form and process become intertwined, leaving a lasting aesthetic imprint and blurring the boundaries between design, construction, and crafting (fig. 7).

In all three cases, engagement and participation extend far beyond the completion of the project. The buildings continue to offer the community opportunities for ongoing collaboration. At the METI School in Rudrapur, for example, the earth and bamboo structures require regular maintenance by the local community, allowing them to re-engage and relive the collaborative process that initially brought the school to life.[40] Similarly, in the Rohingya refugee camps, authorities allowed only temporary structures, enforcing restrictions such as no brick walls taller than 2 feet (61 centimetres), no reinforced-concrete floors, and no corrugated sheets, while placing a focus on low-cost materials. These materials and structural constraints serve as daily reminders of an uncertain future. Yet rather than expressing a deferred hope for development, the temporariness often fosters a self-reflective search within the community. Looking back at a shared past and forwards towards healing in unfamiliar terrain. One such instance occurred in Camp 25, where young refugee girls led an art programme and male community members repainted and refurbished the interior space as part of their effort (fig. 8).

Conclusion

The projects discussed in this essay position architecture as an autonomous pedagogical tactic. The social engagement approach shifts the focus from individual actions to a broader socio-material network of people, objects, and stories. It emphasises that human actions are not driven by individual agency alone but emerge from material interdependencies and a web of discursive tools that span legal, geographical, cultural, and economic realms. Rather than merely serving as physical spaces, these buildings actively engage in recodifying and reinscribing knowledge, challenging the conventional educational discourse of Bangladesh. They encourage new forms of interaction within classrooms and reshape the region's historical understanding of school architecture. The buildings, reminiscent of exhibition pavilions, convey time-bound lessons to their audiences, reflecting a paradigmatic shift in architectural discourse in Bangladesh.

Negotiation between structural conditions – such as the country's education system – and the community's role and contribution to the project is central to the pedagogical nature of these three projects. Hence, these initiatives embody a certain ambivalence: on the one hand, the architects acknowledge the constraints imposed by structural forces; on the other, within the micro-spaces of *amāna* or the broader context of *sangath*, the projects create and preserve opportunities for change. This dynamic fosters a space where the structural condition can be decoded and reinscribed, enabling the continuous evolution of the design by those who engage with it. Acting as caregivers and micro-entrepreneurs, reliant on foreign donations and private charity, these architects underscore architecture's role in both facilitating and critiquing the "teaching machine". While the role of architecture in supporting neoliberal charity is open to debate, it is essential to recognise its transformative power as both a facilitator and a critique within this system.

Acknowledgements
I am grateful to the architects Saif Ul Haque and Rizvi Hassan for generously sharing their time and their insights on the discussed projects. All information about these projects has been gathered from interviews with these two individuals, unless otherwise noted.

1. Mahatma Gandhi's Ashram and Rabindranath Tagore's Shantiniketan offered subversive pedagogical environments that challenged the colonial "teaching machine". Both used architecture as a medium to express alternative epistemologies, promoting lifestyles that diverged from colonial modernity. In the postcolonial context, Gandhi and Tagore, though being celebrated as symbols of moral alternatives, were also criticised as impractical, elitist, and idealistic. On this, see Mohammad A. Quayum, *Rabindranath Tagore's Journey as an Educator: Critical Perspectives on His Poetics and Praxis* (London: Routledge, 2023); Michael Mann, ed., *Shantiniketan – Hellerau: New Education in the "Pedagogic Provinces" of India and Germany* (Heidelberg: Draupadi Verlag, 2015); and Dennis Hardy, "Mahatma Gandhi and His *Ashram* Experiments: Non-Violence in Intentional Communities", *International Journal on World Peace* 38, no. 1 (March 2021), pp. 69–94.

2. The postcolonial states under Jawaharlal Nehru in India and Mohammad Ayub Khan in Pakistan initiated several programmes focused on youth development or urban and village community development linked to the networks of new educational buildings. For a critical review and history, see Padma Sarangapani and Rekha Pappu, *Handbook of Education Systems in South Asia* (Singapore: Springer Nature Singapore, 2021) and Gayatri Chakravorty Spivak, *Outside in the Teaching Machine* (New York: Routledge, 1993).

3. Spivak, *Outside in the Teaching Machine*.

4. Willy Maley et al., "Reviews", *Textual Practice* 10, no. 1 (1996).

5. Lisa Rosén Rasmussen, "Building Pedagogies: A Historical Study of Teachers' Spatial Work in New School Architecture", *Education Inquiry* 12, no. 3 (2021), pp. 225–48, https://doi.org/10.1080/20004508.2020.1857495.

6. Joel Spring, *How Educational Ideologies Are Shaping Global Society: Intergovernmental Organizations, NGOs, and the Decline of the Nation-State* (Hillsdale, NJ: Lawrence Erlbaum Associates, 2004). In this book, Joel Spring explores three key educational ideologies shaping global society: neoliberal education, human rights education, and environmentalism. This creates a conflict between free-market advocates and those focused on human rights and environmental education.

7. Basic information about the project has been gathered from the following website: https://archello.com/project/handmade-school-in-bangladesh.

8. See Dipshikha's statement on its pedagogical approach here: http://www.meti-school.de/daten/metischool_e.htm. See the online entry of the METI School in the book *Montessori Architecture: A Design Instrument for Schools*, https://montessori-architecture.org/repertoire/meti-primary-school/.

9. For a review of the modern use of adobe and rammed-earth architecture and its relationship with the discourse of development and eco-consciousness, see Nicholas Coetzer, *An Architecture of Care in South Africa: From Arts and Crafts to Other Progeny*, vol. 1 (Abingdon, Oxon: Routledge, 2024) and Albert Narath, *Solar Adobe: Energy, Ecology, and Earthen Architecture* (Minneapolis: University of Minnesota Press, 2024).

10. This quotation is taken from the website *Handmade School in Bangladesh*, http://www.meti-school.de/daten/schulung_e.htm.

11. For a discussion of the relationship between voluntary labour and self-help, see Ijlal Muzaffar, *Modernism's Magic Hat: Architecture and the Illusion of Development without Capital* (Austin: University of Texas Press, 2024). For a specific discussion of how the labour-intensive, rammed-earth structure was considered as a political strategy in the UN-sponsored self-help architectural programme, see Farhan Karim, "Reinventing Mud in the Age of Development", in *Architecture in Development: Systems and the Emergence of the Global South*, ed. Aggregate Architectural History Collaborative (New York: Routledge, 2022), pp. 237–55.

12. A critical discussion of the disciplinary "modern" space of Bangladeshi schools is yet to be undertaken: for some examples, see Shaheen Islam and Tanmi Akhter, "Magnitude and Effect of Punishment on Psychosocial Development of Urban and Rural School Children in Bangladesh", *Indian Journal of Positive Psychology* 6, no. 3 (2015), pp. 326–30; Md. Hasan Reza et al., "Child Maltreatment in Bangladesh: Poverty, Social Class, and the Emotional Abuse of Elementary School Children by Teachers", *Children and Youth Services Review* 116 (2020), p. 105195; Md. Saiful Malak et al., "'Can I Really Teach without My Magic Cane?': Teachers' Responses to the Banning of Corporal Punishment", *International Journal of Inclusive Education* 19, no. 12 (2015), pp. 1325–41; Farhan Karim, "Standardized Citizens: Education Reformation of East Pakistan", in *The Delos Symposia and Doxiadis*, ed. Mantha Zarmakoupi and Simon Richards (Zurich: Lars Müller Publishers, 2025).

13. See more information about the Arcadia Education Project on the website of the Aga Khan Award for Architecture, https://the.akdn/en/how-we-work/our-agencies/aga-khan-trust-culture/akaa/arcadia-education-project.

14. Manon Mollard, "Arcadia Education Project (2016–2020): Demolition Postcard", *The Architectural Review*, 22 August 2023, https://www.architectural-review.com/essays/arcadia-education-project-2016-2020-demolition-postcard.

15. Ruin is an important element in contemporary Bangladeshi architectural discourse, and a detailed critical discussion is still lacking. However, a brief note is relevant here that Bangladeshi architects have been fascinated with the use of bare-faced brick buildings as a way to recreate the image of ruins as an operative notion for history, and Louis Kahn was obviously a central motivational figure in this respect. See Kazi Khaleed Ashraf, "Taking Place: Landscape in the Architecture of Louis Kahn", *Journal of Architectural Education* 61, no. 2 (2007), pp. 48–58; see also Farhan Karim, "Sculpted Landscape: The Unbuilt Public Square of Islamabad", in *Contemporary Urban Landscapes of the Middle East*, ed. Mohammad Gharipour (New York: Routledge, 2018), pp. 90–119.

16. I'm referring to Rahul Mehrotra's idea of "impermanent architecture". We could also consider the twelfth-century earthen Great Mosque of Djenné, which requires regular community participation to maintain its life.

17 Giorgio Agamben, *The Use of Bodies*, trans. Adam Kotsko, from the series *Meridian: Crossing Aesthetics* (Stanford: Stanford University Press, 2016).

18 Shahirah Majumdar, "How Not to Be a Useless Architect: Talking to Architects Rizvi Hassan and Khwaja Fatmi at the Dhaka Art Summit", *Dhaka Tribune*, 14 February 2023, https://www.dhakatribune.com/seminars-and-interviews/304899/how-not-to-be-a-useless-architect.

19 For more information, see "Aga Khan Award for Architecture 2022 Honors Community Spaces in the Rohingya Refugee Response", published on the BRAC website: https://bracusa.org/the-2022-aga-khan-award-for-architecture-honors-community-spaces-in-the-rohingya-refugee-response-an-initiative-of-brac-and-actionaid-in-bangladesh/.

20 Giorgio Agamben, *Homo Sacer: Sovereign Power and Bare Life*, trans. Daniel Heller-Roazen (1995; repr., Stanford University Press, 1998).

21 Adnan Morshed, "Modernism as Postnationalist Politics: Muzharul Islam's Faculty of Fine Arts (1953–56)", *Journal of the Society of Architectural Historians* 76, no. 4 (2017), pp. 532–49.

22 Kazi Khaleed Ashraf, ed., *Muzharul Islam: An Architect of Tomorrow; Architecture and Nation-Building in Bangladesh* (Novato: ORO Editions, 2025). Also see Nasreen Hossain and Mahmudul Anwar Riyaad, *Fifty Years of Architecture in Bangladesh* (Dhaka: University Press Limited, 2021).

23 Weaker governance and increasing NGO development narrative served to influence the citizenship narratives and their expression in many cultural sectors. On this, see Naila Kabeer, "Citizenship Narratives in the Face of Bad Governance: The Voices of the Working Poor in Bangladesh", *The Journal of Peasant Studies* 38, no. 2 (2011), pp. 325–53. Also see Naomi Hossain, *The Aid Lab: Understanding Bangladesh's Unexpected Success* (Oxford: Oxford University Press, 2017).

24 Fathy viewed communities as spaces for individuals to exercise their unique decision-making powers, thereby fulfilling the covenant (*amāna*) referred to in the Quran (al-Ahzāb 33:72).

25 Hassan Fathy, *Architecture for the Poor: An Experiment in Rural Egypt* (Chicago: University of Chicago Press, 1973), p. 11.

26 *Balkrishna Doshi: Architecture for the People*, trans. Mark Willard et al., interview by Hans Ulrich Obrist (Weil am Rhein: Vitra Design Museum et al., 2019).

27 For a review of Aranya Community Housing, see James Steele and Balkrishna V. Doshi, *Rethinking Modernism for the Developing World: The Complete Architecture of Balkrishna Doshi* (New York: Whitney Library of Design, 1998).

28 For a review of Giancarlo De Carlo's work and his magazine, see Matteo Sintini, "Criticism of the Architectural Culture since 1978", in *Spazio e Società* magazine, and the conference Theory's History, 196X–199X: Challenges in the Historiography of Architectural Knowledge, session "Thinking the Social", Brussels, 9–10 February 2017.

29 Farhan Karim, "Postscript: How and When Was Architecture Socially Engaged?", *The Routledge Companion to Architecture and Social Engagement* (New York: Taylor & Francis Group, 2018).

30 Alberto Franchini, "Giancarlo De Carlo: Participation Depends", *Architectural Theory Review* 27, no. 2 (2023), pp. 161–87; Marianna Charitonidou, "Revisiting Giancarlo De Carlo's Participatory Design Approach: From the Representation of Designers to the Representation of Users", *Heritage* 4, no. 2 (2021), pp. 985–1004.

31 Laurence Davis and Ruth Kinna, *Anarchism and Utopianism* (Manchester: Manchester University Press, 2014).

32 Michael Löwy, *Morning Star: Surrealism, Marxism, Anarchism, Situationism, Utopia* (Austin: University of Texas Press, 2009).

33 Melani Cammett and Lauren M. MacLean, eds., *The Politics of Non-State Social Welfare* (Ithaca, NY: Cornell University Press, 2014).

34 Shin'ichi Shigetomi, ed., *The State and NGOs: Perspective from Asia* (Singapore: Institute of Southeast Asian Studies, 2002); Margaret Sutton and Robert F. Arnove, *Civil Society or Shadow State? State/NGO Relations in Education* (Greenwich, CT: Information Age Publishing, 2004).

35 Karim, "Standardized Citizens: Education Reformation of East Pakistan".

36 Since its independence, Bangladesh has endured several dictatorships, including two military regimes, and most recently a fifteen-year period under what is widely regarded as one of the most brutal fascist regimes, which ended in 2024. The current interim government continues to face significant challenges in establishing stability and ensuring democratic elections.

37 I use the "master-salve" term from Hegel's master-slave dialectic, presented in his 1808 work *Phänomenologie des Geistes*, published in English as: Georg Wilhelm Friedrich Hegel, *The Phenomenology of Spirit*, ed. and trans. Terry Pinkard (Cambridge: Cambridge University Press, 2018). The dialectic illustrates that power is not static or one-sided; it involves a dynamic, relational process in which both parties – the dominant and the dominated – are shaped by their interactions. This dialectical framework provides the main framework for modern Western intellectual culture, including architectural thought.

38 Participation or engagement introduces a way of thinking about architecture that resembles Deleuze's concept of *assemblage*, which refers to a complex, dynamic system of interconnected elements – a fluid collection of diverse components, both human and non-human – that interact, adapt, and evolve over time. See Kevin Grove and Jonathan Pugh, "Assemblage Thinking and Participatory Development: Potentiality, Ethics, Biopolitics", *Geography Compass* 9, no. 1 (2015), pp. 1–13.

39 The construction was awarded to Pran Bollov, the family carpenter of Razia Alam. Bollov assembled a team of construction crews from adjacent villages and other places.

40 James Morris and Suzanne Preston Blier, *Butabu: Adobe Architecture of West Africa* (Princeton, NJ: Princeton Architectural Press, 2004).

Building Earthbound: Notes from Accra and Freetown

Katherine Dawson

Earthly Entanglements

The Kamanar Secondary School in Thionck Essyl, Senegal, appears like a set of earthly mounds, with rounded edges, sandy hues, and patterns of light which shoot through the many slats and squares that embellish the structures. The school might be understood as the materialisation of a self-conscious binding with the Earth. Its very materiality owes its form to the clay-rich ground that once lay beneath it; and the vaulted catenary domes which frame the trees and sky from the classroom modules – or *awlas* – are a product of the kinds of shapes and pressures such clay can accommodate. The clay walls and wooden lattices of the *awlas* work as evaporating coolers, such that no artificial air-conditioning is required – a cornerstone of managing heat in a warming and carbon-constrained world. This self-conscious binding with the Earth can be understood as a kind of thoughtful entanglement with earthly materials and processes. It is an aspirational kind of entanglement that offers a blueprint for building in ways that remain wilfully anchored to time and place. Yet the school also serves as a reminder that the built world is always an earthly entanglement – an inevitable bind with materials and processes of the earth, be those sand, stone, rock, wind, chemical reactions, or erosion. It is a reminder that a building is what I call *earthbound* – the outcome of variable, though incessant, human bindings with earthly substance and force.

Understanding buildings as earthbound means attuning ourselves to how earthly materials and forces are deeply entangled with human thought and movement. This perspective invites a view of the built world as *geosocial*, a term that Nigel Clark and Kathryn Yusoff use to describe the constant interplay between a dynamic Earth and socio-political life.[1] Thinking of the built world as earthbound resonates with Clark's conception of cities as *planetary*, where planetary expresses the multitude of forces that constitute the Earth as a dynamic, shifting planet.[2]

In my own work, I have reckoned with the built world as earthbound – and, indeed, geosocial and planetary – by tuning in to the specificities of one core constituent of built form: sand. As a fundamental component of concrete, sand is the granular backbone of the built world and is increasingly recognised as a foundational substance of life and economy across the planet. Often referred to as a scale of earthly material that inhabits the category between silt and rocks, sand is a material with its own stories, forces, and constant (un)becomings. Outside of its role in concretising the planet, sand moves across mountainous, riverine, and coastal environments, providing landscapes for human and more-than-human lives to play out. Increasingly, it is positioned as a critical infrastructure for protecting coastlines from the effects of a climate-changing world marked by coastal erosion and by increased intensity and frequency of severe weather events. In this essay, I think across the sandy worlds of Accra and Freetown. I turn to the piles of sand sitting in depots, stations, trucks, and boats, thinking through the particularities of place and people to enliven these sandy formations. As I show, these piles of sand take their shape through contested relationships with resources, landscape, and futures. In this way, stories of people, place, and matter augment an understanding of the built worlds of Accra and Freetown as contested *earthbound* formations.

Notes from Accra, Ghana

Greater Accra is a region of more than 5 million inhabitants,[3] witnessing significant population growth across the twentieth century.[4] Historically, the bulk of the region's population has lived in the Greater Accra Metropolitan Area (GAMA), and while this is likely still the case, suburban and peri-urban areas beyond the traditional urban core have witnessed significant growth in population, with inhabitants making a home where land is considered both available and more affordable.[5] Concrete is a ubiquitous material found across the built worlds of the wider region of Accra. It forms the backbone of large residences with multiple rooms and extensive grounds, grand offices in the central districts of Accra, as well as modest one-storey homes and small commercial enterprises across the city's central, suburban, and peri-urban landscapes. This concrete ubiquity reflects the collective aspirations for concrete form, shared across income divides, with concrete underpinning the infrastructural desires of elite city dwellers, a growing middle class, and low-income residents.[6] This is a phenomenon expanding well beyond Accra, as Armelle Choplin remarks on the growing number of concrete buildings across the wider West African urban corridor, captured in what Choplin calls a "cementing" process.[7] In my own work, I have sought to understand the ways these concrete desires remain bound to the earth in distinct ways and, indeed, the way these materialisations bear on people and places in often uneven ways. In particular, by turning to sand, I have grounded these cementing aspirations to the earthly forms that constitute them. Indeed, like elsewhere in the world, sand is a cornerstone of Accra's concrete formation. Sand is uplifted from grounds at the edges of the expanding city and transported across the region. It lands in depots, from where it is redistributed to consumers across the city, or it may be taken directly to the point of sale, most often a new residential development. Sandy grains are then mixed with water, cement, and sometimes quarry dust to form concrete blocks, which become the homes, shops, schools, and offices that make up the growing city. Meanwhile, piles of these concrete blocks are found on plots across the city, symbolising a building yet-to-come.

By moving with the trucks that transported sand across Accra, I came to know the expanding concrete city through the mobilities of sand. Indeed, as part of my PhD and postdoctoral research (2017–21), I spent months between trucks and sand extraction zones, or "pits", moving from the north-westerly edges of the city to a more central node, Awoshie Junction, where I had

met a number of sand-truck drivers who kindly offered to host me on their trips around Greater Accra.[8] Sand emerged not only as an urban material, but as a way for drivers to express their intimate knowledge of the city's changing landscape. Places from where sand was once extracted, and which were thus likely to have been the city's peri-urban edges, were now seen to be turning into the city, consolidating their urban form into community units of homes, schools, shops, and places of worship. As we moved through these more recent suburban areas of Greater Accra, en route to the newest edges of an expanding city, drivers would point out of the window and express this shifting dynamic, something like "all of this was sand here, but it's now become the city".

Spending time on the trucks enlivened the sand piles and concrete blocks littered around the city. These seemingly inanimate forms became fleshed out with the stories, struggles, and aspirations of those employed, often precariously, in the sand transportation economy. Some of these drivers I came to know well, and, over time, they started sharing their thoughts with me about what life was like on the sandy road. Work on the truck was laborious. At the peri-urban edge and into the sand pit itself, the truck drivers had to navigate uneven roads, some of which were potholed by the movement of the sand trucks themselves. Traversing these uneven roads was an embodied process, requiring skill, attention, and physical movements that sought to secure the body in place. For the mate, an assistant or helper who works with the truck driver in the sand transportation economy, directing sand on and off the truck and subsequently securing the sand in place once on the truck was a deeply embodied practice, and it exposed these workers to heat, dust, and fumes on an almost daily basis. This was a tiring, time-consuming job, prompting reflections from drivers and mates, such as "if you have a wife, they will not know you".

Work on the truck was also stressful, requiring constant calculations to ensure that the correct sums of money would reach the truck's owner on a weekly basis, accounting for both expected and unexpected costs, like police stops, repairs or illness. Through conversations on and off the truck, I was told that those owning the trucks fell into a category of significant privilege. Requiring huge sums of upfront money to import a truck, ownership of such a vehicle was limited to Accra's elite, who, as the drivers suggested, were likely connected to business and/or politics. The work was precarious, and becoming a "driver" was a matter of promotion from other roles on the truck, such as a "spare driver" or the "mate". But becoming a driver was also a matter of luck. Drivers spoke of their loss of access to a truck, for reasons not entirely clear to me. Securing a long-term driver role was thus difficult and a constant process of negotiation. Gaining an insight into the lives of the drivers who were responsible for moving sand around the city served to enliven the city's materiality and revealed it to be more than inanimate matter.

This unevenness was also reflected in the experiences of those living in Greater Accra's peri-urban regions, from where sand was often extracted. During interviews with residents in these zones, people lamented having lost access to their agricultural land to make way for the sand extraction organised by the landowner. The loss of crops was also accompanied by the depletion of nutrients from the topsoil, affecting the land's long-term fertility. Compensation for the resulting crop failure varied, with some citing experiences of massive deprivation. The reduction in income affected people's ability to send children to school, while other residents reflected on the impact of sand extraction on water sources, requiring smaller incomes to be spent on purchasing privately sourced water.

Turning to sand and its entanglements with people and places provides a lens on to Accra's materiality as earthbound in distinct ways. Indeed, it reveals the city – and its many buildings in the making – to be a process marked by uneven human experience and encounter with a dynamic earth. As the concrete city takes shape in one place, elsewhere land and livelihoods are pulled apart. And as sand moves from zones of extraction towards places of consumption, the hopes, anxieties, and embodied experiences of drivers also move with the grains.

Notes from Freetown, Sierra Leone

Freetown wraps around a peninsula of the Atlantic coastal edge of Sierra Leone, providing a home for more than 1 million inhabitants.[9] This number is set to grow, with current projections estimating a doubling of that figure to reach a population of 2 million by 2040.[10] After a sustained period of urban segregation in the colonial period (1807–1961), the city's population expanded in the post-independence era, reaching 1 million by the turn of the twenty-first century (increasing from 100,000 at the opening of the twentieth century).[11] The devastating civil war (1991–2002) contributed to the expanding population, as hundreds of thousands of displaced people who sought temporary refuge in Freetown remained in the city following peace.[12] They were accompanied by ex-combatants, who stayed or moved to the city after the end of the war. More recently, further migration to the city was driven by the closure of the nation's iron ore mines, which resulted in significant job losses.[13] As the city's population has continued to grow, the urban landscape has also transformed, with an expanding population making their homes and lives at the edges of the city, on both steep mountainous terrain and reclaimed coastal land.[14]

Like elsewhere, concrete has continued to underpin a significant part of material urban transformation in Freetown, with homes, roads, shops, and social institutions visibly built with concrete. In other settlements, households might be required to wait to obtain the financial resources in order to shift from corrugated-iron structures to concrete homes.[15] Thus, like Accra, concrete transcends income divides, giving form to a diverse Freetown of elite residences,

incremental homes, hotels, offices, and roads. Also, like Accra, sand sustains these concrete manifestations; it is lifted from beaches of the Western Area and surrounding coastal landscapes and moved towards centres of building in urban and peri-urban landscapes.

Yet the sands used in Freetown's construction economy are not uniform, and this diversity gives rise to more subtle differences in the concrete landscape. In Freetown, different grades of sand are available according to their salt content, where sand with significant salt content is understood to corrode the metal rebar in the structure, and thus its use in the production of concrete compromises the integrity of the building. Given its limited salt content, river sand is of the highest quality and therefore commands the highest prices, while the price of unwashed sand harvested from the shallow ocean floor is lower.[16] In this way, while people across income divides might build with concrete, their relative income dictates the kind of sand undergirding the concrete and thus the long-term structural integrity of their building. In this way, by attuning to the earthbound nature of Freetown's built world and its sandy underpinnings, a sense of urban concrete ubiquity gives way to a landscape of uneven risk and resilience.

Turning more closely to the extraction of sand extends an understanding of the concrete city as earthbound. The extraction of sand in Freetown has a long history. My conversations across the city with coastal inhabitants and lorry drivers spoke to this history, highlighting the significant role that beach sand had played in the building of the capital, with coastal places like

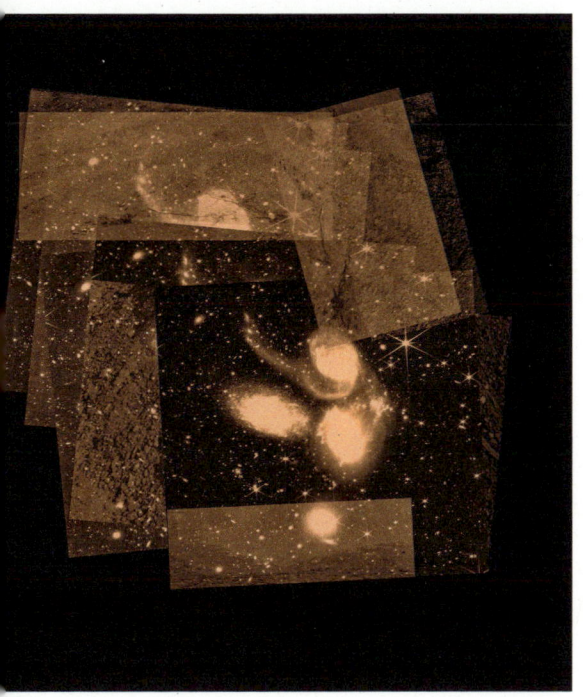

Worlds in Grains is an image series which takes its name from William Blake's oft-cited phrase, from 1863, "to see the world in a grain of sand". I use this as a provocation to think about the worlds which inhere in grains of sand as they traverse planetary socio-ecologies. The series uses images taken of sandy landscapes and formations in both Accra and Freetown, where sand plays a contested role in changing urban environments as beach, seabed, and building. These photographs are presented next to cosmic collages, which include grainy textures from the images made in Accra and Freetown, in dialogue with images captured through the lens of the James Webb Space Telescope. Pieced together, I hope to incite reflection on the vast worlds contained within grains of sand – as both earthbound and always cosmic. The formats of the collages are inspired by a picture produced in the "Countdown to the Webb Telescope's First Images" taken by the Webb's Fine Guidance Sensor (FGS) (nasa.gov, 2022). The speculative nature behind the use of the FGS alludes to the always imperfect attempt to capture worlds, while the visual format, which layers image upon image, evokes a sense of incessant multiplicity in the universe. Both of these notions appealed as a way of representing the worlds in sand grains – speculative and multiple.

Hamilton noted as significant sources of sand for the city. As someone working in the city's sand industry remarked, "without Hamilton, there would be no Freetown".

Today, sand is extracted from a range of beaches that stretch across the Western Area as it juts out into the Atlantic Ocean. The most significant and well known of these is John Obey Beach,[17] which is a zone of extraction presently authorised by the government for sand mining. But John Obey is just one of many spaces from where sand is extracted, with places like Lakka also forming critical resource zones, though not necessarily authorised in the same way. Shovels, buckets, trucks, tarpaulin, paper, pens, bodies, and vast amounts of socio-natural knowledge provide the critical infrastructure for extracting sand from such shorelines, offering vital lines of income for a growing urban population. But it is not without contestation. As I have been learning through my work with the Sierra Leone Urban Research Centre (SLURC),[18] sand extraction in Freetown, like elsewhere, is a process marked by struggles over landscape and resources.

The mining of sand from beaches is experienced as erosion further down the coast, with communities such as Bureh, which rely heavily on tourism, struggling to secure their shoreline. On islands nearby, communities lamented the effects of sand mining on their fishing-dependent livelihoods. In a community interview with inhabitants of the town of Oku on Tasso Island, residents recounted the recent history of sand mining as it has intensified since 2018, after which time the price of sand has been notably increasing. Today, as many as seventy-five boats pass the island each day, heading towards Rokeh River to extract sand. Residents have complained of collisions between their fishing boats and the sand-bearing boats, damaging the wooden structure of the boats and the fishing nets. In 2018 alone, seven or eight boats were destroyed, with residents sharing the severe stress experienced by those navigating debt from the cost of boat repairs. The collisions were also dangerous to people, with injuries and loss of life reported. Collisions were recounted as happening daily, sometimes twice a day, and the likelihood of collision was compounded by the limited number of sand boats using lights in the evenings. The community pointed to rising water levels around the island, due to the loss of sand from the banks surrounding the coastline. Buildings were lost and drinking water affected, with people pointing to the impacts on a long-standing water well.

Significantly, their catch was affected. The engine noise of the boats drove fish away, while the extraction of sand from sandbanks in the water affected feeding grounds and habitats for fish. Explaining that "sand is where the fish feed . . . they've cleared the sand", residents recounted the loss of oysters, cockerels, sea snails, and other species from their regular catch. The mounting challenge of sustaining a livelihood built on fishing was reshaping labour, life, and ecology in Oku, with more people turning to the forest to support charcoal production. As one resident remarked: "more of us are going into the bush." The residents of Oku were not alone in their struggles over sustaining a livelihood from fishing. For many across the city and the region's wider shoreline landscapes, the prospect of making a living from fishing was understood as increasingly challenging, citing overfishing from large commercial trawling activities and climate-changing conditions. This, it was argued, was driving coastal inhabitants to take up a livelihood in the sand economy. Such transitions prompted a Freetown port officer to remark: "the boats used to be full of fish; now, the boats are full of sand . . . it's really strange to me." Or, as the Head of Fisheries noted in an interview, the coastal wharves "used to be fishing grounds; now they are for sand mining". This gradual landscape change from fish grounds to *san san*[19] grounds can thus be understood as indicative of the shifting geologies, ecologies, and socio-economies of Freetown, shaping and shaped by the city's earthbound built world.

Building Earthbound

In this essay, I have attended to the built world as an earthbound formation. By earthbound, I mean to express the inevitable human bindings to planetary materials and forces that inhere in built environments. Whether a building is constructed with clay, straw, limestone, chalk, plastic, concrete, or glass, it remains bound to the earth and (non-)human labour and life. In this essay, I have thought about this bind by attending to the sandy material which underpins concrete transformations across Accra and Freetown. I tuned into the sands of Accra and Freetown and traced just fractions of their elaborate networks of relation with people and places – webs of connection which shape livelihoods and landscape in often uneven ways. Hence, by turning to the grains which constitute urban form, the city's landscape is read as a contested materialisation.

To paraphrase William Blake's oft cited notion of "to see the world in a grain of sand", this essay has opted to see the urban world in piles of sand and concrete blocks. Either way, to see worlds in grains of sand requires us first to see *sand in the world* – and in the city. This, I contend, remains possible with an astute commitment to reading the built world as ever earthbound.

1. Nigel Clark and Kathryn Yusoff, "Geosocial Formations and the Anthropocene", *Theory, Culture & Society* 34, nos. 2–3 (2017), pp. 3–23.
2. Nigel Clark, "Planetary Cities: Fluid Rock Foundations of Civilization", *Theory, Culture & Society* 39, no. 2 (2021), pp. 177–96.
3. Ghana Statistical Service, "Population by Regions: Greater Accra", https://www.statsghana.gov.gh/regionalpopulation.php?population=MTM0NTk2MjQzOS4yMDE1&&Greater%20Accra&regid=3.
4. Richard Grant and Paul Yankson, "Accra", *Cities* 20, no. 1 (2003), pp. 65–74.
5. Divine Mawuli Asafo, "Fragile and Compromised Housing: Implications of Land Conflicts on Housing Development in Peri-Urban Accra, Ghana", *Housing Studies* 39, no. 5 (2024), pp. 1340–63.
6. Ian E. A. Yeboah, "Demographic and Housing Aspects of Structural Adjustment and Emerging Urban Form in Accra, Ghana", *Africa Today* 50, no. 1 (2003), pp. 107–19.
7. Armelle Choplin, "Cementing Africa: Cement Flows and City-Making along the West African Corridor (Accra, Lomé, Contonou, Lagos)", *Urban Studies* 57, no. 9 (2020), pp. 1977–93.
8. Katherine Dawson, "Geologising Urban Political Ecology (UPE): The Urbanisation of Sand in Accra, Ghana", *Antipode* 53, no. 4 (2021), pp. 995–1017; Katherine Dawson, "A Share in the Sands: Trips, Pits and Potholes in Accra, Ghana", *Africa* 93, no. 1 (2023), pp. 40–59.
9. Alexandre Apsan Frediani, "An Introduction to the City of Freetown", in *Urban Transformations in Sierra Leone: Knowledge Co-production and Partnerships for a Just City*, ed. Joseph M. Macarthy, Braima Koroma, Andrea Rigon, Alexandre Apsan Frediani, and Andrea Klingel (London: UCL Press, 2024), pp. 19–31.
10. Ibid.
11. Kenneth Lynch, Etienne Nel, and Tony Binns, "'Transforming Freetown': Dilemmas of Planning and Development in a West African City", *Cities* 101 (2020), p. 102694.
12. Ibid.
13. Alexandre Apsan Frediani, "An Introduction to the City of Freetown".
14. Ibid.
15. Camila Cociña, Marcella Mardon, and Alexandre Aspan Frediani, "Building Resilient Homes in Informal Settlements: Understanding Access to Building Materials in Freetown and Harare", *IIED*, 25 June 2024, https://www.iied.org/building-resilient-homes-informal-settlements.
16. Notes from fieldwork with Ansumana Tarawally.
17. Abdul Brima, "Mining Cash for Sand in Sierra Leone Is Costing the Environment", *Dialogue Earth*, 21 November 2023, https://dialogue.earth/en/ocean/mining-sand-for-cash-in-sierra-leone-is-costing-the-environment/.
18. In particular, the notes from Freetown are the product of field interviews with Ansumana Tarawally.
19. *San san* is the Krio word for sand.

Building Learning Spaces with Communities

In Conversation with Anna Heringer and Christian Paul Zigato Agboada

This conversation between the German architect Anna Heringer and the Ghanaian engineer Christian Paul Zigato Agboada, moderated by Deen Sharp, explores how education, materials, and cultural identity intersect through architecture. The discussion is centred on their collaboration on the Earth Campus in Tatale, Ghana, which is a vocational training centre that aims to further sustainable development through education and practical skill-building in a local rural setting. The conversation explores the transformative power of building with mud and reflects on honouring local knowledge systems and rethinking what educational spaces can, and should, be.

Deen Sharp (DS) This book features educational design projects that go beyond the boundaries of the physical building. They respond not only to the needs of individual learners in the classroom, but also to the broader communities and environments that support them. Your project in Tatale, Ghana, is a compelling example of this kind of holistic approach. Could you begin by telling us how this collaboration began and what you set out to achieve?

Anna Heringer (AH) It happened quite naturally. Right, Zigato? In Bangladesh, when working on the METI School in Rudrapur, I was very familiar with the context, the culture, even the language. I spent a lot of time there during a period of seven years before building. But in Ghana, I felt like a cultural beginner. I would have been completely lost without Zigato's support as a partner. It's been an interesting process: coming with initial ideas to the site, then developing them further while there, and creating structures that really adapt to the local context. We started building with a local technique called *atakpame*.[1] We are constructing an educational campus that includes a vocational campus focused on sustainable agriculture, construction techniques (including earthen construction), electrical training, and life skills. The latter includes training women in how to sustainably run their families. There will also be housing.

Another focus of this project is to disrupt the rigid grid pattern that you can see so clearly from the air. The influence of decades of development aid and colonisation are visible, as are the spatial patterns established based on discipline, control, and efficiency. But there is also another spatial pattern that exists which is more complex, a community layout that Zigato is better placed to elaborate on.

Christian Paul Zigato Agboada (CPZA) One of our main concerns was how to create an environment that reflects the local way of living, rather than imposing a foreign layout like the rigid grid system. The initial design we received resembled a military camp – very rigid and not reflective of local African living. We wanted something which embodied family and community life, and which reflected how they live. Anna proposed a design that met all of our criteria. During

Figure 1. Initial design of the Don Bosco Campus in Tatale, Ghana, and the Claystorming Studio by Anna Heringer

stakeholder engagement, 90 per cent of the community loved Anna's design because it resonated with how they build (fig. 1).

We're now using four traditional construction methods:
1. *Atakpame* (called cob building in the West)
2. Adobe sun-dried blocks (with unstabilised earth)
3. Wattle and daub (sticks as framework, mud as envelope)
4. Rammed earth (less known in Ghana, but common historically in Senegal, Mali, and Niger)

We've completed nine buildings so far at Tatale using *atakpame* and adobe sun-dried blocks. Next, we'll build with rammed earth. Then we will conclude with the wattle and daub.

Anna's approach resonated with me immediately. She arrived at a time when climate change was being widely discussed, yet many industry solutions were expensive – carbon credits, battery technologies – and thus not accessible to most people. But sustainable construction, especially with local materials, is an effective and affordable way to combat climate change (fig. 2). It's not always recognised as such, but it should be. I embraced Anna's design immediately because I saw it as the surest way to combat climate change. I saw this project as being a reference point for building sustainably throughout Ghana.

In government, and under the engineering department which I head, is a section called the Rural Housing and Cottage Industry Unit. This unit is mandated to put into policy projects and programmes to increase access to safe, decent, and affordable housing in rural and peri-urban areas. It also disseminates creative and innovative research findings in the production and use of Indigenous building materials. Working with Anna on this project is a very good way of solving this issue, as we are doing tests on site and then reporting back to the government. What can improved, what cannot? So meeting Anna was such a godsend, because her approach fits very well into my department and the broader activities of the government in respect to providing low-cost housing. And it is a very cool way, from my perspective, of fighting climate change.

AH Going back to the point about the grid system with the master plan, what is important is that the knowledge used here is an oral tradition based on storytelling. We do a lot of storytelling on the site – Zigato is a true master at that – and some kind of vision and wisdom is wrapped up in a beautiful story that we love to listen to in the evening, when we all gather in one of the campus courtyards. And it is something that we feel has been missing on many educational campuses. Is the layout based on discipline and control? Or is it one that encourages storytelling, where you want to cultivate this traditional transmission of know-how? That is something that we wanted to integrate into the master plan. You can only do this if you are able to have a close engagement

Figure 2. Local workers constructing the Earth Campus in Tatale, Ghana, designed by Anna Heringer. *Atakpame* walls are formed by sticking balls of wet, moulded earth to each other.

Figures 3 and 4. A woman shapes clay with her fingers on the Earth Campus structure (left), while a man applies clay to the wall, illustrating the hands-on construction process.

with the context. We are working in a very traditional area. It is a town but very rural. What struck me was how space naturally encourages gathering – bonfires, shared meals, community life. The oral tradition is a very precious one that is about to be lost, also because of architecture, and the way we tend form our campuses and master plans. This is something that, coming from the West, we are not aware of.

We began with very local techniques, just hands shaping mud. And the collaboration works like this. I come as a European architect based in Germany and might plan a window with sharp corners, but on the site, women come and plaster with their hands in round shapes. The result is deeply authentic – something that AI or a CAD tool can't replicate. This is real cooperation coming out of the process.

Being on site is essential. You see potential you would miss from afar. These buildings evolve organically, not because we're trying to make something special, but because the process allows them to emerge.

But this process isn't always accepted. Our clients had all been educated in concrete structures and were resistant to the organic shapes. The workers liked it, but the middle class gave us clear directions: "no more curves!" They wanted straight walls and straight corners. That was also a learning process for me, and I have to accept that feedback. So, we introduced the second technique, the adobe bricks, unstabilised, which looked more "modern" while still using earth.

The adobe was a compromise – it looked like cement, had sharp corners, and was cheap because it used excavation soil. But what people started to do when they copied it was plastering it with cement to make it look more like concrete. That led us to think: How can we highlight the uniqueness of clay? We began using finger-made ornaments and moulded furniture – things you can only do with a natural, non-toxic material. That helped to reclaim clay as something beautiful, not just as a "cheap" alternative.

Of course, I learned a lot. I tried to study African ornament patterns intellectually but couldn't grasp them. Then we just started with one simple element, and it flowed naturally. Children joined in, women led the work, and eventually the men, too – it became communal, meditative, and powerful. This building process is transformative. Working with earth affects you – it's calming, grounding. The designs that emerge from it don't strive to be special; they just are. And that kind of authenticity comes only through process (figs. 3 and 4).

DS You mentioned the tensions that can emerge between different stakeholders. How do you navigate these dynamics – especially when trying to balance community expectations with your commitment to sustainability? Where do you draw the line when bottom-up demands conflict with your core values or principles?

CPZA It's about managing expectations. Some things are negotiable – like door alignments – but others aren't. Traditional buildings weren't built with precise measuring tools; they were shaped by hand and eye. There are no "instrumental" straight lines. That's part of our culture.

We tell clients: "This is your identity. Don't replace it with someone else's." There's no "instrumental" straightness in our vernacular buildings. But we find a balance – some straight parts, some traditional flow. People usually accept that.

AH We also frame it through inclusion. For example, when we say we want to create jobs for women, people understand why the work might look a certain way – plastered by hand, not tools. That builds acceptance. I have to, as a designer, respect limits, and that is why having a partner like Zigato is so essential, someone who understands the users' perspective, and who tells me on certain aspects, "not now, maybe in three years, but not now."

But we're strict on materials. Sustainability isn't negotiable. The design might adapt, but not the principle of using regenerative materials and our commitment to sustainability. In Bangladesh, when I built the METI School, the client wasn't excited about using mud and bamboo. They accepted it out of trust because I became like a family member. I felt guilty imposing my values, because what I learned from working with the NGOs is that you should never impose on the community, that everything has to come from the ground. But I come with my values, too. And I've come to see that those values matter – especially when it comes to planetary limits.

DS There are important principles here of equity, but also translation. Anna, you have mentioned that you bring the lessons you have learned from Bangladesh, and now Ghana, back to European contexts. What elements have been transferable and translatable?

AH First of all, I build with earth in Europe, too – with more tools, but with the same material. The biggest lesson is that the process matters as much as the design. We usually focus on outcomes, not how we get there. Building is a part of our human DNA. Every child builds with boxes, sticks, blankets. In the past, also in Europe, people came together to build their homes. In Ghana, if a family builds a new house, the neighbours come to help. That fosters a sense of belonging. People remember the walls they helped raise, the songs sung, the stories shared. It's not just construction – it's community-building (fig. 5).

In Germany, I now design parts of the building where the future users can really participate in construction. It may stretch the letter of the law. But earth is a safe and fantastic material because it's so inclusive – it's non-toxic, touchable, tool-optional. And the deeper issue isn't a lack of material things, but rather a lack of good relationships, of connection. Ghana and Bangladesh are strong in terms of community, and this contributes directly to well-being. We need to restore that in the West. We need to recognise both the spiritual and the technical aspects of materials like earth. That's something I've been learning from Zigato, how materiality connects to culture and spirituality.

CPZA In West Africa, we revere earth as the creator of humans. We see it as protective. In fact, in every chief's palace, there's still a mud building. Within most African traditional settings, before a chief is installed, he is kept in a small room built with mud. The room is without any windows and has only a small door. Within it is complete darkness and silence. That's where the person communicates with the gods or ancestors for them to prepare him for his new role. They spend around seven days in this space, and during this period the person is referred to as being planted in the womb of Mother Earth, awaiting to be reborn into a leadership position. Just like how we

Figure 5. Mud in West Africa is sacred. In every chief's house, Zigato explains, there is a mud building.

have a biological womb where we develop into full human beings and then are born into this world. No matter how modernised a chief's palace may be, there is still that small structure built in mud for that purpose. This spiritual value is part of our tradition. We even say, "Cry to the wall", meaning to speak your burdens to the mud wall in your bedroom – it will listen. These walls have heard more prayers than any church. We often overlook this spirituality when we talk about architecture. But for us, mud isn't just a material – it's a sacred medium.

DS The spirituality of a material is certainly not a part of dominant architectural discourse, and you've powerfully highlighted architecture as something deeply spiritual and nurturing. Anna, your school designs resonate with these concerns in the way they create spaces where children feel safe, inspired, and connected. Could you speak about the principles that guide your approach to designing educational spaces, both physically and pedagogically?

Figure 6. Schools are not just for learning; they are spaces for gathering, storytelling, and connection.

AH In the Bangladesh project, the client said, "Anna, I just want a space that the kids are excited to enter." When children feel well, they become curious and are open to receiving new information. If they feel uncomfortable, they shut down. I tried to remember the spaces I loved as a child, places where I felt safe but also connected to the world. It could be the crown of a tree where the leaves protect you, or under a table covered in a tablecloth, spaces that give you comfort but allow you to see and hear what's going on. That's what I try to create in school design.

At the METI School, we created "caves" – niches for children to retreat to. Not every child learns at the same pace. If someone finishes early, they can grab a book and go to their cave, instead of distracting others. We also built in spaces for meditation, group work, and breakout teams. There are lots of corners that were requested by the teachers for breakout rooms.

In Ghana, we adapted that idea outdoors. I wanted to have it indoors but there were concerns about girls' safety that of course I respect. We created outdoor cosy corners – Zigato calls them "girlfriend corners" – spaces for small confidential conversations, places that feel intimate but are a part of a larger environment (fig. 6). Interestingly, there are lots of walls in Ghana. In the

West, we often want to tear walls down for openness. But in Ghanaian vernacular contexts, walls create cozy niches, shaded spaces for gathering. So, I've used walls to structure outdoor communal areas. The key is that children – and adults – need spaces where they feel safe and relaxed, because that's when learning happens.

CPZA In West Africa, we live communally. We gather together, starting in childhood. If a student isn't in class, we ask, "Where is my neighbour?" We feel a sense of responsibility for one another.

So, a school must support social interaction – places where people can meet, play, tell stories, and just be together. Tatale has many such spaces – like courtyards between buildings, much like family compounds. That's where storytelling happens. It has that family spirit.

Every village has a designated space usually called a market square or village square where people gather and can meet. A school should be similar. It needs to offer spaces where we can gather, not just for instruction. And this was very pronounced in Anna's design.

AH The design that you directed! But it raises a question: What kind of education are we building for? Is it just for white-collar jobs? Or are we cultivating wisdom, connection, and the tools to address injustice and environmental collapse? We need an education of the heart, the hands, and the mind – and architecture can help foster that. It's not only about form; it's about creating spaces for new ways of being together.

Editor's Note
This interview has been edited and condensed. Portions of the conversation have been paraphrased and rearranged to enhance clarity and flow, while maintaining the accuracy of the participants' perspectives.

1 *Atakpame* walls are formed by sticking balls of wet, moulded earth to each other. It is also the name of a town in the northern part of Togo, and it is said that the building method got its name from a group of builders from this town, who then spread the method.

LEARNING

ECOLOGIES

Architecture's Ecology: Translation, Participation, Collaboration

Lesley Lokko

The social ecology that enables a robust architectural culture is relatively easy to map out: educational opportunities, a thriving culture of architectural critique, local and international awards, publications, significant exhibitions, in-depth scholarship, and established state, public, and philanthropic institutions that promote dialogue and discourse. Wherever great architecture is produced, healthy ecologies are invariably already in place, characterised by dynamic interactions and interrelations among these components. Underpinning these ecologies are practices of translation, inclusive participation, and equitable collaboration. The translation (of languages, expertise, culture[s], and materials) across diverse – and often unequal – contexts into meaningful architecture is a complex process, requiring careful and thoughtful attention.

For it to be truly effective, it must account for imbalances in power that determine whose voices are heard, whose contributions are valued, and what knowledge counts. Participation must be inclusive, ensuring that all stakeholders – not just those with power or resources – have a meaningful voice in shaping outcomes. Central to inclusive participation is recognition justice, which involves acknowledging and valuing the unique identities, knowledge, and contributions of diverse participants. Finally, equitable collaboration – between architects trained locally and abroad and the communities they engage – must be built on legitimacy and trust, as it strengthens both engagement and outcomes.

Figure 1. George W Bush Highway in Accra, Ghana, where the unlikely spectre of winning millions sits uneasily alongside makeshift taxi ranks

Figure 2. L'Ecole Africaine des Metiers de l'Architecture et de l'Urbanisme (EAMAU)

In Africa, the ecological infrastructure to support a thriving architectural culture is seriously impaired (fig. 1). Africa has the least number of professional schools of architecture of any continent – by an enormous margin. In many countries, there is simply no school: the whole of Francophone West Africa, an area encompassing nearly 25 per cent of Africa's land-mass and over 400 million people, has just one officially accredited school in Togo, L'École Africaine des Métiers de l'Architecture et de l'Urbanisme (EAMAU) (fig. 2). Private schools do exist, but without state or public support they are tenuous and fragile, often too vulnerable to truly make a difference. Wealthier parents send their children overseas to study. They often return to their home countries with world-class degrees and burning ambition but face an uphill struggle to find space in which to practise both their ideals and their hard-won knowledge. In societies without such opportunities and platforms, one must look elsewhere for the resources and spaces in which to explore alternatives and best practice. Nadine Gordimer, in *The Essential Gesture*, quotes the eloquent words of Pablo Neruda: "Every artist, in any society, has to struggle through what the poet Pablo Neruda calls the 'labyrinths' of his [or her] chosen medium of expression; that is a condition of his [or her] being."[1] The labyrinth of architecture is ecology: to a greater extent than other arts, it exists not in isolation but in *constant dialogue with others* – with clients, developers, users, institutions, civil society, and the state. Its tools are shaped by these encounters, yet it also shapes the very nature of the encounter itself. To overcome the "resource-deficit" model of engagement that characterises almost every encounter with African architecture, a different approach is urgently needed.

It is in this context that award programmes such as the Aga Khan Award for Architecture play such an important – and often overlooked – role. Especially international ones like the Aga Khan Award serve many purposes, some of which are more readily apparent than others.

Peer recognition, increased visibility, and a sense of personal and professional accomplishment are self-evident, but at a deeper, more structural level, awards can bring about significant cultural, social, and even political change. Their real power lies not in the nomination or evaluation processes, but in their potential to sustain and nourish hope. While it is certainly not the role or responsibility of an award programme to tackle the many challenges brought about by weak or weakened social ecologies, each award cycle is nevertheless a significant moment in which questions may be raised, debated, and often answered, even if not in the ways one might expect.

The recent collaboration between the Aga Khan Award for Architecture and the Accra-based African Futures Institute, titled Critical Workshop Dakar, brought together winners, funders, organisers, architects, critics, scholars, and students in a series of conversations over three days in October 2024 (figs. 3 and 4). It facilitated a level of honest, challenging, and critical interaction between locals and foreigners that is rarely experienced in Africa outside the two regions where healthier ecologies exist: some parts of North Africa and across South Africa. In this dialogue, participants raised the spectre of the profound and distinct challenges facing the profession of architecture in Africa, where extreme economic and demographic pressures

Figures 3 and 4. Critical Workshop Dakar, a joint initiative of the Aga Khan Award for Architecture and the Accra-based African Futures Institute

intertwine with planetary transformations – such as urbanisation and climate change – that are impacting the continent with particular force. The participants noted the struggle to translate between the global realm of architectural knowledge and expertise and the lived realities of most Africans.

A common theme among participants was the need for a new global narrative and approach towards African architecture and architects, one that acknowledges the community they are meant to serve and contributes to the effort to build the socio-ecological infrastructure necessary for meaningful architecture to be produced. A new orientation is needed that acknowledges the two-way reciprocal nature of the colonial–postcolonial–paracolonial relationship. This new orientation is not simply a rejection; it is a commitment to setting up a new, creative, and essential relationship between the past and the present based on something more than the rejection of Eurocentric culture or oppression.

One possible response to this provocation by the critical workshop participants may lie in the way we approach international awards, not merely as signs of individual excellence but in terms of their ability to generate meaningful change. The unspoken but powerful design language that international juries both recognise and reward often obscures the harsh realities of architects working in contexts where the ecologies that support excellence are either weak or non-existent, which in turn amplifies the "resource-deficit" framework where only foreign or foreign-trained architects stand a chance. An emphasis on translation, participation, and collaboration requirements for eligibility, beyond the level of the manual labour required to physically build, would provide opportunities for local architects to engage *as equals* and to acquire the skills needed to invest in and build a homegrown ecosystem (or at least components of it), which in a generation's time may significantly alter the imbalances we all grapple with. Exhibitions, workshops, seminars, and publications (both digital and physical) are all opportunities for growth, because training in the skills required to take part in constructing one's built environment neither begins nor ends in the university at a formally accredited programme.

Of all the international awards, the Aga Khan Award for Architecture stands out for its explicit search for projects that advance the role of social and environmental concerns across a wide spectrum of architectural activity – design, planning, landscape, historic preservation, and adaptive reuse. As with all global initiatives, finding common ground in terms of the meaning and importance of the criteria is the first, and perhaps greatest, challenge. The term "preservation" may have multiple meanings – and impact – in different places. Likewise, "history", "landscape", even "building". Semantics aside, these differences matter. In so many ways, the ability to think beyond existing definitions and to conceptualise alternative meanings and outcomes is the first step – though it may be unclear whether this leads to a dead end or a new beginning. Here,

Figure 5. Hawkers along one of Accra's main streets, selling everything from live puppies to spare car parts

the words of Nadine Gordimer are instructive. She describes "relevance" and "commitment" as concepts that "become the text claimed by artists [architects] who, individually, understand different things by them; they also become the demands made upon the artist [architect] by his [or her] people. Relevance and commitment pulse back and forth between the artist [architect] and society."[2]

In the messy, fraught labyrinth of the myriad contradictions and challenges that make up Africa's contemporary architectural "space", relevance has another demand (fig. 5). Whilst struggle and/or freedom may have been the state of collective consciousness during the independence eras of the 1950s, 1960s, and 1970s (coinciding with the explosive growth of African cities), it is no longer the only or overriding paradigm. For the African architect, at this point, commitment must take over from within, and the right to search out a new spatial, material, and technological vocabulary which breathes new life and courage into society needs to be asserted. It is vital to create new forms and norms out of, and for, a people already in the process of recreating themselves.

No small feat, make no small plans. We are all catalysts for a future we cannot afford to ignore.

1 Pablo Neruda, quoted in Nadine Gordimer, *The Essential Gesture: Writing, Politics and Places*, ed. Stephen Clingman (New York: Alfred A. Knopf, 1988), p. 135.

2 Gordimer, *The Essential Gesture: Writing, Politics and Places*, p. 136.

Creating a School for Architecture

Mamadou Jean-Charles Tall

Figure 1. Street view of the Collège Universitaire d'Architecture de Dakar

In 2005, my architectural colleagues Annie Jouga, Mouhamadou Naby Kane, and I gathered in Dakar to discuss the challenges facing our profession. A key issue was the lack of qualified staff. We often hired polytechnic graduates and trained them in the workings of an architectural firm. Despite their understanding of project management – organising on-site work and supervising construction – they struggled to translate their skills into designing space that met project requirements. To address this, we began meeting regularly to explore ways to improve the quality of our respective staff and the outcomes in our offices. Over time, it became clear that we were making the mistake of trying to transform our private architectural practices into schools of architecture. This was neither their purpose, nor something we were equipped to sustain. After three years of discussion and planning, we realised that what we truly needed was our own school of architecture (fig. 1). We began formalising the idea, drawing on our experiences as both practitioners and educators to shape its foundation.

However, we soon recognised a key limitation. As teachers, our perspective was often shaped by our specific fields of instruction. We focused on the subjects we taught, without fully considering the broader needs of students in their training. Yet, in an architecture studio, staff required more than just technical skills. They needed a deeper understanding of architecture as

Figure 2. Mamadou Jean-Charles Tall presenting a clay model

a discipline. Many of our students believed that becoming an architect simply meant mastering architectural software to produce 3D images. However, those who lacked drawing skills often became constrained by the rigid and formulaic aesthetics of computer-assisted design. The real challenge of pedagogy, therefore, lay in fostering creativity. Hand-drawing classes became a cornerstone of our curriculum, reinforcing the importance of sketching as a fundamental tool for architectural expression, even in the digital age. To counter students' overreliance on computers, we prohibited their use in design studios during two years of study. An architect must certainly know the techniques that he or she is using, but good design is not merely about adapting such methods to a given context; it requires the ability to translate creative vision into form (fig. 2). Just as jazz musicians "forget" musical structures to improvise within them, architects must internalise design principles while maintaining the freedom to explore beyond them. This led us to poetry. To nurture creativity within the structured constraints of architectural education, we encouraged students to design buildings based on poems they had composed themselves. However, this artistic approach had to be balanced with the practical demands of the profession. While fostering creativity was essential, students also needed to stay proficient in industry-standard software to remain competitive in the job market.

Beyond technical skills, what about architectural culture? All three of us had been trained in Europe, and upon returning to Senegal, we were struck by how different the realities of architectural practice at home were from what we had learned abroad. The challenges, constraints, and possibilities of designing in our own country demanded a different kind of architectural education, one rooted in local context rather than reliant only on imported frameworks. We had learned all the basics at foreign architecture schools – acoustics, heat exchange, lighting – but somehow something essential still felt as if it were missing. How could we connect these skills to the realities of our country, where urban architecture was largely produced by draftspeople who unquestioningly accepted any design originating from "the West" as superior? How do you teach students that the materials in their own houses – glass, steel, and cement – are not the only materials capable of producing good architecture? How can you teach students coming from a village that the mud bricks in their own community, which they are so eager to replace, might, in fact, be more effective at regulating heat than the supposedly "modern" cement bricks? More broadly, how do you deconstruct the idea of "modernity" in a country that endured 300 years of colonial rule, where the very concept of modern architecture remains tightly bound to Western, urban aesthetics?

To provide the best possible training for our students, we realised that we needed to rethink what architecture meant in – and for – our country and context. Architecture students often seek role models to inspire their work. However, the references they were relying on seemed overwhelmingly Western – Mies van der Rohe, Bauhaus, postmodernism – while their knowledge of African architecture was limited, and their understanding of architectural production in neighbouring countries was almost non-existent. Even more concerning, the students lacked exposure to architectural theory. It quickly became evident that few theoretical frameworks had been developed for architecture in Africa. The only one we were familiar with in Senegal was "asymmetrical parallelism", a concept embedded in Senegalese national architectural law (Law 78–44). Yet, to those trained in Euclidean geometry, this notion seemed perplexing. The poet who introduced it as the foundation of Senegal's architectural framework lacked the technical background to articulate how an alternative geometry could shape architectural thinking and practice.

It took us some time to encounter the concept of fractal geometry and to realise that moving away from Euclidean geometry could offer a much clearer understanding of space in Africa.

The work of the American mathematician Ron Eglash, and particularly his book *African Fractals: Modern Computing and Indigenous Design*, was instrumental in this shift.[1] Eglash explored the expression of art and space in various African cultures, arriving at the conclusion that African geometry is predominantly based on fractural principles rather than Euclidian geometry. This insight led us to recognise that to study and produce space in our country, we needed to rethink our approach to architecture. By embracing this new perspective and adopting different tools, we could help students think differently about architecture and its relationship to space.

The first aspect our students had to grasp was that they need to overthrow the old tools and methods (fig. 3). Colonialism cannot be dismantled using colonial frameworks. If asymmetrical parallelism proved effective in this struggle, then we should apply it to analysing the structures of our spaces. This also required questioning the very notion of architectural heritage. In our countries, "architectural heritage" has long been equated with colonial heritage, as colonisers dismissed our capacity to build or create anything worth preserving. However, viewing our history through a different lens transformed our architectural past into critical lessons. We realised that studying our spaces meant looking beyond form and aesthetics to understand what truly defines their specificity and genius.

Then we then noticed something so obvious that it had almost gone unmentioned. The cabins and huts built in our villages required no air-conditioning, which, in any case, was beyond our means to provide. Yet, these traditional structures offered far greater thermal comfort than modern buildings. This realisation led us to integrate the study of Indigenous past architecture into our lectures as a way of introducing the concept of comfort. At the same time, we recognised that studying architecture in isolation made little sense without understanding the broader context in which it is produced. As a result, we made the study of urbanism a mandatory component of architectural education. Students needed the tools to understand a social environment, to be able to question different situations that they would face in their lives and profession. We developed various ways of understanding the reality of our societies and gave the students some tools to really know what they were dealing with.

The greatest challenge, however, in establishing and developing our school was not designing a pedagogy or selecting teaching tools. Instead, it came from within our own professional community, the body of architects in our country. To our surprise, the fiercest opposition arose from some of our own colleagues. We were publicly attacked in newspapers, accused of being frauds who were deceiving parents by claiming to offer proper training. Naturally, we sought clarity from the board. What criteria determined recognition by the Architects' Association? What specific aspects of our curriculum or teaching methods needed adjustment to meet their standards? We sought to engage constructively, yet the path to official recognition remains

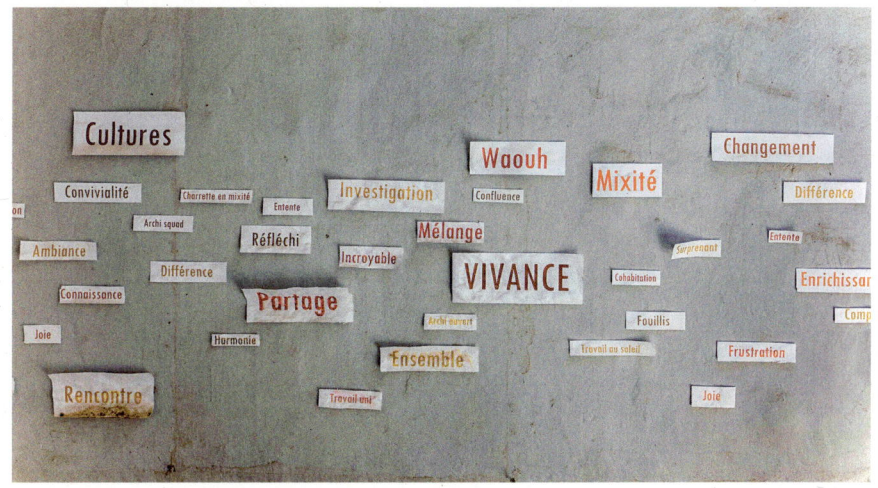

Figure 3. A wall in the school displaying a collection of brainstorming ideas

uncertain. To this day, we have received no written response to our inquiries. However, in practice, architecture studios across Senegal continue to hire our graduates, entrusting them with design work they were supposedly never trained to do. Now, after seventeen years of training architects, the issue of recognition has become less pressing. Some members of the National Board of Architects have even pledged to support the full accreditation of our school. More tellingly, our own colleagues now entrust us with their children's education, enrolling them in our College of Architecture. Furthermore, our graduates consistently secure jobs within three months of completing their studies, a testament to the quality of their education.

The journey of our school underscores a broader transformation – one that moves beyond inherited models to cultivate an architectural pedagogy deeply rooted in local knowledge, climate realities, and cultural specificity. As African architects continue to redefine their discipline, they are not only shaping new ways of designing but also fostering a generation of professionals who understand that architecture is both an art and a responsibility. Across the continent, the momentum is building: new schools, innovative research, and a growing recognition of local design principles are laying the foundation for a more responsive, sustainable, and confident architectural landscape. With each graduating class, we move closer to an architectural future that is distinctly African, one that honours the past while embracing the challenges and possibilities of the present.

1   Ron Eglash, *African Fractals: Modern Computing and Indigenous Design* (New Brunswick, NJ: Rutgers University Press, 1999).

Structures of Hope: Architecture, Education, and African Futures

In Conversation with Christian Benimana

Christian Benimana is a Rwandan architect dedicated to transforming architecture into a catalyst for social equity and sustainable development across Africa. Born in Rwanda, he pursued his architectural studies at Tongji University in Shanghai, China, earning a Bachelor of Science in Architecture in 2008. Upon returning to Rwanda in 2010, Benimana joined MASS Design Group as a Global Health Corps design fellow. He has since risen to the role of co-executive director and senior principal, leading the firm's Africa Studio and overseeing impactful projects such as the Rwanda Institute for Conservation Agriculture (RICA), the Ellen DeGeneres Campus of the Dian Fossey Gorilla Fund, and the African Leadership University campus (all in Rwanda). In 2015, Benimana co-founded the African Design Centre (ADC) in Kigali, a field-based apprenticeship programme aimed at cultivating a new generation of African designers equipped with socially focused design principles.

In this conversation, Benimana discusses how architecture can be a tool for dignity, equity, and transformation across Africa. Speaking with Deen Sharp, he reflects on MASS Design Group's trajectory in Rwanda and beyond, with a particular focus on educational infrastructure. He traces his own journey from a design fellow to a principal shaping MASS's African projects, highlighting the importance of architecture that responds to community needs and local materials. The interview ultimately underscores the role of architecture in imagining and building more just futures, rooted in context, history, and hope.

Deen Sharp (DS) Christian, to begin, could you please introduce your role at MASS Design Group, and its work with educational institutions?

Christian Benimana (CB) I joined MASS in 2010 as a design fellow at the entry level, and I have worked here at MASS for the past fifteen years. I'm now one of the co-executive directors and senior principals. I am responsible for our work in Africa.

In the space of education, we have not only worked with educational institutions but have also done a number of initiatives. MASS has engaged extensively with a range of partners in education, from ministries of education to universities and research institutions to design learning environments, which we believe are contributing to learning objectives and outcomes desired by these institutions, supporting educational goals and pedagogical practices. We've also invested deeply in understanding the systemic barriers that prevent the realisation of high-quality, inspiring educational spaces, especially the disconnect between curricular ambitions and the standardised designs typically implemented.

Moreover, we've placed a strong focus on teaching and learning about architecture. Many staff members at MASS, including myself, helped to establish the first architecture school in

Figure 1. The participants from the African Design Centre are driven by a strong commitment to move from words to action, and to demonstrate that change is possible.

Rwanda [in 2009, at the Kigali Institute of Science and Technology (KIST)].[1] I taught there as my first job before joining MASS. Additionally, MASS has invested in a design fellowship for young architects and designers that asks how architects can go beyond spatial planning to think of space as a lever that helps these organisations, like those in the education space, to achieve their intended outcomes and goals.

DS Within MASS Design Group, and as part of this broader work, there is the initiative that you instigated, the African Design Centre. Could you tell us about this centre and how it emerged?

CB The African Design Centre is a MASS initiative developed and implemented as part of our broader vision. MASS Design Group is a mission-driven practice – our name stands for "Model of Architecture Serving Society". That mission manifests differently in each place we work. But the unifying factor is that MASS invests in design solutions that create a future where both people and the planet can flourish. We fundamentally believe that the built environment is a powerful tool to help us achieve this aim.

Our approach involves not just designing beautiful buildings, but demonstrating that these spaces uplift communities and contribute meaningfully to equity, belonging, and shared prosperity. We contribute to other people's efforts to improve the current conditions. To achieve this, we do projects which show that it is possible to do what we are saying. Otherwise, it is just preaching. We have done about fifty projects all over the world to demonstrate the different aspects of our philosophy. To focus our efforts, we organise thematic "design labs". These labs are the platforms through which we turn the insights gleaned from these projects into sustained movements of change. We consolidate learnings from our projects across Africa, for example, and ask ourselves what we can focus on in terms of interventions and initiatives. If we apply ourselves to such projects with the maximum resources we can gather, and for as long as possible, then we are able to move the needle in the right direction. The African Design Centre is one such design lab (fig. 1).

Each lab has three workstreams:
1. **Research** – Studies focused on understanding the contexts, barriers, and opportunities for design-led change, but also on mobilising resources from philanthropy to support these initiatives so that it is not left to the research-and-development budgets of successful firms that just do it on the side.
2. **Catalyst projects** – Real-world implementations which prove that alternative models are possible.
3. **Systems change** – Efforts to amplify impact beyond MASS, such as our design fellowship and public engagements like my TED Talk in 2016.[2]

DS What does the African Design Centre aim to change within the African context?

CB Africa is at the epicentre of global population growth and urban development. Unfortunately, many past development interventions – often led by people who are not from Africa, at every level from financial planning to the implementation stages – have led to displacing communities and erasing cultural identities, because there is an idea of what modernity is supposed to be, and, in places like South Africa, this has deepened inequalities. Many of these are mistakes we can see repeating themselves. And if we are not able to overcome the challenges of that system and innovate, then we cannot respond to today's unprecedented growth.

In our view, there's a tremendous opportunity to chart a different path. Because much of the necessary infrastructure hasn't been built yet, there is an opportunity to do something fundamentally different and to leapfrog many of these predictable challenges. We are able to innovate with contextually appropriate, resilient, and inclusive approaches from the outset. Development does not need to exist in conflict with many of the other ideals we hold, especially when you are starting with a more or less blank canvas as far as infrastructure is concerned.

What we are trying to do at the African Design Centre is precisely this – through research, projects, and training that interrogate the root causes of inequitable development in healthcare, climate vulnerability, education, and economic opportunity, and that propose how locally driven solutions can change this, through a design lens. The catalyst projects are there to prove that it is feasible in practice, so our ideas do not remain theoretical. We work very hard to show how much we can change if only we could work with a different set of circumstances and opportunities. And through the third workstream, "systems change", our biggest initiative involves the fellowship programmes (figs. 2 and 3). Our special ADC fellowship programme within MASS makes sure that young professionals from Africa know and understand how to do this work. It provides them with confidence and experience to go forward independently.

DS A key part of the work you are doing at MASS involves educational projects. Let's talk about one of those projects – the Ruhehe Primary School in Ruhengeri, Rwanda. How did it come about? And how did you integrate this school into the work of the African Design Centre?

CB Ruhehe Primary was designed by our first ADC fellowship cohort in 2016. We had eleven fellows working with us for two years, investigating barriers to quality education in Africa, and particularly in Rwanda.

One issue is that, in the need to optimise and standardise school-rolling-out programmes, we have often found that our Ministry of Education has narrowed down the material pallet which is used to build classrooms, and which then becomes the basis for planning out building programmes for schools. What ends up happening is that the standard becomes a free-for-all interpretation at the local level; and even though everything is supposedly standardised, the structures are all very different when finished. So one of the things we've been looking at is how we can start from the material pallet that people know how to work with, so that we don't get challenged by questions of scale – and so that we are still able to challenge the models we've observed across the country and the continent as to how they perform, or not, in relation to the curriculum and pedagogy that the education ministries are actually putting forward.

Ruhehe Primary School presented an interesting case study, because in Rwanda we had changed the basic education system from a knowledge-based to competency-based curriculum that promotes more activities with students and is less about absorbing knowledge. Teachers needed to find new configurations for using the space in their classrooms, one that is more aligned with this competency-based curriculum. The problem was that they were not working

Figures 2 and 3. Participants of the ADC fellowship programme doing fieldwork

Figure 4. View of a classroom at Ruhehe Primary School in Ruhengeri, Rwanda

with the available spaces for a number of reasons. Some were not built to the right measurements at the minimum standards. For instance, if they say in the guidelines that the maximum number of students should be thirty, but in reality few of the classes in practice had less than forty-five students. So the space and the desks they were using were not functioning for the competency-based curriculum.

Our aim and challenge was to create a scalable, adaptable alternative model that supported the pedagogical shifts Rwanda was making – while remaining rooted in local realities. This is what we posed to the fellows, who came to understand the context and the constraints through extensive research. We had the benefit of a partnership with one district here in Rwanda that was also interested in this initiative. All of this translated into the creation of Ruhehe Primary School, where we looked at the material pallet that is standardised and localised, and at how it can be done better (figs. 4 and 5). We reviewed the competency-based curriculum and what it prescribes, and then we challenged the size of the classrooms and the lack of accessibility, as well as the role that such schools play in these communities. Schools are also civic infrastructure

Figure 5. View of the school's terraced outdoor area

and space, and on the weekend they turn into multi-use spaces, for cooperatives, church choirs, or football teams. Thinking about how we can design for all of these different dynamics is what drove the Ruhehe Primary School.

DS And in terms of materials, there are often tensions between sustainability and aspiration. How did you navigate that?

CB The conversation about materials is very interesting and complex. I find it problematic when Indigenous architecture in Africa is reduced to mud huts or earth construction. It's not that it's wrong, but this viewpoint is incomplete. It is only a partial – and often romanticised – narrative.

Every construction decision is a trade-off between resource utilisation and desired outcome. Instead of asking whether we're using "modern" or "traditional" materials, we should ask questions like: Are we achieving the outcomes we set out to deliver? Are we investing adequately in schools so they can fulfil their educational promise?

We celebrate building cheaply, but rarely do we ask whether the spaces support learning. We don't question enough whether the investment was sufficient to achieve the necessary learning outcomes. We need to design for actual performance – not just affordability or aesthetics. It is the idea of balance: What are the ideas that will make this feasible and possible? What do we think will lead to desired learning outcomes as we have promised? The material deduction, for me, is a simple exercise of what ticks the boxes, rather than being hell-bent on what sounds romantic, yet without achieving a practical solution to the problem, or the scale required. The right material is the one that enables the desired outcome within real-world constraints.

DS What are the key skills you are trying to instil in the ADC fellows?

CB Many architecture programmes in Africa still train students to solve problems of the Global North. The result is graduates who are technically competent but poorly equipped to address local challenges.

Through the African Design Centre, we want to build a movement of architects who start by asking the right questions: What problem are we solving, and for whom? Fellows should leave with the tools and confidence to design within their given context, and with the criticality to challenge systems that limit good design.

We also recognise that market forces and corruption often constrain architects, no matter their talent. The African Design Centre provides a support system – so fellows don't just learn to work differently; they also have the backing to take risks and challenge the status quo.

DS Last questions: Are you hopeful? Do you believe in a future where Africa is more often designed by architects trained and based in Africa?

CB Yes, I'm hopeful. While there are still many foreign architects working across the continent, I don't think that's inherently a problem. Diversity in perspectives can be valuable.

What's crucial is that Africans define what excellence in architecture means for our context. We're seeing a new generation of architects – especially in East Africa – rejecting imported models and seeking design that truly serves local communities.

When I studied architecture in China, everyone referenced iconic, expressive buildings from star architects. Today, many students in Africa are citing local projects by architects like Francis Kéré, Sumayya Vally, or Mariam Kamara. That shift in values is significant – and it gives me real hope.

Editor's Note
This interview has been edited and condensed. Portions of the conversation have been paraphrased and rearranged to enhance clarity and flow, while maintaining the accuracy of the participants' perspectives.

1   See Matthew Barac, "Pedagogy: KIST, Kigali, Rwanda", *The Architectural Review*, 25 October 2013, https://www.architectural-review.com/essays/pedagogy-kist-kigali-rwanda.

2   Christian Benimana, "The Next Generation of African Architects and Designers", *TEDGlobal 2017*, 30 August 2017, https://www.ted.com/talks/christian_benimana_the_next_generation_of_african_architects_and_designers?language=en.

Designing Education: Reflecting on the Aga Khan Award for Architecture

Christian A. Hedrick

"I have come to the conclusion that there is no greater form of preparation for change than education. I also think that there is no better investment that the individual, parents, and the nation can make than an investment in education of the highest possible quality."

—His Late Highness Aga Khan IV, Osh, October 2002[1]

Unlike other awards that primarily recognise prominent architects and buildings, the Aga Khan Award for Architecture (AKAA) highlights often overlooked projects that address pressing social, cultural, and environmental challenges. By expanding categories beyond aesthetic excellence, the Award draws attention to architecture's deeper role in shaping communities and advancing critical global issues. One of the most significant of these matters is education – a theme that resonates far beyond the Award and its recipients. Architecture's role in shaping learning environments is widely acknowledged, yet few awards have consistently illuminated this relationship. This essay explores the intersection of architecture and education through the lens of the AKAA, examining how its award-winning educational projects have contributed to innovative learning spaces while integrating sustainable and socially responsive design.

Since the inception of the Aga Khan Award for Architecture, numerous shortlisted projects with an educational component have gone on to receive the Award.[2] Although all of them are worthy of discussion, there is little room here to do so. Nonetheless, it is important to acknowledge the rich diversity found within just this category alone. His Late Highness the Aga Khan IV himself prioritised education and articulated the fundamental need to recognise education as a vehicle for peace and prosperity – not only in the developing world, but beyond.[3] Indeed, when one considers the breadth and depth of involvement of the Aga Khan Development Network (AKDN) in education – from the Aga Khan Academies (AKA), which alone reach over 2 million K-12 learners, to the establishment of the Aga Khan University to support higher education, to the additional support and education of teachers – the AKDN's commitment to education is clear.[4] The Award then goes beyond the AKDN's own efforts in order to call attention to and recognise efforts around the world that prioritise education in Muslim majority contexts.[5] It is in this vein that nine award-winning projects have been chosen and brought together here to highlight the role that education plays within Islamic cultures. Each of these projects, despite their geographical and temporal diversity, reveals different facets of the Aga Khan Award and deserves to be acknowledged for celebrating the myriad different ways architecture can play a contributing role in local communities. Moreover, beyond the formal characteristics that often define a project lies the true importance of the Award, which acknowledges the variety of people and organisations that came together to produce a particular building that was needed at a specific point in time for or by a defined group of people. In this essay I demonstrate both the incredible diversity and unity that has come to characterise this unique architectural award by examining specific award-winning projects (across all cycles) which share and celebrate the programme of education.

Education and Architecture: A Symbiotic Relationship

Over the decades, the AKAA has identified and honoured a wide range of educational institutions. Even within the educational model there is great diversity. However, we can begin to organise them into three primary models of learning: Classical (formal education), Praxis (learning by doing), and Exemplar (learning by example). These models, though by no means mutually exclusive, provide a framework by which we can begin to understand the profound impact of architectural interventions on pedagogical approaches as they ultimately relate to community engagement. After all, education is the continuous communication of a culture's knowledge and identity from one generation to the next. These taught and learned cultural practices can certainly be communicated in a myriad of ways; however, these three particular learning models have emerged as clear themes expressed and celebrated through the AKAA over the course of its lifetime.

The Classical Model: Institutions of Higher Learning

The first of these categories expressed in the Aga Khan Award for Architecture is the Classical Model, which we can understand as a formal educational instructional model such as that found in universities and research centres. The University of Technology Petronas (Malaysia), the Issam Fares Institute for Public Policy and International Affairs (Lebanon), and most recently the Alioune Diop University Teaching and Research Unit (Senegal) are all representative of this category. These institutions not only serve as centres of higher learning, but also integrate architectural innovations that foster and promote collaborative research, social interaction, and environmental sustainability.

The University of Technology Petronas, designed by Norman Foster + Partners and completed in 2005 (recipient, 10th Award Cycle), is a significant example of the relationship between architecture and education in a Classical Model by its integration of spatial planning and sustainability (fig. 1). The campus layout fosters academic collaboration, with buildings arranged radially around a central park, facilitating interdisciplinary engagement to enhance learning and research while ensuring accessibility and future expansion. The climate-responsive design creates a comfortable learning environment by integrating crescent-shaped canopies, shaded walkways, and natural ventilation to counter Malaysia's heat, while passive cooling techniques and a centralised gas-fired chilled water system enhance energy efficiency.[6] Architectural elements, such as locally sourced materials, ceramic tiles, and woven silk panels, reflect regional

Figure 1. View of the main building of the University of Technology Petronas, Bandar Seri Iskandar, Malaysia

Figure 2. View of the Issam Fares Institute for Public Policy and International Affairs on the campus of the American University of Beirut, Lebanon

craftsmanship and enhance durability and cultural identity within an academic setting at the same time.[7] Additionally, rainwater collection systems contribute to resource efficiency, promoting environmental responsibility.

By merging educational functions with ecological awareness, the campus serves as a model for academic infrastructure, embodying Malaysia's commitment to technological advancement and industry-linked education.[8] The university's architecture not only supports pedagogical objectives, but also demonstrates the role of the built environment in promoting innovation, collaboration, and long-term sustainability.

The second example within the Classical Model, the Issam Fares Institute for Public Policy and International Affairs, Beirut, Lebanon (recipient, 13th Award Cycle) was designed by Zaha Hadid Architects, completed in 2014, and also exemplifies the integration of architecture and education through the Classical Model of higher education, promoting intellectual exchange and research while respecting the historical and ecological context (fig. 2). Its cantilevered design minimises the building's footprint, preserving open spaces and historic trees, thus reflecting an academic ethos that values progress alongside conservation and heritage. The spatial organisation enhances collaboration and accessibility, with multiple entry points and circulation ramps weaving through the trees, creating a learning environment that extends beyond the enclosed spaces.[9] Constructed with in-situ reinforced concrete and partially pigmented glass partitions, the design balances openness and privacy, fostering collaborative and independent learning, while positioning the institute as a regional leader in public policy and international affairs research.[10]

The third Classical Model example can be found in the Alioune Diop University Teaching and Research Unit, Bambey, Senegal (recipient, 14th Award Cycle) (fig. 3). This relatively recent project, completed in 2017, exemplifies a continuing trend that highlights architecture's innovative approach to academic buildings within a rural context. Conceived to accommodate the institution's growing student population, the design integrates functionality, environmental sensitivity, and cost efficiency. The single-storey structure consolidates key academic facilities – including a 500-seat lecture hall, multiple classrooms, laboratories, offices, and meeting rooms – into a cohesive architectural mass, distinguishing itself from the pre-existing dispersed campus blocks.[11]

The university exemplifies the essential connection between architecture and education, demonstrating how thoughtful design can enhance learning environments while addressing climate, sustainability, and social needs. By consolidating academic facilities into a single, cohesive structure, the design fosters a sense of institutional identity and improves functional efficiency.[12]

Figure 3. View of the eastern facade of the Alioune Diop University Teaching and Research Unit in Bambey, Senegal

The Praxis Model: Learning Through Craft and Restoration

The Praxis Model highlights educational projects where students and community members engage in hands-on learning, often through construction and restoration activities. This Praxis Model not only results in a useful building; it also provides employment and fulfils a didactic function: invaluable training that those involved can take with them. The Amiriya Complex (Yemen), the Agricultural Training Centre (Senegal), and the Arcadia Education Project (Bangladesh) exemplify this approach by integrating education with local craftsmanship and building practices.

The Amiriya Complex, Rada, Yemen (recipient, 10th Award Cycle) was originally constructed in 1504 as a madrasa and was restored between 1982 and 2004 under the guidance of the conservator Selma al-Radi (fig. 4). The project highlights the integration of education and historical preservation by employing local labourers and craftspeople who learned traditional

Figure 4. Street view of the Amiriya Complex in Rada, Yemen

Yemeni building techniques, including how to use *qudad* (a traditional Yemeni lime plaster).[13] This process revitalised a significant heritage site that needed repair, and it also provided vocational training to the community, ensuring the continuity of Indigenous construction skills.[14] The restoration of the Amiriya Complex highlights the significant relationship between architecture and education, particularly within the context of preservation. Moreover, the transmission of traditional building knowledge situates it firmly within the Praxis Model of education.

By the 1980s, the building had fallen into severe disrepair, necessitating an extensive restoration effort. Due to the scale of the project, the restoration became an educational initiative, ultimately providing training for over 500 local craftspeople and artisans in traditional building and craft techniques. Skills such as carved gypsum plasterwork, traditional *qudad* waterproofing, and mural restoration were revived, ensuring the preservation of Yemeni architectural heritage while equipping a new generation with specialised expertise. Many artisans later applied these skills to other restoration projects, strengthening cultural conservation efforts throughout the region.[15] Beyond its historical and artistic value, the Amiriya Complex serves as a model for architectural conservation, demonstrating how restoration projects can function as educational platforms, fostering both skill development and community engagement. By relying on local

Figure 5. View of a classroom at the Agricultural Training Centre in Nianing, Senegal

labour, materials, and expertise, the project reinforced the sustainability of traditional construction methods, ensuring their continued relevance in modern restoration practices.

Completed in 1977, the Agricultural Training Centre, Nianing, Senegal (recipient, 1st Award Cycle), was developed with support from UNESCO and the Senegalese Ministry of Education (fig. 5). The project focused on teaching agricultural techniques and sustainable building practices to local communities, hence its pertinence and relevance to the Praxis Model of education. Constructed using local materials and labour-intensive methods, the training centre enabled local populations to gain practical skills while fostering self-sufficiency in food production and rural development.[16] The training centre is an educational facility designed to support learning and community development in a rural setting.[17] The architecture of the centre emphasises environmental responsiveness, sustainability, and the use of locally available materials and simple yet efficient techniques to ensure cost-effectiveness and ease of maintenance.

Figure 6. Arcadia Education Project, South Kanarchor, Bangladesh; general view of the building during the dry season

The design incorporates passive cooling strategies essential for the region's hot climate. Structures are arranged to maximise cross-ventilation, and shading elements are integrated to reduce solar heat gain.[18] Functionally, the centre is organised to facilitate agricultural education and practical training, comprising classrooms, demonstration fields, and storage facilities. The spatial configuration promotes interaction between students and instructors, fostering a hands-on learning environment. Additionally, water management strategies, including modelling rainwater harvesting and irrigation systems, support the centre's agricultural activities and contribute to its self-sufficiency.

Although the construction methods were developed by a UN agency and introduced to the area for this project, they were considered easily learned by a master mason who could quickly teach others.[19] Built with didactic construction techniques meant to teach its users, while promoting modern educational agricultural methods, the Agricultural Training Centre serves as a model for sustainable rural development and education. Its architecture goes beyond meeting the functional requirements of an agricultural institution to also align with the broader goal of promoting ecological resilience and community engagement in agricultural practices.

Another example of an awarded project that can be utilised to further expand on the understanding of the Praxis Model is the Arcadia Education Project, South Kanarchor, Bangladesh (recipient, 14th Award Cycle), designed by Saif Ul Haque Sthapati and completed in 2016 (fig. 6). The project is an innovative "amphibious school" that adapts to seasonal flooding.[20] Commissioned by the Maleka Welfare Trust under the leadership of Razia Alam, the project addresses the challenge of building in a flood-prone region by employing a floating structural system for approximately five months out of the year due to the monsoon season. The school consists of three classrooms, an office, a toilet facility, and an open platform, all connected via a single corridor. Constructed using locally sourced bamboo from neighbouring villages, and steel drums for buoyancy, the design ensures minimal environmental impact yet simultaneously maintains resilience against monsoon conditions.[21] Traditional construction techniques, such as rope-tied bamboo joints and natural waterproofing using gaab fruit extract, contribute to its durability and sustainability.

The project demonstrates climate-responsive architecture by integrating floating mechanisms that allow the structure to rise and fall with the river's water levels. As such, its success extends beyond education by serving as a physical prototype for resilient, low-cost, and adaptable architecture in vulnerable communities, educating both architects and non-governmental organisations (NGOs). Functioning as a shelter for the purpose of education, the building itself is also a paradigm of how to create educational facilities like this in what may at first appear to be an inhospitable location such as a flood zone. The initiative has received international

Figure 7. METI Primary School in Rudrapur, Dinajpur, Bangladesh

recognition for its sustainability, social impact, and innovative use of materials, highlighting the potential for scalable solutions in flood-prone regions.

The Exemplar Model: Schools as Catalysts for Social Change

Projects within the Exemplar Model serve as beacons of transformative architecture, demonstrating how schools can become catalysts for broader societal change. The METI School in Rudrapur (Bangladesh), the Kamanar Secondary School (Senegal), and the Primary School in Gando (Burkina Faso) all illustrate how architectural design can empower communities to create innovative learning environments. The Exemplar Model is unique in that it is not just about a community participating in erecting their own building. The project extends much further than the local or regional context to become a model of development for similar contexts throughout the world.

The METI School in Rudrapur, Dinajpur, Bangladesh (recipient, 10th Award Cycle), designed by Anna Heringer, Eike Roswag Architects, and completed in 2005, exemplifies the relationship between architecture and education, demonstrating how contextually responsive design enhances learning environments while promoting sustainability and community engagement. Constructed using traditional materials and local craftsmanship, the school embodies hands-on learning and participatory design, reinforcing the educational philosophy of Dipshikha, the NGO that oversaw the project. The design process actively involved architects, local craftspeople, students, parents, and teachers, ensuring that the building itself became a tool for education – not just a place for learning, but a model for sustainable construction techniques. The integration of earthen materials such as loam and straw with lighter elements like bamboo reflects a commitment to the environment, teaching students about resourcefulness and ecological balance (fig. 7).[22]

Figure 8. One of the vaulted classrooms at the Kamanar Secondary School, Thionck Essyl, Senegal

By adapting vernacular building techniques with modern refinements, the METI School not only improves comfort and functionality but also provides a model for upgrading rural housing standards.[23] This approach fosters a sense of ownership and empowerment among the community, supporting the idea that education extends beyond the classroom into the built environment to embrace sustainability and craftsmanship. Ultimately, the school's architecture mirrors its educational philosophy, promoting creativity, self-sufficiency, and community development through both its structure and its purpose.

Kamanar Secondary School, Thionck Essyl, Senegal (recipient, 15th Award Cycle), a secondary school designed to focus on community engagement and sustainable practices, completed in 2020, fits under the Exemplar Model due to its success as a contextually responsive educational facility. Designed by Dawoffice and funded by the associated NGO called Foundawtion, the school addresses the urgent need for an increase in educational infrastructure in this rural region.

The school consists of nineteen modular classrooms arranged around open courtyards that incorporate existing vegetation, creating shaded communal areas – all upon an adaptable grid layout that allows for future expansion (fig. 8).[24] Built with on-site compressed earth bricks, the design ensures thermal regulation, minimising artificial cooling needs. Catenary vaulted classrooms enhance airflow, and wooden lattice facades facilitate cross-ventilation and control sunlight. A metal roof, supported by wooden trusses, offers protection from the heavy rainfall typical of this tropical savanna climate. The design prioritises student experience, community engagement, and sustainability, resulting in an institution that harmonises with its surroundings and encourages an environment conducive to learning at the same time.

Finally, the Primary School, Gando, Burkina Faso (recipient, 10th Award Cycle), designed by Francis Kéré and completed in 2001, is a community-driven architectural project that embodies the Exemplar Model through its use of local materials and its thoughtful climate-responsive design. Faced with the deteriorating state of the village's original school, Kéré, the first person from Gando to receive higher education abroad, initiated the project.[25] He was motivated to design a school because when he was a child there was no school in Gando and he had to travel some 40 kilometres to attend a school with poor lighting and ventilation (fig. 9).[26] He secured funding through the organisation Schulbausteine für Gando, a German-based association, as well as government support. Further, he mobilised local villagers to participate in the construction, ensuring both skill development and community ownership.[27]

The school was constructed primarily from locally sourced compressed earth blocks, significantly reducing reliance on imported materials; and it incorporates passive cooling strategies, such as cross-ventilation. The structure's modular layout allows for future expansion, while

Figure 9. Gando Primary School, Gando, Burkina Faso

pilasters provide additional stability on the exterior and niches for convenient storage alcoves on the interior. The school has significantly impacted education in the region, attracting students from neighbouring villages and setting a precedent for similar initiatives. The project demonstrates how vernacular building methods, community participation, and contemporary architectural knowledge can converge to create resilient, context-sensitive educational infrastructure in resource-constrained environments. As such, it epitomises the Exemplar Model of education celebrated by the AKAA.

Conclusion

By utilising the categories of Classical, Praxis, and Exemplar Models, this essay has demonstrated how architecture shapes both learning environments and community development. Whether through advanced technological campuses, hands-on vocational training centres, or transformative primary and secondary schools in rural areas, the AKAA continues to highlight the profound impact that architecture makes on education. The recognition of these projects underscores the vital role of architecture in celebrating educational environments that have become models of learning. As global challenges in education intensify, the principles embodied in AKAA-winning projects offer valuable insights for future architectural endeavours. By prioritising user experience, local engagement, pedagogical innovation and environmental sensitivity, these projects serve as enduring models for the future design of educational institutions. The Aga Khan Award for Architecture's continued support for educational projects underscores the transformative power of architecture in shaping the future of learning and community development worldwide.

1. Opening ceremony of the Aga Khan School by His Late Highness Aga Khan IV, Osh, Kyrgyz Republic, 30 October 2002.
2. I count here the projects whose main programme is dedicated to education. There are many shortlisted and award-winning projects that include educational components, but the focus for this essay is on those solely dedicated to the enterprise of education.
3. See "5 Ways Education Can Nurture Peace", AKDN website, https://the.akdn/en/resources-media/whats-new/spotlights/5-ways-education-can-nurture-peace. See also the Stephen Ogden Lecture at Brown University by His Late Highness Aga Khan IV, Providence, Rhode Island, 10 March 2014.
4. See the AKDN website, https://the.akdn/en/what-we-do/developing-human-capacity/education.
5. See Rebecca Nichols, ed., *Case Studies: Addressing Needs and Aspirations Through Education* (Geneva: Aga Khan Trust for Culture Education Programme, 2022).
6. "University of Technology Petronas Project Brief", compiled by the Aga Khan Award for Architecture (Geneva: Aga Khan Award for Architecture, 2013), p. 10.
7. Ibid.
8. Ibid., pp. 1 and 11.
9. "Issam Fares Institute for Public Policy and International Affairs On-site Review Report", edited by the Aga Khan Award for Architecture, 2016, p. 6.
10. Ibid., pp. 6 and 10.
11. "Alioune Diop University Teaching and Research Unit", in *Architecture in Dialogue*, ed. Andres Lepik (Berlin: ArchiTangle, 2019), p. 221.
12. Ibid.
13. Selma Al-Radi, GOAMM, Yahya Al Nasiri, "Restoration of Amiriya Complex", in *Intervention Architecture: Building for Change*, ed. Pamela Johnston (London: I.B. Tauris, 2007), p. 86.
14. "Restoration of Amiriya Madrasa On-site Review Report", edited by the Aga Khan Award for Architecture, 2007, p. 12.
15. Al-Radi et al., "Restoration of Amiriya Complex", p. 84.
16. "Agricultural Training Centre Project Brief", compiled by the Aga Khan Award for Architecture (Geneva: Aga Khan Award for Architecture, 1980), p. 3.
17. Renata Holod and Darl Rastorfer, "Agricultural Training Centre", in *Architecture and Community*, ed. Renata Holod and Darl Rastorfer (New York: Aperture, 1983), p. 70.
18. Ibid., p. 71.
19. "Agricultural Training Centre Project Brief" (see note 16), p. 6.
20. "Arcadia Education Project On-site Review Report", edited by the Aga Khan Award for Architecture, 2019, p. 1.
21. Ibid., p. 4.
22. "Hand-Made School On-site Review Report", edited by the Aga Khan Award for Architecture, 2007, p. 20.
23. Ibid., p. 19.
24. "Kamanar Secondary School On-site Review Report", edited by the Aga Khan Award for Architecture, 2022, p. 4.
25. "Primary School Project Brief", compiled by the Aga Khan Award for Architecture (Geneva: Aga Khan Award for Architecture, 2004), p. 1.
26. "Gando Primary School / Kéré Architecture", *ArchDaily*, 22 April 2016, https://www.archdaily.com/785955/primary-school-in-gando-kere-architecture.
27. Philippa Baker, ed., "Gando Primary School", in *Architecture and Polyphony: Building in the Islamic World Today* (London: Thames and Hudson, 2004), p. 34.

Please scan the QR code to view the Aga Khan Award for Architecture visual portraits of the Kamanar Secondary School, Thionck Essyl, Senegal (AKAA 2022), Alioune Diop University Teaching and Research Unit, Bambey, Senegal (AKAA 2019), Arcadia Education Project, South Kanarchor, Bangladesh (AKAA 2019), Issam Fares Institute, Beirut, Lebanon (AKAA 2016), University of Technology Petronas, Bandar Seri Iskandar, Malaysia (AKAA 2007), METI School in Rudrapur, Dinajpur, Bangladesh (AKAA 2007), Restoration of Amiriya Complex, Rada, Yemen (AKAA 2007), Primary School, Gando, Burkina Faso (AKAA 2004), and Agricultural Training Centre, Nianing, Senegal (AKAA 1980).

Epilogue
Souleymane Bachir Diagne

At the beginning of the twentieth century, France entrusted a young education inspector named George Hardy with the task of devising a school policy for its West African colonies. In 1884–85, the division of Africa among European colonial powers had taken place in Berlin, and ten years later, in 1895, France had grouped its West African possessions into a federation called Afrique-Occidentale française (French West Africa, known by the acronym AOF). Hardy, who had graduated from the prestigious École normale supérieure with an *agrégation* in history and geography, translated his enthusiasm for the mission into a book he published in 1917 entitled *Une conquête morale: l'enseignement en AOF* (A Moral Conquest: Education in AOF). The message was clear: the physical conquest of the colonies could not be a lasting victory unless it was also a "moral conquest", for which education was the means. The French school in Africa was thus not just a colonial institution, but colonialism itself. The native pupils who entered this colonial school entered physically into a space built and implanted according to colonial architecture, and mentally into a colonial world where they were taught, in the language of the coloniser, that their ancestors were Gauls.

It is not just for secular France that the school was a tool for moral conquest. That was the case for the missionaries too. Ola Uduku reminds us that missionaries were pioneers in introducing Western education to Africa, from the teaching of catechism to the establishment of institutions of higher learning, such as Fourah Bay College in Sierra Leone, founded in 1827 by the Anglican Church Missionary Society, or the Lovedale and Tiger Kloof missions in South Africa.

But education is a means of emancipation: knowledge is freedom. Therefore, school is also the "miraculous weapon", in Aimé Césaire's words, that the colonised can turn against the coloniser, using it as a tool for decolonisation. This decolonisation movement would be twofold: to provide the school that opens up access to the most modern human knowledge; and to inscribe it in the living, social, cultural, spiritual, and environmental reality of the context. In this movement of inscription, an architecture that manifests rootedness and openness plays the essential role of making the school an IWACU, to use the name of the Centre in Kigali, Rwanda, presented here by Justicia C. T. Kiconco. This name, IWACU, which means "our home", is truly emblematic of *Learning Ecologies in Architecture* and can be applied to all the examples cited in this volume, all of which illustrate this notion of rooting the school in its natural and cultural environment.

It certainly applies to the Kamanar Secondary School (CEM) in Thionck Essyl, Senegal, whose architects wanted it to be the work of the entire community, built according to local aesthetics and using local materials. It's hardly surprising, then, that the inhabitants of Thionck Essyl have taken full ownership of a building that reflects the "local way of life", making the school both a place of community life and an educational space.

The name applies to the learning spaces created in the Rohingya refugee camps. Schools designed to educate children from the Rohingya exile have thus turned the ban on durable construction into an opportunity for making creative use of natural, ecological, and lightweight materials such as bamboo and wood.

As far as materials are concerned, special emphasis must be placed on the ecological significance of clay. Clay is living substance that gives a sense of organic continuity between the natural environment and the architectural construction. It's no coincidence that mud as a source of life is a universal theme in human spirituality everywhere. In Deen Sharp's conversation with Anna Heringer and Christian Paul Zigato Agboada, we find this statement by Zigato expressing the spiritual significance of mud: "This spiritual value is part of our tradition. We even say, 'Cry to the wall', meaning to speak your burdens to the mud wall in your bedroom – it will listen. These walls have heard more prayers than any church. We often overlook this spirituality when we talk about architecture. But for us, mud isn't just a material – it's a sacred medium."

Being part of the environment and not unduly burdening nature: this is an Islamic principle that must be held to be universal. When the Quran states that the "servants of God are those who walk on the earth in humility" (25:63), such a command to take care of our footprints also applies to human constructions. This is why, while the Aga Khan Award for Architecture has always honoured a wide variety of buildings, it has often encouraged the development of educational projects that also reflect a demanding ecological philosophy. This volume manifests why.

The light- and air-permeable wooden lattices of the *awlas* at Kamanar Secondary School. Like clay and bamboo, wood as a building material is natural, sustainable, and inspiring in its creative use.

Echoing the tradition of gathering under trees, the Alioune Diop University Teaching and Research Unit features slender metal trunks with V-shaped branches that support an expansive external roof, creating shaded spaces.

A delicate wire structure for flowers echoes the distinctive arches of the Kamanar Secondary School.

The *awla* is softly illuminated at night.

Contributor Biographies

Jonathan Kplorla Agbeh is an architectural researcher, educator, and writer from Ghana with a strong focus on sustainable urban development. He holds a Bachelor of Architecture from Central University, where he is a research and teaching assistant at the School of Architecture and Design. Agbeh is the co-founder of the Inspo7 Development Group, an architecture and planning firm committed to environmental sustainability and urban resilience in sub-Saharan Africa. His work explores the intersections of architecture, planning, and climate justice, with a focus on community-centred development. Beyond academia and practice, Agbeh plays an active mentoring role as a patron and advisor to the Architecture Students Association of Ghana at Central University. He is also a member of Docomomo Ghana, contributing to the preservation of Ghana's modern architectural heritage.

Christian Paul Zigato Agboada is a Ghanaian construction engineer who heads the Engineering Department of the Ada East District Assembly in Ghana. He also serves as a technical consultant for the Salesians of Don Bosco, a Catholic religious order known for its work in education and youth development. His work spans two Salesian provinces: the Anglophone West Africa Province (AOS), which includes Ghana, Togo, Ivory Coast, and Sierra Leone; and the Nigeria-Niger Province (ANN). Zigato is currently collaborating with Anna Heringer on the Earth Campus in Tatale, a teaching, learning, training, and production centre located in northeast Ghana near the Togo border. The Earth Campus is run by the Don Bosco Mission and is part of a broader effort to promote locally grounded education and climate-sensitive construction.

Christian Benimana is a Rwandan architect dedicated to transforming architecture into a catalyst for social equity and sustainable development across Africa. Born in Rwanda, he pursued his architectural studies at Tongji University in Shanghai, China, earning a Bachelor of Science in Architecture in 2008. Upon returning to Rwanda in 2010, Benimana joined MASS Design Group as a Global Health Corps design fellow. He has since risen to the role of co-executive director and senior principal, leading the firm's Africa studio and overseeing impactful projects such as the Rwanda Institute for Conservation Agriculture, the Ellen DeGeneres Campus of the Dian Fossey Gorilla Fund, and the African Leadership University campus. In 2015, Benimana co-founded the African Design Centre, a field-based apprenticeship programme aimed at cultivating a new generation of African designers equipped with socially focused design principles.

Katherine Dawson is a lecturer in environment, politics, and society at University College London (UCL). She is interested in the relationships between society, space, and geological materials. Dawson holds a PhD in human geography and urban studies from the London School of Economics (LSE) (2015–20). Her thesis focused on the ways in which sand became part of the city of Accra – thinking about sand's materiality, expansive economies, and shifting ecologies. Before joining UCL, Dawson held an ESRC Postdoctoral Fellowship at LSE (2020–21), where she developed a series of creative outputs and engaged with the growing policy space surrounding sand's global governance. She also worked as part of an interdisciplinary team of geographers and geologists on the project "Mining for Meaning: The Geoethics of Extractive Industries", funded by the British Academy.

Farrokh Derakhshani is the director of the Aga Khan Award for Architecture and has been associated with the Award since 1982. Derakhshani trained as an architect and planner at the National University of Iran and later continued his studies at the School of Architecture in Paris (UP1). His main field of specialisation is the contemporary architecture of Muslim societies. He lectures widely and has organised and participated in numerous international seminars, exhibitions, colloquia, workshops, and international competitions. He has served as a jury member at various international competitions and schools of architecture and collaborated on a large variety of architecture-related publications.

Souleymane Bachir Diagne is a renowned Senegalese philosopher and public intellectual whose work bridges African philosophy, Islamic thought, and Western traditions. Born in Saint-Louis, Senegal, he studied at the École Normale Supérieure in Paris and earned his PhD under the supervision of Jacques Derrida. Diagne is currently a professor of French and philosophy at Columbia University in New York, where he also directs the Institute of African Studies. His scholarship explores themes of pluralism, translation, decolonisation, and the global circulation of ideas. Notable works include *African Art as Philosophy* (Other Press, 2023), *Open to Reason: Muslim Philosophers in Conversation with the Western Tradition* (Columbia University Press, 2018), and *The Ink of the Scholars: Reflections on Philosophy in Africa* (CODESRIA, 2017). Diagne's writing is widely recognised for its intellectual clarity and ethical engagement with questions of universality, language, and the postcolonial condition. A leading voice in global philosophical conversations, Diagne has been awarded the Édouard Glissant Prize and elected to the American Academy of Arts and Sciences. He advocates for a pluriversal vision of knowledge that honours the complexity and interconnection of philosophical traditions across cultures. Diagne served on the Master Jury of the Aga Khan Award for Architecture in 2010 and is a member of the 2025 Steering Committee.

Christian A. Hedrick is an architectural historian, educator, and consultant based in the Boston area. His research examines the many ways that cultural exchange has shaped architecture. His early work, supported in part by grants from the American Research Center in Egypt (ARCE) and the Deutscher Akademischer Austauschdienst (DAAD), focused on how European interpretations of Islamic architecture informed nineteenth-century German design and contributed to the emergence of the modern movement. His more recent research explores how the long arc of cultural exchange in architecture has shaped contemporary design and regional identity, particularly as today's policy- and decision-makers grapple with the complex legacy of the past. His work has appeared in the journals *Thresholds* and *JSAH*, and in the edited volume *Expanding Nationalisms at World's Fairs: Identity, Diversity, and Exchange, 1851–1915* (Routledge, 2021). He earned his PhD from the Massachusetts Institute of Technology (MIT) in the HTC and AKPIA programmes and his MArch from the University of Michigan, Ann Arbor. Hedrick has taught architectural history at Boston Architectural College, Northeastern University, and MIT, and was the Digital Humanities Research Associate at MIT's Aga Khan Documentation Center, where he initiated a new research project focused on the pedagogy of architectural history.

Anna Heringer is a German architect and activist whose work centres on the use of natural materials and community-driven design. She began her engagement with sustainable development in Bangladesh at the age of nineteen, working with the NGO Dipshikha. This formative experience shaped her architectural philosophy: to trust in local resources – both environmental and social – as the most resilient and empowering foundation for building. In 2005, she put this approach into practice with her diploma project, the METI School in Rudrapur, Bangladesh, designed in collaboration with Eike Roswag. The project won the Aga Khan Award for Architecture in 2007. Today, Heringer continues to work across Asia, Africa, and Europe, including a recent collaboration with Zigato on the Earth Campus in Tatale, Ghana. She holds the UNESCO Chair of Earthen Architecture and has developed the "Clay Storming" design method with Martin Rauch, which she teaches at institutions such as ETH Zurich, TU Munich, and Harvard GSD.

Farhan S. Karim is an architectural historian and educator whose research explores the intersections of modernism, decolonisation, and social engagement in South Asia. He is an associate professor in The Design School at Arizona State University, where he teaches architectural history and theory. Karim earned his PhD in architectural history from the University of Sydney and holds bachelor's and master's degrees in architecture from the Bangladesh University of Engineering and Technology. Karim is the author of the book *Of Greater Dignity than Riches: Austerity and Housing Design in India* (University of Pittsburgh Press, 2019), which examines how economic scarcity influenced architectural modernism in postcolonial India. He also edited *The Routledge Companion to Architecture and Social Engagement* (2018), offering critical perspectives on socially engaged architectural practices, and co-edited *The Making of Modern Muslim Selves through Architecture* (Intellect Books, 2024) with Patricia Blessing. Additionally, he is co-editing *Architectural Pedagogy in the Global South*, exploring educational practices in architecture. His scholarly articles have appeared in *Fabrications, Planning Perspectives, Architectural Theory Review*, and the *International Journal of Islamic Architecture*. Karim's research has been supported by various institutions, including the Graham Foundation, Canadian Centre for Architecture, Aga Khan Program for Islamic Architecture at MIT, Mellon-Volkswagen Fellowship, and Getty Research Institute.

Justicia C. T. Kiconco is a senior graduate architect and architectural researcher with a strong background in practice, research, and academia. She currently works with FBW Architects and Engineers in Kigali, Rwanda, where she develops innovative design strategies tailored to diverse project needs. Her work bridges design and research, with a focus on health, education, and architectural history. Previously, Tegyeka worked at MASS Design Group, gaining experience in socially engaged design and community-centred architecture. Her approach combines design, visual representation, and textual analysis to understand and innovate within the built environment. Before moving to Rwanda, she practised in Kampala, Uganda, and taught architectural history at Uganda Martyrs University. Tegyeka holds both a Bachelor of Environmental Design and a Master of Architecture (Professional) from Uganda Martyrs University. Her ongoing work contributes to critical conversations at the intersection of architectural practice, research, and education in East Africa.

Timothy Latim is a Ugandan architect and photographer whose work investigates the relationship between people, architecture, and place. With a strong presence on construction sites, Timothy explores both traditional and contemporary building practices through visual and spatial research. He currently works with Terrain Architects, a design firm founded in Tokyo that operates across Uganda, and also with Flexi-Home, a Uganda-based design-build company. His photography complements his architectural work, serving as a method for documenting and reflecting on local contexts and construction cultures. Outside of architecture, Latim is deeply committed to environmental conservation and outdoor exploration. He is an avid hiker and climber and serves on the committees of Mountain Slayers Uganda and the Mountain Club of Uganda, where he advocates for responsible engagement with nature. His cross-disciplinary practice brings together design, research, and environmental advocacy to reflect on the changing built environment in East Africa.

Lesley Lokko is a Ghanaian-Scottish architect, academic, and novelist renowned for her transformative contributions to architectural education and discourse. Lokko earned her BSc(Arch) and MArch from the Bartlett School of Architecture, University College London, and completed a PhD in architecture from the University of London in 2007. Lokko made history as the first Black curator of the Venice Architecture Biennale in 2023, with her exhibition *The Laboratory of the Future* focusing on themes of decolonisation and decarbonisation. Her accolades include the 2020 RIBA Annie Spink Award, the 2021 Ada Louise Huxtable Prize, and the 2024 Royal Gold Medal for Architecture, making her the first African woman to receive this honour. Additionally, she is a best-selling novelist, having authored several novels that explore themes of cultural identity and belonging. Lokko served on the Master Jury of the Aga Khan Award for Architecture in 2016 and is a member of the 2025 Steering Committee.

Tubi Otitooluwa is associate director at James Cubitt Architects in Lagos, Nigeria, where he leads the firm's work on digital innovation in design and construction. He holds a diploma in architectural technology from the Federal Polytechnic Ede, a bachelor's and master's in architecture and environmental design from the University of Lagos, and an Erasmus double master's in BIM from Politecnico di Milano and the University of Minho. Otitooluwa is deeply involved in architectural conservation and heritage documentation. He volunteers with the Adunni Olorisa Trust Foundation (AOTF) on the conservation of the Osun Osogbo UNESCO site, serves on the restoration committee of Legacy 1995, and is the principal investigator of the Endangered Wooden Architecture Programme (EWAP) 2023 grant, which documents colonial wooden railway buildings in Lagos using photogrammetry, building information modelling, and ethnographic research. A fellow of the Shared Heritage Africa (SHA) initiative, Otitooluwa contributed to exhibitions in Lagos, Kigali, Accra, and Frankfurt am Main, and co-authored *Modernism in*

Africa (Birkhäuser, 2023). His work has been published in *Docomomo Journal*. Otitooluwa's practice brings together technology, heritage, and design, advancing innovative approaches to architectural preservation and education in West Africa.

Deen Sharp is an LSE Visiting Fellow in human geography and environment at the London School of Economics and Political Science in the Department of Geography and Environment. Sharp holds a PhD in earth and environmental sciences (geography) from the City University of New York (CUNY) Graduate Center. He was previously a postdoctoral fellow at the Aga Khan Program for Islamic Architecture at the Massachusetts Institute of Technology and the co-director of the Terreform Center for Advanced Urban Research. Moreover, he is the co-editor of *Beyond the Square: Urbanism and the Arab Uprisings* (Urban Research, 2016), *Open Gaza: Architectures of Hope* (American University in Cairo Press and Terreform, 2022), and *Reconstruction as Violence in Assad's Syria* (American University in Cairo Press, 2025). Sharp has published in top-ranking journals, including *Progress in Human Geography* and *Urban Studies*, and contributed to several books. He has written for publications such as *Jadaliyya*, *Portal 9*, *MERIP*, *Arab Studies Journal*, and *The Guardian*. Sharp has worked for the United Nations, including UNDP and UN-Habitat, as well as for various governments and international NGOs.

Mamadou Jean-Charles Tall is a Senegalese architect, educator, and advocate for sustainable, context-driven architecture in West Africa. A graduate of the École nationale supérieure d'architecture de Marseille-Luminy, Tall has dedicated over four decades to promoting environmentally responsive and culturally grounded design. He is the co-director of J&T Architectes et Associés, a Dakar-based firm he leads with Annie Jouga. Their work emphasises bioclimatic principles and the use of local materials, challenging the dominance of concrete in Senegalese urban development. Tall has been a vocal proponent of earth-based construction techniques, advocating for their thermal efficiency and cultural relevance in the face of climate change. In 1990, Tall co-founded the Collège Universitaire d'Architecture de Dakar. This institution, which he chairs, offers an alternative model of architectural education that integrates theory with practical engagement in urban and rural contexts. The college has trained students from across West and Central Africa, fostering a generation of architects attuned to local needs and contexts.

Ola Uduku is the Roscoe Chair and Head of the Liverpool School of Architecture at the University of Liverpool. Prior to that, she was a research professor in architecture at the Manchester School of Architecture (2017–21). From 2011 to 2017, she was a reader in architecture and Dean for Africa at Edinburgh University. Her research focuses on modern architecture in West Africa and the evolution of educational spaces across the African continent. In 2018, she authored *Learning Spaces in Africa: Critical Histories to 21st Century Challenges and Change*, a seminal monograph on school-building practices. Uduku is deeply committed to equity and heritage preservation, promoting the documentation of African modernist buildings through Docomomo in Africa. She has also played a key role in the Shared Heritage Africa project coordinated by Docomomo Germany, and as part of this initiative co-edited the *Docomomo Journal* special issue on "Buildings for Higher Education in Africa" (2023).

Image Credits

All copyrights belong to the respective owners listed below, to whom we are grateful for the honour of presenting their work in this book.

Aga Khan Schools: p. 49; Aga Khan Trust for Culture / Amir Anoushfar (photographer): pp. 24-25, 232; Aga Khan Trust for Culture / Andreas Perbowo Widityawan (photographer): p. 51; Aga Khan Trust for Culture / Anne de Henning (photographer): p. 226; Aga Khan Trust for Culture / Asif Salman (photographer): pp. 163-64, 168-69; Aga Khan Trust for Culture / Cemal Emden (photographer): pp. 222-23; Aga Khan Trust for Culture / Chérif Tall (photographer): p. 81; Aga Khan Trust for Culture / Christopher Little (photographer): p. 227; Aga Khan Trust for Culture / Inan B.K.S. (photographer): pp. 158-59, 231; Aga Khan Trust for Culture / Nadia Siméon (photographer): p. 199 (left); Aga Khan Trust for Culture / Patrick Bingham-Hall (photographer): p. 221; Aga Khan Trust for Culture / Sandro di Carlo Darsa (photographer): pp. 167, 228-29; Aga Khan Trust for Culture / Siméon Duchoud (photographer): pp. 234-35; Aga Khan Trust for Culture / Sylvain Cherkaoui (photographer): pp. 6-9, 14-15, 77, 84 (bottom), 87 (bottom), 203-04, 207; Iwan Baan: pp. 214-15; Rubén P. Bescós: pp. 112-13, 119; Alizée Cugny / Studio Anna Heringer: p. 186; Dawoffice: pp. 28-29, 117-18, 121, 123, 125-27, 138-55, 241; Kate Dawson: pp. 177, 180-81; Don Bosco: p. 192; Magdalena Dussel: p. 133; École Africaine des Métiers de l'Architecture et de l'Urbanisme (EAMAU): p. 198; Anna Enrich: pp. 134-35, 244-45; IDOM: pp. 96-107; Festus Jackson Davis: pp. 197, 201; Justicia C. T. Kiconco: pp. 63-65; KNUST Development Offices, Archives: pp. 72-73; Timothy Latim / *Docomomo Journal* 69 (2023), pp. 61-69: p. 71; Timothy Latim: pp. 67-70; Katharina Lehmann / Studio Anna Heringer: p. 187; Lesley Lokko (copy); Fred Swart (graphic design); Festus Jackson Davis (photographer): p. 199 (right); MASS Design Group: pp. 210, 213; Claudia G. Mauriño: pp. 20-21, 122; Seun Oduwole: p. 52; Aitor Ortiz: pp. 12-13, 82-83, 242-43; Tubi Otitooluwa: pp. 58-61; Federico Pardos: pp. 84 (top), 92; Noemí de la Peña: pp. 26-27, 111, 116, 124, 129; Francesco Pinton: pp. 10-11, 16-17, 78-79, 89-91, 94-95, 225; *Présence Africaine*: p. 87 (top); Marcos Sagna: p. 131; Saif Ul Haque Sthapati / Hasan Saifuddin Chandan (photographer): p. 160; Studio Anna Heringer: pp. 188, 191; Ola Uduku: pp. 45, 47; Jara Varela: pp. 18-19, 22-23, 136-37; Wikimedia Commons, GNU Free Documentation License: https://commons.wikimedia.org/wiki/File:Badagry,_school_children.jpg: p. 43; Wikimedia Commons, public domain: https://commons.wikimedia.org/wiki/File:ACHIMOTA_SCHOOL.jpg: p. 46

Learning Ecologies
in Architecture

With contributions by Jonathan Kplorla Agbeh, Christian Paul Zigato Agboada, Christian Benimana, Katherine Dawson, Dawoffice, Farrokh Derakhshani, Souleymane Bachir Diagne, Christian A. Hedrick, Anna Heringer, IDOM, Farhan S. Karim, Justicia C. T. Kiconco, Timothy Latim, Lesley Lokko, Tubi Otitooluwa, Deen Sharp, Mamadou Jean-Charles Tall, and Ola Uduku.

Editor: Deen Sharp

Project management: Silke Martini, Nadia Siméon, Cristina Steingräber

Image editing: Isabelle Griffiths, Silke Martini, Deen Sharp

Copyediting: Dawn Michelle d'Atri

Art direction: Julia Wagner, grafikanstalt

Production: Sonja Bröderdörp

Reproductions: Optische Werke Hamburg GbR, Germany

Printing and binding: DZA Druckerei zu Altenburg GmbH, Germany

© 2025 Aga Khan Award for Architecture, ArchiTangle GmbH, and the contributors

Aga Khan Award for Architecture
P.O. Box 2049
1211 Geneva 2
Switzerland
www.akdn.org/architecture

Published by
ArchiTangle GmbH
Meierottostrasse 1
10719 Berlin
Germany
www.architangle.com

ISBN 978-3-96680-036-5

Scan the QR codes throughout the book to access additional digital content.